Museum Ethics

A number of developments in the museum movement during the last few years have forced museums to give greater attention to ethical issues. Members of a profession are increasingly regarded as constituting an ethical community. Every person within such a community must have a sense of personal obligation as well as a responsibility for others to assure ethical achievement. This volume firmly places notions of ethics in the field of action.

Museum Ethics considers the theoretical and practical elements of the philosophy of conduct in relation to critical contemporary issues and museums. This discussion encompasses the procurement of artifacts, the rights of indigenous peoples, repatriation, the politics of display, the conservation of objects and the role of education, as well as the day-to-day management of a museum. All persons active in museum matters, whether custodian, curator, or trustee have an ethical obligation to the museum profession and the public. This volume will allow the professional and student to work towards a more responsible and responsive museum community.

Gary Edson is Director of the renowned museum training program at Texas Tech University and a course lecturer, as well as Executive Director of the large university museum. He has travelled extensively and has recently given museum-related training workshops in Ecuador and Paraguay. He is co-author of *Handbook for Museums* (1994), and editor of the *International Directory of Museum Training* (1995).

The Heritage: Care–Preservation–Management programme has been designed to serve the needs of the museum and heritage community worldwide. It publishes books and information services for professional museum and heritage workers, and for all the organisations that service the museum community.

Editor-in-chief: Andrew Wheatcroft

Museum Ethics

Edited by Gary Edson

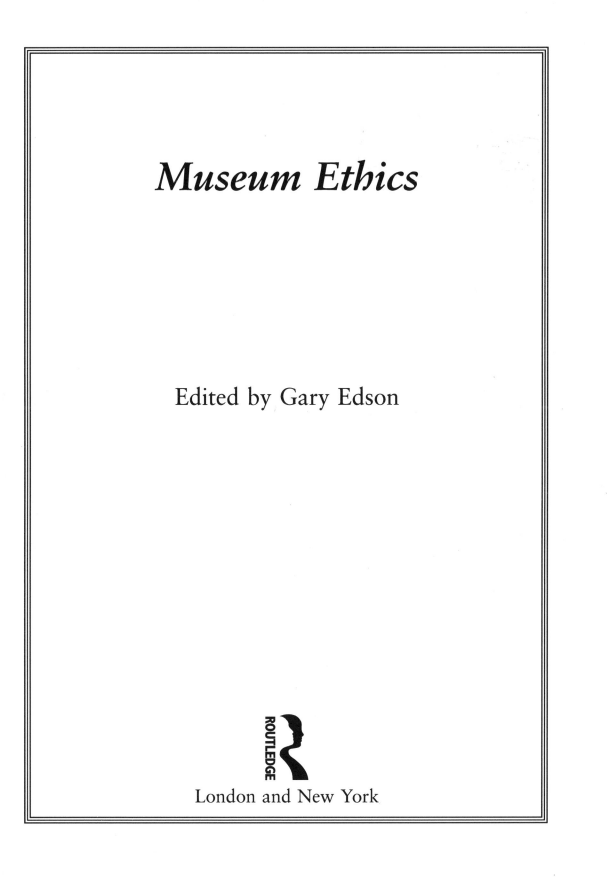

London and New York

First published 1997
by Routledge
11 New Fetter Lane, London EC4P 4EE

Simultaneously published in the USA and Canada
by Routledge
29 West 35th Street, New York, NY 10001

Typeset in Sabon by Keystroke, Jacaranda Lodge, Wolverhampton
Printed and bound in Great Britain by TJ International Ltd, Padstow, Cornwall

British Library Cataloguing in Publication Data
A catalogue record for this book is available from the British Library

Library of Congress Cataloging in Publication Data
Edson, Gary, 1937–
Museum ethics / by Gary Edson.
p. cm.
Includes bibliographical references and index.
1. Museums—Management—Moral and ethical aspects. I. Title.
AM121.E37 1997
174′.9096—dc20 96–41629
CIP

ISBN 0–415–13811–6 (hbk)
0–415–15290–9 (pbk)

To: M

Contents

Figures

Contributors

Robert E. Child, head of conservation, National Museum of Wales, Cardiff, Wales.

Robert Child has a Bachelor's degree from the University of Exeter and is a fellow of the International Institute for Conservation, and a fellow of the Society of Antiquaries. He is actively involved with a number of national and international professional organizations including: the United Kingdom Institute of Conservation, the International Institute of Conservation, ICCROM, and the Society for the Preservation of Natural History.

Robert Child has been visiting lecturer at the University of Wales, University of Durham, the Institute of Archaeology, ICCROM, and the Science Museum. He has organized courses on, among other topics, the Care of Collections, Biodeterioration, and Lighting for Conservation and Display. His conservation activities include being an adviser on pest control to the National Trust, adviser on preventive conservation to English Heritage, the National Museum of Ireland and other museums and galleries, and conservation consultant to overseas governments through the British Council including: Sri Lanka, Bophuthatswana, and Northern Cyprus.

David K. Dean, associate director for museum facilities and programs, and an adjunct professor in the Museum Science Program at the Museum of Texas Tech University, Lubbock, Texas USA.

David Dean earned a Bachelor of Science degree in 1974, with a double major in Art and Biology, and a minor in Education from Hardin-Simmons University, Abilene, Texas. He was awarded a Master of Arts degree at Texas Tech University after completing the Museum Science Program in 1976. He currently teaches the Museum Interpretation and Communication course in the Museum Science Program and team-teaches in the program's Professional Development course. In his role as associate director, he oversees the museum's exhibitions, security, education, and facilities divisions. He has been involved in exhibition design and production for twenty years in the respective roles of preparator, designer, production manager, and administrator.

David Dean has participated in national and international workshops, seminars, and professional development programs throughout his career. He has given workshops and taught seminars in such places as Ecuador, and in subjects ranging from museum management and exhibitions development, to computer use in museums.

He has authored and co-authored several publications, including *An Ancient Watering Hole: The Lubbock Lake Landmark Story* (1990), *Tales of the Ancient Watering Hole – Book 2: Protohistoric Life on the Southern Plains* (1994), and the textbook *Museum Exhibitions: Theory and Practice* (1994). He is also the co-author, with Gary Edson, of *The Handbook for Museums* (1993).

Gary Edson, executive director of the Museum of Texas Tech University, director of the Museum Science Program, and professor of Museum Science.

Gary Edson has a Bachelor's degree in Fine Arts (BFA) from the Kansas City Art Institute and a Master of Fine Arts degree from Tulane University. He has been an administrator and teacher at the University level for thirty years and currently teaches Museology and Museum Administration. He is an active member of the International Council of Museums (ICOM) through the activities of the training committee (ICTOP), and serves on the board of AAM/ICOM, the US national committee of ICOM.

Prior to joining the faculty at Texas Tech University, Gary Edson was a professor of art at West Virginia University, the Herron School of Art in Indianapolis, and Northwest Louisiana State University. Before beginning an academic career, he ran a pottery, served as a Peace Corps volunteer in Ecuador, and worked for the US government in Korea as a crafts supervisor.

Gary Edson has traveled extensively, lecturing and presenting workshops in various locations nationally and internationally. He is author of *Mexican Market Pottery* (1979), co-author of *The Handbook for Museums* (1993) with David Dean, and editor of the *International Directory of Museum Training* (1995).

Amareswar Galla, convener, Cross Cultural Heritage Management, National Centre for Cultural Heritage, University of Canberra, Australia.

Dr Galla is a cultural equity and cross cultural heritage specialist from South Asia whose education, work research, and community cultural development work span South Asia, Europe, Australia, New Zealand, South Africa, and North, South, and Central America. During 1986–91, he established a national affirmative action program for indigenous Australians through the Museum Studies and Cultural Heritage Management Programs at the University of Canberra. He is currently the convener of Cross Cultural Heritage Management at the same university. A member of the Asia Pacific Executive Board and coordinator of the Cross Cultural Working Group of the International Council of Museums, he also chairs the Joint Heritage Committee of the Cultural and Heritage Councils in the Australian Capital Territory.

Amareswar Galla is also the national convener of the Arts, Culture, and Heritage Coalition of the Federation of Ethnic Communities Councils of Australia. He has responsibility for the development of the National Cultural

Advocacy Strategy of the Federation. The most recent work in his extensive publication record is entitled *Heritage Curricula and Cultural Diversity* (Office of Multicultural Affairs, Canberra, 1993).

Johanne Landry, conseillère technique en muséologie, Jardin Botanique de Montréal, Montréal, Canada.

While preparing a doctorate degree in Biology in Québec, Johanne Landry shifted her field of interest toward popularization of science. After further studies in History and Socio-politics of Science in Montreal, she went to California to analyze the scientific museums in the United States. From 1984 to 1990, she worked at La Cité des Sciences et de l'Industrie, in La Villette, in Paris. She returned to Montreal in 1990 to be part of the team building the Biodôme of Montreal, the new museum of environment where she was director of public programs until 1994. She is presently museology advisor for the scientific museums and the parks of the City of Montreal.

Silas Okita, professor of Museum Studies, Center for Nigerian Cultural Studies, Ahmadu Bello University, Zaria, Nigeria.

Silas Okita was a former member of the Governing Board of the Nigerian National Commission for Museums and Monuments. Currently, he is president of the Museum Association of Nigeria and chairman of the Nigerian National Committee of the International Council of Museums (ICOM). He is a member of the Board of the International Committee on Training of Personnel (ICTOP), and was a visiting professor on the Exchange Visitor Program at the Museum of Texas Tech University in Lubbock, Texas. There he conducted a study on African Collections and the American Audience, as part of his research interest in museums and multiculturalism.

Paul N. Perrot, museum consultant, Sarasota, Florida, USA.

Paul Perrot was educated at the École Sainte Marie in Paris, the Scuole Pie in Florence, Italy, and the College de Betharram. He also studied at the École du Louvre and the Institute of Fine Arts of New York University. In 1982, he was named a *Cavalier de l'Ordre des Arts et Letters* in France, received the Katherine Coffey Award from the Mid-Atlantic Association of Museums in 1986, the ICCROM Award from the International Center for Conservation in Rome in 1990, and was elected to honorary membership in the American Institute for Conservation in 1990.

Paul Perrot served as director of the Santa Barbara Museum of Art from 1991 to 1994, and as a consultant for that institution. From 1984 to 1991, he was director of the Virginia Museum of Fine Arts and prior to that, he was assistant secretary for museum programs at the Smithsonian Institution in Washington, DC. He is chair of the Advisory Committee of the World Monuments Fund and has served as vice-president and member of the ICOM Council in Paris. He is past-president of the International Center for Conservation in Rome and a member of the International Institute for Conservation of Historic and Artistic Works.

Piet J. M. Pouw, director, Reinwardt Academie, Amsterdam, The Netherlands and chairman of ICTOP.

Piet Pouw studied Literature and Philosophy at the State University of Leiden. He has been lecturing at the Reinwardt Academy Department of Museology of the Amsterdam School of Arts since 1976, and in 1981 he was appointed director. Piet Pouw has made several presentations and has published work on the training of museum personnel and on professional ethics. He was elected chairman of ICTOP (ICOM's International Committee for Training of Personnel) in 1989. He is also a member of the Ethics Committee of ICOM.

Piet Pouw serves as a board member and advisory committee member for Dutch museums, and on behalf of ICOM, he has been advisor for international training programs.

Tereza Cristina Scheiner, director, School of Museology, UNI-RIO, Rio de Janeiro, Brazil.

Tereza Scheiner received a Bachelor in Museology (1970), with a Major in Science Museums from the School of Museology, National History Museum. She received a Bachelor and License in Geography (1976–77), major in Human Geography – Institute of Geosciences, State University of Rio de Janeiro (UERJ), and has earned credits in Anthropology, Method and Theory in Archaeology, Cultures of the Pacific, and Museum Techniques (1968–69) at the George Washington University. She completed a specialization in Methodology of Teaching for University Level in 1974 at the School of Education, Federal University of Rio de Janeiro (UFRJ), and the Masters course on Political Science, IUPERJ (1985–86).

Tereza Scheiner has worked in Museology since 1972 and has published works on Museology and Human Ecology. She is a member of the editorial board of specialized periodicals in Museology, a member of ICOM, vice-chairman of ICOFOM, and a member of ICTOP. With Nelly Decarolis of Argentina, she coordinates the regional ICOFOM Group for Latin America and the Caribbean (ICOFOM/LAM). She is a member of AAM, CMA and ABM (Brazilian Association of Museums) and a consultant ad hoc of the National Council for Scientific Research (CNPq) in the field of Museology.

Tomislav Sola, lecturer in Museology, University of Zagreb, Zagreb, Croatia.

Professor Sola was born in Zagreb in 1948. He obtained a BA degree in History of Art and carried out postgraduate studies in Journalism and Information Sciences at the University of Zagreb. He also attended a postgraduate course on Contemporary Museology at the Sorbonne and earned a PhD in Museology from the University of Ljubljana. Sola has participated in many international meetings and conferences. He worked as curator at the Gallery of Primitive Art in Zagreb and as director of the Museum Documentation Center in Zagreb. Currently, he is lecturer in Museology at the University of Zagreb. Sola is a former Chairman of ICOM Yugoslavia, former Secretary of ICOM-ICOFOM, and former member of the Executive Council of ICOM. Presently, he serves as a member of the Advisory Editorial Board of *Museum international*, UNESCO, and is a lecturer in the postgraduate study of Museology, University of Zagreb. He regularly lectures at the International Summer School of Museology, University of Brno, and at Centre Europeu del Patrimoni in Barcelona, Spain.

Stephen L. Williams, assistant professor of Museum Studies, Baylor University, Waco, Texas, USA.

Stephen Williams is the collections manager of the Strecker Museum Complex and an assistant professor in the Department of Museum Studies of Baylor University. He has a BS and MS in Zoology and an MA in Museum Science. Williams was collections manager at the Carnegie Museum of Natural History in Pittsburgh from 1976 to 1990. During that time, he participated in the development of the Society for the Preservation of Natural History Collections, the Bay Foundation pilot training program in Los Angeles, and various initiatives with the Institute of Museum Services and the National Institute for Conservation. In 1990, he went to Texas Tech University where he managed the operations of the vertebrate research collections and taught collection-related courses in the Museum Science Program. In 1995, he moved to Baylor University where he manages collections of cultural history and natural history, publishes on collection management and care, and teaches undergraduate and graduate courses in preventive conservation, modern management of collections, and principles of museum registration.

Foreword

La méthode suivie par Gary Edson et son équipe apparaît à la fois comme une approche pertinente des résultats des recherches théoriques jusqu'ici entreprises (la bibliographie est impressionnante) et comme une revue des problèmes quotidiens auxquels sont confrontés les responsables des professions muséales.

Il ne s'agit pas pour les différents auteurs, d'asséner des principes mais de réfléchir aux réactions possibles face à des situations simples ou complexes en se référant toujours aux exigences d'une éthique professionnelle rigoureuse. Nul doute qu'un tel travail vienne à son heure et soit utile sinon indispensable tant à l'étudiant néophyte qu'au professionnel chevronné.

Le Code de déontologie du Conseil international des musées (ICOM) dont on trouvera ici le texte, est maintes fois cité, analysé ou commenté; la démarche de ses rédacteurs fut différente: il ne s'agit pas là de réflexions personnelles ou collectives mais de principes généraux qui engagent formellement ceux qui ont volontairement adhéré à l'ICOM où un "Comité de déontologie" a été chargé non pas de légiférer ou de prendre des décisions en lieu et place du Conseil exécutif, mais de veiller à l'application du Code, d'informer le Conseil en lui soumettant des avis motivés et, s'il l'estime nécessaire, de demander la publication des dits avis.

La saisine du Comité peut émaner soit du Conseil lui-même désireux de voir étudié un problème complexe, soit de tout adhérent à l'ICOM, le Comité ayant la possibilité de se saisir lui-même de tel ou tel cas particulier.

D'expérience les dossiers examinés jusqu'ici ont été peu nombreux et relativement faciles à traiter; ils ont le plus souvent concerné des situations particulières qui relevaient plus de la politique de l'ICOM que de l'éthique proprement dite, preuve peut être que l'interprétation du Code n'a soulevé qu'un minimum d'interrogations.

Gary Edson a justement signalé qu'un Code comme celui là se devait d'être évolutif et c'est là une évidence. Le Comité s'est cependant refusé jusqu'ici à toute modification estimant qu'il fallait laisser "du temps au temps" et ne proposer de modifications que si tel ou tel article s'avérait obsolète ou si tel autre paraissait s'imposer.

Que l'on nous permette néanmoins une remarque: ni le Code de l'ICOM ni le présent livre n'ont abordé la question de la protection des biens culturels en cas de conflit armé. L'UNESCO s'est efforcé de convaincre les Etats membres de la nécessité d'une politique commune en la matière, politique dont les bases ont été définies lors de la Conférence Générale tenue à La Haye en 1954. Depuis cette date, que de conflits! Que de biens culturels de première importance ont été volés, pillés, détruits, perdus à jamais et cela dans une indifférence quasi générale. Comment ne pas évoquer enfin le malaise ressenti tout récemment encore face aux séquelles de la Guerre mondiale plus de cinquante ans après la fin des conflits ...

Une réflexion éthique s'impose également en ces domaines. Un beau sujet pour un nouveau livre aussi bénéfique que celui-ci ?

Hubert Landais
Président
Comité de déontologie de l'ICOM

(Translated from French by Luc Lithwinionek.)

The methodology adopted by Gary Edson and his colleagues stands both as a well-founded approach to the results of current theoretical research (the bibliography is impressive evidence of this) and as a review of the daily problems encountered by museum professionals.

The aim of the various authors is not to establish principles but to consider possible responses to different situations, whether simple or complex, within a constant framework of rigorous professional standards. There can be no doubt that such an endeavor is long overdue and will prove as useful, if not indispensable, for the novice student as for the experienced professional.

The *Code of Ethics* of the International Council of Museums (ICOM) as found in the text, is often cited, analyzed or commented upon. However, the objectives of the editors are different: the intent is not to present personal or collective reflections but to state general existing principles that formally commit members who have voluntarily adhered to ICOM. As such, the "Ethics Committee" was appointed not to legislate or make decisions in place of the Executive Council, but to watch over the application of the Code, to inform the Council by submitting justified opinions and, if necessary, to demand publication of these opinions.

The Committee's authority can come either from the Council itself wishing to look at a complex problem, or from an individual member of ICOM, as the Committee has the capacity to examine individual cases.

Up until now, the cases examined have proved to be few in number and relatively simple to address. Generally they have dealt with particular situations related more to the politics of ICOM than to ethics *per se* – proof perhaps that the interpretation of the Code raises only a minimum of questions.

In this sense, Gary Edson underlines the fact that such a Code should be always evolving, and rightfully so. However, the Council has up to now refused to acknowledge any change, believing that time is the best asset and that modifications should only be imposed when an article becomes obsolete or is superseded.

However, let us underline one point; neither ICOM's Code, nor this current book addresses the question of the protection of cultural resources in case of an armed conflict. UNESCO has tried to convince the member states of the necessity of establishing standard policies in this matter, as defined at the General Conference of La Haye in 1954. Since that date, how many conflicts have occurred! How many cultural resources have been stolen, pillaged, destroyed, or forever lost, and this in a context of general indifference. How not to conjure up in that sense the unrest still recently felt in the aftermath of the Second World War, fifty years after its end . . .

An ethical reflection is therefore equally overdue on the subject. An interesting topic for another book as beneficial as this one?

Hubert Landais
President
Ethics Committee of ICOM

Acknowledgments

A number of people gave special assistance to form both the idea for this book and the book itself. They are: Robert Child, United Kingdom; David Dean, USA; Amareswar Galla, Australia; Johanne Landry, Canada; Silas Okita, Nigeria; Paul Perrot, USA; Piet Pouw, The Netherlands; Tereza Scheiner, Brazil; Tomislav Sola, Croatia; and Stephen Williams, USA. Each of these people contributed stellar chapters included in the "Ethical Perspectives" part of this book. All did a great job. Their material gives valuable insight into the ethical issues that confront museums on a daily basis.

Also a special thanks to Elisabeth des Portes, secretary general of ICOM and Hubert Landais, president of the ICOM Ethics Committee for allowing the inclusion of the ICOM *Code of Professional Ethics*. It is this document that is the base of much of the book, and without their authorization, it could not be included in its entirety.

In developing this text, I took the opportunity to read, re-read, review, and digest a number of books on ethical theory, and to each of those authors I owe a note of appreciation and thanks. Many of the books are included in the bibliography and each warrants careful reading.

The first phase of this book was the result of teaching duties in the Museum Science Program at Texas Tech University. The students listened to the lectures, asked questions, and challenged the ideas. They contributed the necessary elements of discussion and argument to test the ethical issues as they relate to museological situations. For their role, they deserve a measure of recognition and appreciation.

I also wish to acknowledge the advice, energy, and good counsel of Andrew Wheatcroft, editor-in-chief, *The Heritage: Care–Preservation–Management* program of Routledge. Andrew reviewed an early draft of this book and made a number of insightful recommendations. Our visits always leave me inspired and enthusiastic about many things, but most of all the value and importance of the written word.

Finally, my greatest debt of gratitude goes to Miriam Edson for her support, encouragement, and patience. She read and re-read thousands of words searching for errors and helping to find order in chaotic word patterns. Throughout the ordeal she maintained a sense of humor (most of the time) and a ready word of support. Thank you M!

Gary Edson
Museum of Texas Tech University
Lubbock, Texas USA

Every one of our acts has, as its stake, the meaning of the world and the place of man in the universe. Through each of them, whether we wish it or not, we set up a scale of values which is universal. And one would want us not to experience dread and anguish in the face of such a momentous responsibility!

(Jean-Paul Sartre, *Action*)

Introduction

Fresh milk is often slow to curdle; so sinful [unethical] actions do not always bring immediate results. Sinful [unethical] actions are more like coals of fire that are hidden in the ashes and keep on smoldering, finally causing a greater fire.

(Bukkyo Dendo Kyokai 1966: 185)

Contrary to common assumption, telling right from wrong is not always easy to do. It can also be equally difficult to know which right answer is the more right for a particular situation. The study of ethics aids in defining both the question and the answer to these kinds of concerns. Why? Because everyone makes decisions, and decisions are about values. There are profound philosophical and ethical questions about the nature of museums, particularly as they redefine their obligations to the public.

The International Council of Museums *Statutes* (1989: 3) defines a museum and includes a number of additional institutions that fall under the general classification of "museums." One other publication (Burcaw 1983) includes fifteen definitions for "museum." However, with only a few exceptions, most countries of the world have no restriction on the use of the word "museum" as an identifying name. There are often rules or regulations that establish criteria for an entity to receive benefits as a "museum," but beyond those limits, almost anything can be called a "museum." The difference between those buildings that *claim* to be museums and those that *are* museums is the people that work for the good of society and of its development – the museum profession. A necessary part of the profession is a code of ethics.

Museum ethics is not about the imposition of external values on museums, but about an understanding of the foundations of museum practices. Considering the important role of ethics to the museum profession, it was with a great deal of trepidation that this book was undertaken. However, as there are very few books that address the subject of museum ethics, and there is a very obvious need for more information on this topic, the project demanded attention.

As this is a book about museum ethics, it is therefore about museums and museum workers. It was conceived primarily to assist people working in museums, including trustees and volunteers, to understand the importance of ethics as a guidance concept. Too many trustees forget basic ethical principles by assuming attitudes of self-importance, just as too often museum workers lose sight of professional objectives in favor of personal achievement or gain. Neither may be fundamentally "bad," sinful, or unethical, but by acting irresponsibly, both violate public trust and potentially compromise their museum.

To address the challenging subject of museum ethics, this book is divided into two parts. The first part considers the theoretical foundation of museum ethics and the second is composed of ten chapters relating to ethical issues from the international museum community. The general format of the book is question and answer. This method was selected because there is a feeling, certainly among students of ethics, that too many ethical questions are left unanswered. By using this approach to the information exchange process, it is hoped that specific issues can be addressed and clarified.

Museum ethics is about more than a code of ethics, it is primarily about self-understanding. It is also about responsible stewardship, honesty, and "doing the right thing." It is not about formulas or recipes for the ethical issues encountered in the everyday activities of the museum.

In forming the material into sections and chapters, there is an amount of redundancy necessary for explaining certain ideas as they relate to particular ethical theories, and because some questions require similar answers. However, the positive aspect of this process is that readers may select topics of special interest and refer to that section without having to read elsewhere in the book to get relevant information.

The ethical perspectives included in Part II are written by museum professionals from different parts of the world. Each was asked to write on a particular topic. However, except for that request and some basic stylistic editing, no effort has been made to make all commentaries conform to a particular formula or direction of thought. None of the statements has been altered intentionally to favor one opinion as opposed to another. Some of the material challenges the thinking and statements found in the writing of other contributors. Differing opinions about ethical matters are positive in that one of the methods for gaining greater insight into ethics is reflection on diverse ideas. By leaving these seemingly conflicting statements intact, the reader has an opportunity to consider different views of pertinent ethical questions and to gain a more expansive view of ethical issues.

The book is intended to present in simple terms what we know but at times fail to practice. It does not profess by design or desire to provide ultimate truths about ethics. It offers honest thoughts and ideas about the role of ethics as related to the museum profession. It is my hope that it will accomplish two goals. First, it will cause some of those persons entering or already in the museum workforce to gain a new appreciation for ethics, and second, it will cause a number of people to write about museum ethics.

Finally, as this book is also about respect, truth, and good, every effort has been made to present the information in a manner that recognizes the values of all people. No word or phrase has been used knowingly that might convey a meaning other than honest respect and appreciation. Ethics is a personal matter as well as a professional one.

> To utter pleasant words without practicing them, is like a fine flower without fragrance.
>
> (Bukkyo Dendo Kyokai 1966: 184)

Gary Edson
Museum of Texas Tech University
Lubbock, Texas USA
February 1996

Part I
Ethics for museums

1

Ethics

one important service of ethical theory to ethical practice may be seen in cases where a genuine perplexity has arisen as to the authority of conflicting claims. The perplexity, however, must be genuine; it must not be the hesitancy of a mind seeking means to justify itself for some departure from accepted standards.

(Everett 1918: 31)

DOES MUSEUM ETHICS DEAL WITH PRACTICAL ISSUES?

A few years ago, a large metropolitan museum was offered an extraordinary work of aboriginal art that would have been a very important addition to their collection. The curator of ethnology was delighted with the object as it complemented several works already in the museum's collection. The piece was well crafted, had excellent markings, and was a near perfect example of a late-eighteenth-century, post-adolescent initiation figure depicting the dangers of adulthood. To acquire the object was, from the sociological as well as the ethnographical perspective, a once-in-a-lifetime opportunity.

The prospective donor was a local art collector who had given several pieces to the museum in the past. He said he had acquired the object thinking it would be a good addition to his collection, but after having it in his home for a few weeks decided it was not to his liking. He wanted to give it to the museum if they were interested.

The curator of ethnology assured the donor of the museum's interest and sent a request to the Acquisition Committee stating his wish to acquire the figure. The curator stated the important attributes of the piece and assured the Committee of the object's authenticity. He explained the tradition behind the item and how it related to the museum's collection. The curator explained that the piece was so perfect that if he had not tested the colorants by comparing them to similarly dated works, he would have thought it to be of recent production.

The Acquisition Committee shared the curator's enthusiasm and they voted to accept the figure once the documentation was in order. As the object was from another country, the Committee wanted to be reassured of its legal status. The donor indicated that the documentation was requested at the time of the purchase but none had been provided. After several attempts to get the paperwork, the museum initiated an investigation that eventually determined that the item had possibly been removed from its country of origin without the proper authorization.

Following the provisions of their collection policy and the ICOM *Code of Professional Ethics*, "A museum should not acquire, whether by purchase, gift, bequest or exchange, any object unless the governing body and responsible officer are satisfied that the museum can acquire a valid title to the specimen or object" (ICOM 1990: 27), the Acquisition Committee voted not to accept the object. The curator was greatly disappointed with the decision but understood that ethical as well as possible legal issues had prompted the Committee's decision.

WHAT IS THE ETHICAL THING TO DO?

> Suppose you ask me, "What is the right thing to do?" I answer, "Do what a virtuous person would do!" But you counter, "Who is a virtuous person?" To which I reply, "The man [person] who does the right thing."
>
> (Pojman 1990: 123)

Conventional ethical standards evolved under what is called a "primary group" relationship. In that environment, contact between people tended to be of an individual nature, that is, one to one. The people shared common interests and their association was informal and personal. Their ethical expectations gave attention to activities that existed within the primary group (Titus 1947). In contrast, contemporary society lives to a large extent with "secondary groups" where the people are unknown and the relationship is formal. In this more complex relationship the traditional codes provide minimal guidance.

When there was less dependence on others, and most people were self-sustaining, the expectations of social interaction were limited. As human services, health care, technical requirements, and commercial contact increased and became more complex, the requirements and expectations of social exchange grew. Eventually there was a general division of labor and the evolution of specialists.

This separation of work responsibility was of primary importance to the development of modern civilization. By specializing, people gained greater skill, an increased level of achievement, and a higher quality of service. These accomplishments led to a higher standard of living, increased service dependency, and further separated people from a primary group relationship.

The more specialized the service became, the greater the skill, and the less the "consumer" knew about the technology of the work being performed, hence the greater the opportunity for abuse. Because of this situation, the need to establish guidelines for higher standards of conduct was greatly increased. These standards defined the working relationship between persons in the specialization as well as the relations of the specialist with the public. It was from this perspective that the first codes of ethics evolved.

Most museum specialists have a basic understanding of "right" and "wrong." In general, they know the role of museums "in the service of society and of its development" (ICOM 1990: 3). However, it is common knowledge that recent years have been a time of significant change for museums and museum workers. Cultural diversity, educational initiatives, the environment, collection care, international exchange, and repatriation are but a few of the issues that have claimed attention during the past two or three decades. These changes have had an impact upon the museum community in ways that have drawn attention to the need for reinforcing existing standards of conduct.

The museum profession has grown and become more specialized. It has expanded to include a growing number of diverse institutions, programs, and entities. At the same time, it has divided itself into areas that require increased technical skill and further specialized knowledge. As museums have opened their doors to a more representative audience and gained a greater sense of social identity and responsibility, they have increased the need for maintaining high ethical standards.

Contemporary life is influencing the activities of museums and redefining their role and responsibility. These activities have occurred at different rates in different locations, but there can be little doubt that change has taken place. Some may claim that the motivating force for change was self-preservation. Others prefer to believe that an attitude of democratization was the prevailing force. Regardless of the reasons, traditional standards and safeguards are being revised or cast aside.

IS THE CONCERN FOR ETHICS A CONTEMPORARY ISSUE?

Ethics is one branch of philosophy. It is defined as the science of conduct.

> Every form of philosophy – and in different ages philosophy has taken many forms – is built upon some supposition or hypothesis. And the supposition or assumption is always based or supposed to be based upon experience, and is applied to experience.
>
> (Jevons 1927: 77)

The word "philosophy" is said to have been first used by a Greek named Pythagoras who lived in the sixth century BC. It is reported that he spoke of "himself as a 'philosophos' or lover of wisdom" (Fuller 1945: 1). However, it was Plato who gave the word its meaning as used today. From the same environment came the principle of mathematics formulated on the idea that "geometry is inherent in nature rather than part of the framework used to describe nature . . . [the Greeks] believed that their mathematical theorems were expressions of eternal and exact truths about the real world" (Capra 1991: 162). On the basis of this foundation, philosophical theorems were expressed in terms of absolute truths. This thinking has influenced many aspects of Western philosophy and science, including ethics.

With geometric correctness in mind, it was only natural to view ethical attitudes as those life conditions that fit the mathematical equation $x = y$. That is, like situations (x) should always generate the same responses (y). Any act or action that falls outside this equation cannot be confirmed as ethical. This inflexibility has caused many people to deny the possibility of a universal code of professional ethics. However, there are certain principles that, by their broad application, are more universal than might appear at first view.

"Ethics is a human activity" (Brown 1990: xi), and the primary purpose of a code of ethics is to raise the level of professional practice. For the museum profession, this goal is achieved by helping to maintain the professional status of the museum community, and by strengthening the role and responsibilities of museums in society.

DOES ETHICS CONTRIBUTE TO SOCIAL ORDER?

It is natural for humans to join in some kind of group. At first it was for protection and survival in the form of meeting and satisfying communal needs. To accomplish these goals, group communication was a necessity, as was a system of conduct. Undoubtedly, certain acts were viewed with approval while others were considered detrimental to group order. Conduct conflicting with group standards was discouraged and at times punished (Holmes 1992).

As the needs of the group expanded, sub-sets formed to give credibility to special interests. Consequently, as the social order became more complex, the community increased in importance. It was the means of preserving certain common values. As a part of group dynamics, some acts were determined to be "right" and others were "wrong." Although some members of the group might not agree with individual values, all members were expected to abide by the approved ways for the good of the community and its membership.

Over time, the enduring "rights" and "wrongs" were transformed into rules, customs, and practices. Eventually some became laws for maintaining social order, and others were recognized as accepted practices as determined by communal consent.

Contemporary ethics reflects contemporary society in that the ideals and practices change to conform to the actual conditions of humankind. Less complex societies continue to form and maintain groups for the protection and

6

enhancement of the social order. As part of contemporary society, sub-set groups have organized around vocational activities. In certain cases where specialized training and acquired knowledge warrant, vocational groups are recognized as professions.

There is a right way and a wrong way to do most things. It is human nature to seek the correct (right) means for accomplishing an action, act, or deed. To achieve this end, there has been (and is) a search for a model or ideal form of correctness. The quest for an ideal form of correct behavior led to the examination of human conduct, and this investigation is a part of philosophy called ethics.

IS ETHICS ABOUT INDIVIDUAL CONDUCT?

Ethics has been described as, "the study of the criteria of good and bad conduct" (Pepper 1960: 2). From the world-view, the conduct of all museum workers should be to reach a maximum level of museological perfection within the constraints of their environment. This is not to say that every individual act must be perfectly conceived and executed, but that ethics provides a guide of speculative truths about the practical order of acceptable activities.

A code of ethics considers both personal and group activities. Most personal issues involve prudence (discretion), temperance (constraint), conscientiousness (dedication), or judiciousness (probity). These characteristics are usually considered under headings relating to professional conduct and are usually easy to describe and understand. Difficulty may arise in applying available knowledge about proper or correct personal actions, as each circumstance may require contextual decision making.

These characteristics (attributes) relate to virtues and they correspond to principles of conduct. A virtue is an ethically designated quality for expressing the goodness or excellence in human functions.

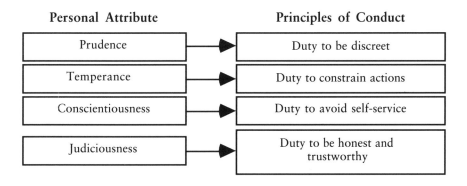

Figure 1.1 The relationship of attributes to conduct

SHOULD MUSEUM PROFESSIONALISM BEGIN WITH ETHICS?

Often the first exposure an employee has to an institution's values (standards) or ethics is at the time of recruitment. A museum has a special identity that includes the standards, values, norms, and philosophies that determine how the institution operates. It may happen that a person's values are only partially consistent with the museum's expectations. The ethical challenge is to determine the common ground for maximizing shared values and to ascertain the means for resolving differences (Guy 1990). Education and training are the normal methods for instilling ethical values. Clear language, practical association, and meaningful reference are important in the process of understanding and using museum ethics.

Adapting to the expectations of an organizational culture is described as socialization, that is, to qualify for companionship with others. Preparation for interaction with a particular group or organization is called "anticipatory socialization" (Guy 1990: 97). For those preparing to enter the museum profession, the socialization process may be accomplished during formal or on-the-job training, informal orientation, or a combination such as an internship or practicum. For those already in the profession, attention must be given to staying current with institutional and community expectations.

Most, if not all, professions face the clear and constant challenge of balancing personal advantage and group dynamics with genuine concern for public service and the interests of society (Tsanoff 1955). The presence of this hazard to professional action can be addressed in two ways: via education and codification. The former is accomplished by a variety of methods, including professional meetings, professional publications, training programs at all levels, informal interaction, and professional expectations. The latter is a code of professional ethics emanating from the profession and endorsed by the general membership.

A code of ethics is a part of the process of creating and maintaining an ethical institution. However, it is only a part of the equation. An ethical museum is one in which all participants acknowledge the core values and where those values

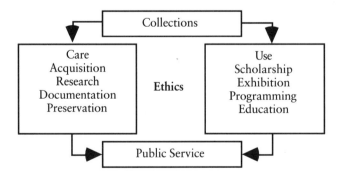

Figure 1.2 The ethical interrelationship of museum activities

are discussed in the context of the museum's mission. A museum's public responsibility revolves around the ethical correctness of museum activities, including both the care and use of collections. Ethical responsibility is evidenced by interaction inside and outside the organization and by the way in which a museum conducts its activities.

There are those within the museum community who believe that ethics is a subject that warrants continued study. They consider ethics to have its own distinctive problems and its own methods for considering and resolving those issues. To the proponents, ethics addresses the fundamental questions of conduct. It asks questions and provides answers. Conversely, there are those who deny that ethics is an appropriate subject for study, not because there are not questions, but because there are no definite answers. For them, because ethics lacks clearly defined answers, it is not a subject worthy of in-depth investigation (Caplan and Callahan 1981).

Ethics is about how people treat one another every day. It is about honesty, accountability, pursuit of excellence, loyalty, integrity, and responsible citizenship (Guy 1990). For the museum profession, ethics also deals with value judgments and the process of decision making. At the risk of making the process of decision making overly simplistic, there are three options possible for every judgment:

1 there is an act or action that a person ought to do,
2 there is an act or action that a person ought not to do, and
3 there are acts or actions that a person may or may not do.

(Fagothey 1972)

The process of decision making applies equally to personal endeavors and to those of others performing the same, or similar, kinds of activities. "This fact, that men [people] do make judgments of right and wrong, is the basic fact of experience from which ethics takes its start" (Fagothey 1972: 3).

The acts or actions a person performs consciously and willingly and for which that person is responsible (accountable) are the province of ethics. The accumulation of those actions within a recognized group may be described as a code of ethics. "A code of ethics should describe a standard of integrity and competence beyond that required by law" (Guy 1990: 19). A code of ethics for museums is a system that details principles of conduct. It should have the general aim of presenting a scheme of action based on the outcome of study rather than a system of speculative goals. Museum ethics defines the principles that underlie practice, so that those working in a particular occupation may better understand and respond to the expectations of the profession.

Laws restrict activities and define methods or means of compliance. They serve as the minimum standards of social behavior. Ethics defines and describes correct actions for persons working in a specialized profession. An institution with a clearly defined code of ethics is less likely to fall into a situation where the correct ethical action becomes a question. A code of ethics aids in defining appropriate actions and serves as a guide for the museum as an institution and to museum personnel as individuals.

DOES PROFESSIONAL EXCELLENCE RELATE TO ETHICS?

A code of ethics may be expected to address two aspects of the museum profession. One is aimed at the internal workings of the museum community and is intended to provide leadership, direction, and a sense of self-worth to those in the field. The other is directed toward those external to the museum community by defining the acceptable conduct and practice (responsibility) of those working in museums. A correctly formulated code of museum ethics must include both elements – a holistic view of the role and responsibility of the museum community.

The first notions of correct or ethical behavior were formulated as duties (Bowne 1892). They related to duties associated with family, friends, community, and jobs. When the museum profession was in its formative stage, workers were assigned duties and responsibilities that were to become the basis for ethical practices. Reflecting that beginning, the first code of ethics adopted by the American Association of Museums was entitled, *Code of Ethics for Museum Workers* (AAM 1925). The canons set forth in that code were founded on practical wisdom and the teachings of experience. However, as the complexities of museums and museum operations advanced, the expectations of ethical practice have become more inclusive. The duties that were accomplished in an acceptable manner for several years no longer met the ethical demands of advancing technology. Many workers learned that the right way to do a particular job was not always the easiest or the most immediately discerned. Instinctive or intuitive behavior gave way to the principles of ethical practice defined and endorsed by the museum profession.

Many ethical issues are of such relevance to the museum community that they are, in one form or another, always present. Although eventually they are incorporated into museological methodology, they need to be rethought by each new generation of museum personnel in consideration of greater technical knowledge and a deeper understanding of the museum as an institution in the service of humankind. Enhanced ethical understanding results in more refined methods of problem solving.

By analyzing the ideas and practices of the museum workforce, a theory of ethics is formed. From that theory, principles of correct conduct can be drawn. In this way, ethics is not deduced from behavior, but formulated to explain it. Logic, reasoning, and speculation do not independently generate ethical judgments but may have a primary role in adjusting that reasoning to meet professional and social needs.

Duty and responsibility are basic to ethical conduct. However, when there is no sense of rational duty there is only a concern for the consequences of acting in a non-dutiful manner. The outcome of such a system of thought is prudence not right judgment. Persons working in museums understand the idea of duty or obligation. In general, the nature of the duty is obvious as it relates to the museum community. Often, due to a failure to emphasize the ideals of duty as defined by a code of ethics, this responsibility degenerates into a system of calculated activities intended to sustain minimum standards. Such a system gives no reasons for conduct but proffers a list of acceptable and unacceptable directives.

Some have argued that ethics is only an expression of positive or negative thinking on a particular subject. However, this idea fails to consider the element of reason and reduces the process of ethical debate to a question of persuasion. In searching for a working arrangement with ethics, one of the methods of evaluating ethical practices is to ask questions and gather answers. By asking questions from different perspectives and accumulating the responses, it is possible to form references based on practice or accepted understanding. This philosophic technique called dialectics, that is, the bringing together of opposing or contradicting ideas and attempting to resolve them through discussion, is associated with the Greek philosopher Socrates (470–399 BC).

In a practical sense, ethics is necessary as a moderating factor between the extremes of intellectual control and impulse. This is not to say that the museum workforce is dominated by either extreme. Direct impulse is ameliorated by reason and *a priori* judgments. The stronger the intellectual influence in the form of conscious purpose, the greater control it exerts over impulse. At the same time, intellectual reasoning may supersede public and fiduciary concerns. Ethics provides guidance for both the impulsive and compulsive.

WHO IS RESPONSIBLE FOR ETHICAL ACTIONS?

Every museum worker is responsible for their decisions and actions within the limits of acceptable museum practice. Almost every decision involves risk. When an object is selected for acquisition, it may be infested, illegal, inappropriate, or a forgery. Preventive conservation is risk-laden as the prevention method may result in greater harm to the object than the problem being addressed. Exhibitions may stimulate or irritate, and in either case there is a risk involved. Every administrative, curatorial, public relations, and fund raising decision includes the possibility of an inappropriate or unacceptable action. The important measure of all decision making is that the seriousness of the risk is never to be out of proportion to the worthiness of the cause or the means of circumvention.

Museum personnel have a duty to consider the ramifications of each decision related to the collections, public, and the profession. Most decisions are made efficiently and accurately as the result of training, education, and experience. Such responses are said to be an inherent part of the profession. It is ethics or an ethical attitude that defines the principles of accepted practice and social responsibility. Training and experience assign those principles to working situations. Ethics also can provide guidance for difficult situations that are unusual, unanticipated, or involve others.

Ethical concerns ought to be common to all areas of the museum. It is naive to assume that ethics is the responsibility of the administration or the board of trustees and not that of the general workforce. Ethical reasoning is a part of every decision, and is fundamental to interaction with others in the museum profession. Problems may arise because individuals have different goals, beliefs, and place greater or lesser value on factors that affect their decision making. This does not mean that a person is unethical simply because they have different beliefs. Rather it points to the importance of a code of ethics to guide decision making at all levels.

IS THERE A PERSONAL OBLIGATION TO A CODE OF PROFESSIONAL ETHICS?

Accepting the obligation to do a particular act or activity implies the ability to complete the act. In contract, some assume that incapacity removes the obligation. This possibility exists. However, the ethical application of this concept does not allow the "incapacity" to mean "unwillingness." That is to say, that the obligation is not removed simply because the person is unwilling to fulfill the obligation (Rescher 1987).

Every act may have some bearing on a person's ethical character, but there is no one specific type of experience that can be described as enhancing or reducing ethical sensitivity and awareness. Of equal importance, every act associated with the museum profession has a related ethical matrix. It is the manner in which daily activities are addressed that defines the integrity and character of the individual and demonstrates the ethical nature of an institution.

Ethical dimensions of a museum worker's professional activities are generating increasing concern. If the principles of professional ethics are to be effective, the thrust cannot be directed toward correcting negative or unacceptable behavior. Instead, the goal must be the further development of professional integrity. A museum code of ethics is important because it serves as a touchstone for guidance and as a reminder of a professional responsibility that exceeds the expedient.

The call for ethics in the museum community did not come from an enraged or demanding public, but from within the profession as a means of establishing standards of "best practices." The aim was not to instruct the profession about the difference between right and wrong but to provide a point of accepted reference to be used when dealing with ethical complexities. The study of ethics and ethical theory assists in defining the museum purpose. A clearer sense of mission allows greater vision to aid in defining and describing future opportunities for the museum community.

WHAT EXACTLY IS A CODE OF PROFESSIONAL ETHICS?

In establishing a code of ethics, it is preferable to develop a set of standards that will have the best possible consequences, that is, provide the best possible guidance and outcome, while causing the minimum of bad consequences.

Ethics is an essential part of museum practice. A code of ethics is not the imposition of external values on the museum community, but a method of understanding the fundamentals of the profession. It is a form of socio/professional responsibility. Given that museums are not abstractions but people working together to achieve a common goal, ethics describes the level of responsibility to be anticipated during that working relationship. Museums often claim to be, and want to be, an essential part of the community in which they exist. To attain that goal requires integrity and a level of mutual trust that must be established based on a code of professional ethics.

It is human nature to make judgments of right and wrong. At times, the decisions are made without reason or consideration. If a person is capable of deciding right and wrong, there must be a reason for making the judgment. The process of careful decision making brings to bear relevant principles of correct action rather than rules that determine outcome. When decisions are arbitrary and inconsistent, they are without principle and indefensible though the results may be acceptable for the particular situation.

The codes of ethics from one hundred top corporations in the United States were collected and analyzed (Guy 1990). They included nine major topics as follows:

1 conflicts of interest,
2 political contributions,
3 relations with customers and suppliers,
4 accurate record keeping,
5 antitrust matters,
6 equal employment,
7 product safety and environmental responsibility,
8 protecting confidential information, and
9 theft by employees.

With only a small amount of manipulation the same topics can be converted for museum use.

There are numerous books written on ethics, and hundreds of organizations have codes of ethics. As already noted, the American Association of Museums published a *Code of Ethics for Museum Workers* in 1925; the document was revised in 1987, and underwent a second revision in 1993/94. Other nations of the world have also developed codes of ethics for museums. New Zealand established a museum code of ethics in 1977. Canada and Israel developed codes in 1979. The Australian code dates from 1982, and the United Kingdom from 1983. The museum association of the German Federal Republic published a translation of the American Association of Museums code in 1984 for the purpose of national discussion. The ICOM *Code of Professional Ethics* was accepted in November 1986 (van Mensch 1989), and since that time, a number of countries have adopted the ICOM *Code of Professional Ethics*, thereby confirming a national and international commitment to professionalism.

In describing ethics, most have looked for complex causes to generate complex results. There is a tendency to compound rather than simplify the cause and effect of ethical conduct. Ethics must be considered as both theoretical and practical. It is theoretical in that it contemplates the truth in acts or actions, and practical as an advocate for correct action.

A code of ethics should be a study guide rather than a prescription for the museum professional. It should stimulate reflection, discussion, and self-assessment by museum workers at all levels. It should address behavioral issues affecting present and future museum workers.

QUESTIONS FOR FURTHER CONSIDERATION

1   Are good ethics good for the museum community?
2   Are most museum workers aware of their ethical responsibility and do they act accordingly?
3   Should museum ethics differ from personal ethics?
4   Is the rhetoric of museum ethics excessive considering the realities of common practice?
5   Should museums provide training on the ethical standards of the individual institution and the museum community?
6   Is there a reason for consistency in ethical practices?
7   Is there a conflict with ethics when museum professionals appraise objects?
8   What ethical principles ought to be valid in all museums in all parts of the world?
9   How do contemporary societies, the museum profession, and museum ethics interact and influence each other?
10 Should institutions and museum personnel be reprimanded for violating established codes of professional ethics?

ETHICAL SITUATION FOR DISCUSSION

Scenario One

Situation

A new curator is hired at your museum who says the rule against dealing commercially in objects related to the collections of the museums is ridiculous.

He says that he can and will collect and sell anything he chooses. He claims his freedom to act is guaranteed by the Bill of Rights and the United States Constitution. He claims that the museum is violating his personal freedom by dictating what he can and cannot do with his own money in his own time.

As a curator in the same museum, you call a meeting of the other curators and ask the new person to present his case. To begin, he reminds everyone that it is a moral obligation to resist rules that you think unjust. He notes that the courts have upheld the right of individuals to protest what they believe to be unjust laws or actions by non-violence. He ends by saying that he is not breaking the law and that he can collect, buy, and sell anything he wishes.

Issues

- What will you say to this individual?
- What ethical principle is involved?
- Are other members of the museum staff allowed or encouraged to collect or deal in objects relating to the collections of the museum?
- Who is to say what is right or wrong in this case?

Comments

> The acquiring, collecting and owning of objects of a kind collected by a museum by a member of the museum profession for a personal collection may not in itself be unethical, and may be regarded as a valuable way of enhancing professional knowledge and judgment. However, serious dangers are implicit when members of the profession collect for themselves privately objects similar to those which they and others collect for their museums.
>
> (ICOM 1990: 33)

> No member of the museum profession should participate in any dealing (buying or selling for profit), in objects similar or related to the objects collected by the employing museum.
>
> (ICOM 1990: 34)

Scenario Two

Situation

Unexpectedly the president of the museum board arrives in your office with her sister. Following a few cordial remarks, the president gets to the point of her visit; her sister has a fine collection of Italian landscape painting from the fifteenth and sixteenth centuries and she wants to exhibit them at the museum.

As director you want to keep the president of the board happy, but this exhibit is totally contrary to the mission of the museum. You mention the mission to the president of the board but apparently she had considered that issue. She suggests it will be a "nice change of pace" for the museum visitors. She feels certain they are tired of seeing the nineteenth- and twentieth-century portraits that are the primary focus of the museum's collection.

The president indicates that her sister might be willing to leave all or some of the paintings on long-term loan to the museum after the exhibit. The loan will depend on whether she decides to sell the paintings. The paintings are currently in a vault but must be removed immediately as the cost of storage is increasing. The president directs you to make arrangements for the exhibit and to "find" room for the paintings to be stored in the museum. She also instructs you to purchase insurance for the collection with museum funds.

Following a few random comments about the weather and how much she enjoys being a part of a progressive museum, the president and her sister leave your office. You are stunned. You are at a loss for what to do, so you take a few minutes to collect your thoughts then you call the exhibits coordinator to rearrange the schedule. You say to yourself, "I happen to like Italian landscape paintings, and she is president of the board."

Concerns

- What are the ethical issues presented in this scenario?
- Which of the two, the president of the board or the director of the museum, is the more unethical in their actions?
- Are there possible legal issues to be considered as well as ethical ones?
- Would this kind of consideration be given to others or only to a person such as the president of the museum board?
- Who is most likely to be held responsible for the inappropriateness of the arrangement?

Comments

A governing body [of a museum] should never require a member of the museum staff to act in a way that could reasonably be judged in conflict with the provisions of this [ICOM] *Code of Ethics*, or any national law or national code of professional ethics.

(ICOM 1990: 26)

Generally, members of the museum profession should refrain from all acts or activities which may be construed as a conflict of interest.

(ICOM 1990: 35)

FURTHER READING

American Association of Museums, *Code of Ethics*, Washington, DC: AAM, 1994.

Brink, David, *Moral Realism and the Foundations of Ethics*, Cambridge: Cambridge University Press, 1989.

International Council of Museums, *Statutes*, Paris: ICOM, 1989.

International Council of Museums, *Code of Professional Ethics* (revised), Paris: ICOM, 1990.

Patterson, Charles, *Moral Standards: An Introduction to Ethics*, New York: The Ronald Press Company, 1949, chapter 3.

Pojman, Louis, *Ethics: Discovering Right and Wrong*, Belmont, CA: Wadsworth Publishing Company, 1990, chapter 2.

Rachels, James, *The Elements of Moral Philosophy*, New York: McGraw-Hill, Inc., 1993, chapter 2.

Taylor, Paul, *Principles of Ethics: An Introduction*, Belmont, CA: Dickenson Publishing Company, Inc., 1975, chapter 2.

Tsanoff, Radoslav, *Ethics* (revised edn), New York: Harper & Brothers, 1955, chapters 1, 2, 3, and 14.

Van Wyk, Robert, *Introduction to Ethics*, New York: St Martin's Press, 1990, chapter 2.

Wheelwright, Philip, *A Critical Introduction to Ethics* (3rd edn), The Odyssey Press, Inc., 1959, chapters 1 and 2.

2

Ethics and the profession

WHAT IS A PROFESSION?

> *A profession consists of a limited group of persons who have acquired some special skill and are therefore able to perform that function in society better than the average person. Or we may say that a profession is a calling in which its members profess to have acquired special knowledge, by training or by experience or by both, so that they may guide or advise or serve others in that special field.*
>
> (Titus 1947: 296)

Professional standing includes a number of responsibilities that must be embraced by all those working in the museum field. All museum personnel, regardless of their status (that is, paid or unpaid staff), have a responsibility to support and perpetuate a standard of quality and service.

The characteristics of a profession, according to McDowell (1955), are:

1 extensive and on-going training,
2 specialized expertise,
3 membership requirements,
4 professional organization,
5 professional schools or training programs,
6 professional journals,
7 code of ethics,
8 self-regulation,
9 relatively high social status, and
10 social recognition as a profession.

DOES THE MUSEUM PROFESSION HAVE AN ETHICAL FOUNDATION?

A primary question for museum professionals is whether those in the profession require special norms and ethics to guide their well-intended conduct. This is a critical question for museum professionals and for those attempting to evaluate their conduct. Any number of decisions are made within the museum community based on the ethical or unethical nature of the activity being considered. Too often the lay person views this attitude as an attempt to elevate museum ethics above normal ethical requirements for the purpose of protecting special interests. At the same time, the lay community expects the museum staff to be honest and accurate in the information presented, trustworthy with donations, protective of the objects held for future generations, and generous with the services provided. The attitudinal variance may be described as "role differentiation" based on the accepted standards of the museum profession.

The premise of role differentiation is that certain jobs (roles) require certain actions as a part of normal practice. The professional has a duty to elevate particular practices, those that are central to the museum profession, to a level of consideration in situations where "normal" ethical perceptions might not prevail. This responsibility explains the special care in handling objects and the inappropriateness of personal collecting by curators.

In anticipation of evolving requirements of the profession, work-related groups within the museum community have developed codes of ethics to formalize standards of conduct. In the United States of America curators, registrars, conservators, museum shop workers, and public relations personnel have developed relevant codes of ethics to provide guidance to persons in or entering the workforce. In the world museum community, similar discipline-based codes are being generated to guide persons with specialized areas of interest.

Ethical issues are those issues that raise normative questions about a number of concerns, including the correctness of an action or the rights and welfare of a person. Normative questions are questions of value. As an example: "Is it ethically correct to deaccession an important painting to fix the hole in the museum roof?" Other kinds of questions are called descriptive. They ask factual questions such as: "Did the museum decide to deaccession the important painting to fix the hole in the roof?" Even though this distinction seems obvious, in the museum profession it is important. Many issues require making value judgments rather than factual decisions.

"In all the world and in all of life there is nothing more important to determine than what is right" (Lewis 1955: xx). Most people want to know what is right for them both as individuals and as members of a group, organization, or profession. To reinforce that understanding, a correctly formulated code of museum ethics supports an attitude of right action and stimulates unification of the thought process related to ethical ideas and actions. Once a basic level of understanding has been achieved, the final goal is an enlightened perception that extends beyond the immediate to the evolving ethical requirements of the museum profession. As professionals, museum workers must be concerned with not only what museums are at a given moment, but what they can be and ought to be.

> The museum professional should understand two guiding principles;
> first, that museums are the object of a public trust whose value to the

community is in direct proportion to the quality of service rendered; and, secondly, that intellectual ability and professional knowledge are not, in themselves, sufficient, but must be inspired by a high standard of ethical conduct.

(ICOM 1990: 30)

To understand better the significance of codes of ethics, attention should be given to related theories and issues, and to a review of their applications to museums or museum work. Ethical theories can help define and clarify the principles involved in an ethical dilemma. However, they can rarely explain what to do. Ethical theories help focus on the principles involved in the decision making process rather than the conclusions. They support the reasoning (that is, the thinking process) that precedes the act rather than the outcome of an action.

A code of ethics is not a catalog of theories that have no practical application. Good ethical judgment is the result of carefully evaluated practice and conscientious review of professional and public responsibilities. Museum ethics must grow out of the profession, be a guide to professional practices, and infuse both the practice and the profession with an overarching concern for responsibility. Strict obedience to past practices without attention to the changing mission of museums is likely to result in a misunderstanding and a misapplication of current ethical concepts. Ethical canons change because new knowledge gives greater insight into practice and technique, as well as the evolving recognition of a more responsible and responsive museum community.

Figure 2.1 Museum ethics: a blend of professional practices and professional and public responsibility

The term "professional ethics" has several meanings. Three that have relevance are as follows:

1 the norms actually followed by most museum professionals,
2 the norms required by the ethical point of view for the work museum professionals do, and
3 the elements of codes of professional museum associations.

It is the combination of these three manifestations of professional ethics that fosters an equanimity among pretensions, practices, and the expectations of society (Kultgen 1988).

WHAT ARE ETHICAL PRACTICES?

Aristotle reportedly asked the question: "What are we doing when we do ethics? And what is the significance of the fact that, in raising and reflecting on ethical questions, we are doing something?" (Aristotle 1985: 1095 a–6). When Aristotle defined the academic discipline called ethics as the pursuit of practical knowledge, he insisted: "that one does ethics properly, adequately, reasonably, if and only if one is questioning and reflecting in order to be able to act – that is in order to conduct one's life rightly, reasonably, in the fullest sense 'well'" (Aristotle 1985: 1095 a–6).

The notion of a universal truth in ethics may be a myth as many believe. Most will say that the customs of different societies create different concepts of "good" or "correct" actions. Some have said that the "right" way is the way of the ancestors, the social practices that have been transferred from generation to generation. Others may agree there are differences between cultures but question the degree of difference. All groups of people have accepted practices. The normal human being places value on following the accepted practices of the group and expects others to act in the same way. It is the motivation to follow and reinforce those acceptable practices that generates ethical canons. Once a standard has been promulgated, the group may determine that something is wrong with an individual who does not follow the approved pattern.

Care must be taken not to evaluate the ethical attitudes of a society by the actions of a group of people within that society. All societies include people who act in a way that can be described as unethical. However, most normal people have a relatively high degree of self-respect and place a value on the composite universe in which they live. All societies are a patchwork of values, practices, and beliefs. In addition to the historically imposed customs, social attitudes are modified by the physical circumstances in which the inhabitants live. Most people would agree that a primary motivating force is survival. An equal number of people may disagree about what constitutes surviving. Some may believe that surviving means a certain level of comfort, security, and social interaction. Others may include fulfillment of their religious belief as a requirement of survival. Another people may be satisfied to be alive. All place a primary value on life but differ in what they believe constitutes living.

To expand on this line of thought, a person on the verge of starvation may steal food and consider himself or herself to be completely honest and principled. A second person may steal because they want greater wealth. That person has no problem with the fact that stealing is against the laws of the land and contrary to traditional values. Neither situation alters the value – the principle of honesty. However, both situations circumvent the value system by superimposing belief (or necessity). "Any number of factors can make the apparent differences between cultures appear to be greater than they are" (Kultgen 1988: 25).

DOES ETHICS PROVIDE ANSWERS?

Too often, inquiries about ethics or ethical action are presented in such general terms that one answer is not possible. Consequently, it may be assumed that no answer exists, or worse, that no answer is necessary. Other ethical concerns are relatively easy to address. The question of doing x or y is usually not difficult to resolve. A number of criteria can be applied to determine the appropriate action, including legal and regulatory directives. Problems arise when two or more ethics come into conflict when analyzing an issue, or when there are no "safe" ethical or legal guidelines on which to rely. Each of the conflicting ethics may have the appearance of equal validity yet they may seem to contradict one another. Instead of right and wrong, the question may be which right is the most correct in this situation? Or, which ethics should take precedence over the other?

For example, consider a circumstance where the registrar at museum ABC is contacted by a museum colleague from museum XYZ to inquire about an artifact in the ABC museum's collection. The inquiring museum worker is researching an object for exhibit and needs specific information related to the artifact in the ABC museum. The registrar wants to assist a colleague, but the donor of the artifact has requested that no information about the object be made available to persons outside the museum. The registrar explains the donor restriction and denies the request. The person from museum XYZ advises the registrar that the ICOM *Code of Professional Ethics*, Section 8, paragraph 8.2. "Professional Co-operation," supports the request for information in that it states, "[professionals are expected] to render their professional services to others efficiently and at a high standard" (ICOM 1990: 34). The registrar con-sults the same document and relies on Section 6, paragraph 6.1. "Acquisition to Museum Collection" which includes the statement, "Negotiations concerning the acquisition of museum items from members of the general public must be conducted with scrupulous fairness to the seller or donor" (1990: 31). The registrar feels justified in refusing the request from XYZ due to a concern for fairness in dealing with the donor and a responsibility to the ABC museum.

> Loyalty to colleagues and to the employing museum is an important professional responsibility, but the ultimate loyalty must be to fundamental ethical principles and to the profession as a whole.
>
> (ICOM 1990: 31)

Obviously this is an excessively simplistic example of an ethical conflict, as the outcome must reflect a commitment of the museum and its employees to the donor's request. In this way, allegiance to the employing institution becomes a factor in the decision making process. A more complex and restrictive ethical conflict can arise when the issue involves opposing ideals drawn from different professional codes. This circumstance may manifest itself in a case of privileged information being shared among lawyers, bankers, or doctors serving on a museum board of trustees. Extreme examples of ethical conflict may jeopardize a person's professional standing.

Figure 2.2 Ethics in conflict

DO PERSONAL AND PROFESSIONAL ETHICS CONFLICT?

One of the major ethical issues facing most individuals is the relationship of personal and professional ethics. Should the individual pursue the most desirable personal outcome or abide by the inclusive ethics of the museum profession? The ICOM *Code of Professional Ethics* addresses the issue of conflict of interest: "privileged information received because of his or her position [museum staff *et al.*] . . . should a conflict of interest develop between the needs of the individual and the museum, those of the museum will prevail" (ICOM 1990: 28). As already noted, the straightforward situation is easy to resolve. Under normal circumstances, professional ethics always supersedes personal beliefs, priorities, or preferences. It is the conflict of seemingly equal principles that creates the dilemma.

Imagine a museum where each curator assumed himself or herself to be in direct competition with every other curator. Collections are gathered in secret to avoid allowing others to know exactly what is being acquired. Accession records are kept in a personal code to prevent anyone other than the collection curator from knowing provenance, description, location, and research significance. Supplies and support materials are hoarded to keep others from using them. None of the collection is exhibited and no research is published to prevent others from knowing the exact nature and research value of the objects. Field notes are maintained as the personal property of the curator and no one is allowed access to the collection. Everyone is viewed as an "enemy."

This kind of situation may be less invasive when there are adequate funds, space, and personnel to accommodate non-communal behavior, but when support is scarce, the secretive attitude is reinforced as each person focuses on acquiring the tokens of power. Success is often measured by the accumulation of material. A museum experiencing these conditions is without order or ethics. Each member of the staff has established his or her own set of rules nullifying the interconnected nature of the museological system.

The problems outlined in the above example are due not to the nonexistence of ethical standards or to a disrespect for ethical practice, but because ethical practices are not directed or defined in a manner to meet the requirements of the museum profession. While this seems an understatement, the attitudes demonstrated by the museum personnel in the scenario are not unlike those thought to be acceptable in other social or commercial activities, that is, accumulation of material wealth. It is when considering those attitudes in relation to the public orientation of museums that they seem unethical and unacceptable. This situation appears to reinforce the concept that a unified code of acceptable (ethical) practices is not only advisable but necessary.

Ethics is described as the theory of right conduct. "Openness and ethics go together" (Guy 1990: 37). While unethical actions often will not withstand scrutiny, the act of being open does not in itself improve the quality of ethical decision making. However, the willingness to work in an open system is the beginning of promoting ethical decision making. Failure to follow ethical standards causes a loss of trust between museum workers and between the museum and the public.

The question may be asked, "Does the museum have the ethical right to impose upon the employee's personal ethics?" The answer has to be "yes" and "no." It depends on the situation and the imposition. Can the museum administration in some way impose upon the individual to perform an activity that is legally or ethically (morally) wrong? No, but assume you are in a position, as a member of a museum staff, to know privileged information about a special object. Suppose someone asks you a direct question about that object and if they have the information, it will be harmful to the museum. Because your personal ethics requires you always to speak the truth, you divulge the privileged information and it compromises the museum. This is a situation when professional ethics must supersede personal ethics.

As a further example of personal and professional ethical interaction, it is appropriate to consider social history. In developing societies, order was regulated by the imposition of one person's will on another – the fear of retaliation. If a person does something unacceptable, not to the society, but to an individual, the retaliation was often swift and at times fatal. As societies organized, the obligation of maintaining order was transferred to public authority. The change was the result of social unity. This transformation can be applied to a professional organization. During the development stage, individual action may result in individual reaction. With the organization of the profession and the establishment of a code of ethical behavior, the role of supervision is transferred to the professional authority. The change is the result of professional unity.

IS ETHICS PRACTICAL?

If the concern about ethics is only an abstract philosophy, it will make no practical difference what answers are found or if no answers are found. The information gained through the study of ethics is practical information. It is a means of focusing on the "correct" working foundation of museology. Aristotle (384–322 BC) notes in speaking of ethics, "the outcome is action, not knowledge" (Aristotle 1985: 1095 a–6). This may be interpreted to mean that although ethics is based on careful and thoughtful analysis, the outcome has a practical application.

It is possible that the definition of "ethics" will aid in the understanding of the ideas, theories, and applications of the principles involved.

> eth•ic noun.
> 1 A principle of right or good conduct.
> 2 A system of moral principles or values.
> 3 ethics (used with a singular verb). The study of the general nature of morals and of the specific moral choices to be made by the individual in his relationship with others.
> 4 ethics. The rules or standards governing the conduct of the members of a profession.
>
> (American Heritage 1991)

The definition appears to be clear, but ethics as a concept is a somewhat vague assemblage of emotional terms such as personal values, limits on activities, and the inner being of a person. In many books about ethics there is a free exchange between the word "ethics" and "morality." The two words, although confused by common use, are valid terms referring to ideals of character and conduct. Morals come from the Latin *moralis* < *mos*, custom; while ethics comes from the Greek word *ethike* < *ethikos*, ethical < *ethos*, character (World Heritage 1991).

Some describe ethics as moral philosophy and use the words interchangeably. Morals can be described as the act of being concerned with the principles of right and wrong in relation to human action. It is morally correct to act in certain ways. Morals relate more to custom and actual practice while ethics refers more to the examination of those practices. It is normal for people to equate ethics and morality. Morals is the broader term that includes any form of voluntary human activity where judgment is involved. Morality includes a range of personal and social conduct. Morals are normally outside the sphere of the law, but may serve as the basis for certain society-regulating rules. It is common also to draw a parallel between morality and religion. Most will claim that right action is the result of "being brought up right." One of the reasons for the link between religion and ethics is the thought that religion provides a reason for doing the "right thing." This idea extended to the concept that those doing the right thing will be rewarded in the afterlife. However, "being brought up right" does not cover all issues.

Too often it is assumed that ethics is about what not to do. This attitude is attached to the morality concept. Morality or moral conduct continues to have a religious connotation. The one-line commandment such as "Do not steal," is typical of the idea of a moral standard. While this idea of not stealing is both a valid and an ethical concern, a code of ethics goes beyond mandated restrictions. Morality is linked to religious belief and recognizes a "greater being" empowered to reward or punish the practitioner for right or wrong acts. Ethics, particularly in the applied form, requires response from the establishing forum (that is, a group, organization, or institution) for validation, alteration, or enforcement.

Most religions provide guidelines for the methods of proper behavior. However, in general these instructions are concerned with morals as they relate to inter-action with humans, inter-social or religious activities. There may also be a conflict between reason (philosophical ethics) and faith (moral theology), and a number of other philosophical viewpoints.

It is possible to describe the difference between morals and ethics as defining what a person is and what a person does. A person may or may not be moral in mind and thought, and may or may not act ethically. A seemingly moral person may act in a way determined to be unethical by a field of applied ethics. There are specialized ethics formulated to address concerns in medicine, law, business, politics, and many other fields, as well as the museum. Persons from these fields establish codes of ethics to aid their members in dealing with complex issues that involve both "right" action and comprehension of the field of specialization.

IS THERE A DIFFERENCE BETWEEN RIGHTNESS AND RIGHTEOUSNESS?

The ethics/morality misapplication related to "rightness" as opposed to "righteousness." The Greek word *dikaiosyne* meaning "justice," is roughly synonymous with righteousness rather than *dike* translated as "right." This confusion has caused great difficulty for the museum community. The quest for the ethically correct action focuses on rightness, while the idea of moral correctness is compounded by righteousness. No matter how morally correct an act may appear to the righteous individual, if it is ethically wrong according to the practices of the profession, then it is still wrong.

An example of this kind of attitude might be embodied by a curator who for moral reasons is opposed to violence and war. The collection for which the curator is responsible includes several Second World War uniforms and, in keeping with the curator's beliefs, the uniforms are removed from the collection. The uniforms are appropriate to the mission of the museum and their removal leaves an obvious void in the collection. The curator justifies the action by claiming that the uniforms represented the horrors of modern warfare and that they would have a negative influence on the youth of the community were they to be exhibited.

While this example may seem extreme, consider not exhibiting, researching, conserving, or protecting objects because they are not morally correct according to the curator's righteous appraisal. Compound the situation by considering that the individual involved in the moral decision making may be anyone from a trustee to a member of the museum security staff.

Again, this situation calls to attention the interconnectedness of things (personnel, objects, research, activities, exhibits, and programs) within the unified whole of museums. It emphasizes the importance of a documented means for maintaining a network of mutual cooperation and understanding within the museological system.

IS IT A LEGAL OR ETHICAL ISSUE?

The ideals of ethics are sometimes interchanged with the law. This relationship is at times confusing to untangle. Laws establish and define a process for maintaining a minimum level of public order. They are a system of rules that set the lowest acceptable standards for the citizenry of a land. They provide a framework for societal interaction that defines the limits of acceptability to avoid civil or criminal liability. Laws are not intended to make people good – only bearable within the limits of a particular social system.

"Many laws are instituted in order to promote well-being and resolve conflicts of interest and/or issues of social harmony." Laws are designed to create or cause a tolerable social situation, "but ethics may judge that some laws are immoral without denying that they are valid laws" (Pojman 1990: 3). There are some aspects of acceptable social behavior that are not covered by law (for example, even though it is generally agreed that lying is usually wrong, there is no law against it). Laws are often based on ethical issues that have evolved from personal concerns to social or civil requirements. On the negative side, the law is sometimes the last resort for those confronted by unethical acts. The defense will inevitably begin with the statement, "But it is not against the law!"

The laws of a group, organization, or society often establish quantitative limits of an ethical concept whereas ethics extends the qualitative limits of the law.

Other ideas associated with ethical thinking are the beliefs and customs of the social environment in which a person exists. In every society, people react according to the examples given to them by their history and the characteristics of their social order. This is true for the economic, social, political, and cultural life of a people. The established patterns of societal behavior can have a subtle or profound impact on the different levels of human existence. When tradition alters ethical behavior relative to time and place, the process is described as ethical relativism.

WHO IS RESPONSIBLE FOR CORRECT ETHICAL BEHAVIOR?

The world of museum people is divided into several strata of ethical comprehension. There are those who have no idea of ethical responsibility and are so ill-informed as to find this void of little concern. Others are conscious of the issue of ethical standards but prefer to disregard ethics as a qualifying element of their existence (usually for personal profit motives). Still others are knowledgeable about ethical behavior but intentionally maneuver around the restrictions of social or professional ethics. There are also those persons who know and respect ethical correctness as a way of life. They attempt to conduct themselves in a manner reflective of their understanding of ethics. Finally, there are those who study ethics and attempt to add to the foundation of ethical practice as it relates not only to professional life but to everyday existence. Between these segments, there are many sub-sets of museum workers interwoven to form this simplified gradation of ethical consciousness. One may or may not be better than the other as ethics may or may not be a factor in their lives or work.

Ethical relativism is based on the assumption that there are no universally valid ethics, rather that ethics is valid relative to some other factor. Relativism contends that different ethical standards apply to different people, societies, cultures, nations, and times. This attitude is opposite to universality or absolutism, which claim there are universal standards and that those standards are absolute, that is, always valid. Unfortunately, those societies that believe their ethical and moral standards are intrinsically right tend to impose them on others.

To apply this thinking to the museum community, the ethical relativist would contend that faced with the same ethical situation a museum worker would probably act differently based on their orientations, values, and experiences. In this situation the relative condition is based on the professional rather than social environment. The point can be made that the degree of difference in the response will depend on the ethics in question and the individual.

One of the confusing issues encountered when considering museum ethics is the commingling of general ethical values and professionally oriented values. Some ethical concepts seem appropriate for everyone and are a part of "common practice." These include the following:

1   a level of honesty,
2   a consciousness of human dignity,
3   a recognition of personal property,
4   a sense of right and wrong, and
5   an awareness of social order.

While not every person in every society endorses these practices equally, there is a consensus that attitudes such as these are requisites for a "civilized" society. When these conditions exist, they are far less obvious than when they do not. These attributes are considered to be a part of a person's "personal integrity," and while they are common to most people, they are more rigidly applicable within the museum profession.

In addition, there are levels of ethical practice that apply only to those within the museum community. (The word "community" is used to include those persons under the supervision of museum professionals, such as volunteers, para-professionals, trustees, and other museum-associated non-professionals.) However, imposition of professional ethics on persons outside the museum profession or removed from professional supervision becomes very difficult and fundamentally inappropriate in most, but not all, situations. There are exceptions, and they are as follows:

1 Board members, trustees, and volunteers ought not to use information gained from within the museum community for

- personal financial profit, or
- self-dealing in any form.

2 Information acquired while working in the museum ought to remain confidential. Information of this kind includes but is not limited to the following:

- donor information,
- object values,
- archaeological site locations,
- acquisition plans,
- deaccessioning plans,
- security arrangements,
- loan agreements, and
- investment plans.

In different parts of the world, museum personnel face ethical problems with common features. They address those problems in different ways by endorsing different ideals. However, within the differences are broad similarities, and out of these responses common principles emerge. The ethical agreements are as significant as the differences giving support to parity as well as commonality of purpose.

ARE ALL MUSEUM ACTIVITIES GOVERNED BY ETHICAL STANDARDS?

It is often the practice in museums to separate functions and responsibilities. Collecting is viewed as being different from exhibiting or programming. Public relations (marketing), is considered as a totally different activity to fund raising (development) or conservation. In the daily activities of museums, the unity (interdependence) of activities is often overlooked. For practical purposes, different duties are assigned to different members of the museum staff. In this way unity is lost or at best diluted. Difficulty arises when the parts are treated in different ways. The interconnection of all parts of the museum should be exemplified by commonality of purpose. The logic of interconnectedness validates the equal application of ethical standards to all parts of the museum. A further extrapolation of this theory will extend across the world community of museums. An ethically correct action or reaction in one location should be equally correct (assuming the circumstances are the same) in other locations.

If groups A and B in the same museum endorse the same ethical standards, and B group follows the same code of ethics as C group in another museum, then groups A and C must support the same ideas and ideals.

If the supposition of this equation is accurate, then it is conceivable that all museums can endorse one set of ethical standards.

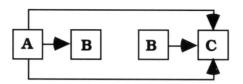

Figure 2.3 Relationship of ethical endorsements

Museum ethics can be described as "professio-centric" in that the ethical issues are profession-wide – they cross social and political boundaries to form a professionally oriented relativism. There are ethical concepts that are universally acceptable to those subscribing to the museum profession. Ethical principles apply to all persons working in a (relatively) similar situation.

The fact that ethics takes a universal point of view does not mean that a particular ethical judgment must be universally applicable. The universality of any idea supposes application greater than personal. In this way an ethical judgment must give equal consideration to all those in a similar situation. Personal interest must be supplanted by the good of many. For example: A curator may have a favorite object in the collection for which he or she is responsible. Because of this special regard for the object, the curator may decide to remove it from the collection and take it for personal use. This act would be described as unethical because it places self-interest before the interest of others by denying access to the particular object.

While the nature of the act may change, the ethical judgment will not change, and from that perspective the application is universal. Words such as "public trust" and "fiduciary" apply to the idea of "service to the many." Ethics is about the choices through which human good is achieved, not instantaneously, but over the long run, and not just for individuals, but for communities and for the whole society (Lovin 1992).

IS RIGHT ALWAYS RIGHT?

The working premise of ethics is to establish principles of right behavior to serve as action guides for individuals and groups. To be defensible on ethical grounds, an action must address an idea larger than the individual. Once a person begins to think in terms of greater self-worth through less self-service, an ethical foundation of universal proportion has been established. The result can be described as good or right in the truest meaning of the words. Self-service is seldom ethically justifiable.

In trying to determine good or right, as an ethical concept, the question must be asked, with whose good or with what good are museological duties concerned? There is a concept of goodness (correctness/rightness) based on traditional standards and customs, and there is a more inclusive concept of what is truly right. This attitude may be defined as just, impartial, and fair – equitable. It aids in understanding the distinction between those issues that are ethical and those that are legal.

It is important to consider whether the rightness or wrongness of an action is or can be determined by the goodness or badness (wrongness) of its outcome. There are those who maintain that the rightness of an action is determined by its conformity to accepted social standards. It is easy to determine correct or right action when dealing with life-threatening situations, as most people have a clearly established concept of life and death. Fortunately, few ethical issues in the museum deal with such extreme situations. However, the answers to some very practical problems relate to the questions of ethical theory.

At times an action that appears to be wrong may be justifiable. The choice does not make the action right, just less wrong than the alternative. This idea is exemplified by some conservation decisions that alter an object for the sake of preservation/conservation. An issue that is very real for many countries is related to the acquisition of objects taken from historic sites by "pot hunters." In most countries there is a ready market for historical material recovered by individuals from public lands. The ICOM *Code of Professional Ethics* (1990: 27) is very clear about museums acquiring by purchase any object unless the governing body is satisfied that a valid title can be obtained. However, if the museum does not acquire the objects, they are sold on the open market and are often transported out of the country of origin.

It is incorrect, by museum standards, for the objects to be removed from the historic site, but the persons doing the pilfering are not obliged to consider museum ethics. It is ethically wrong to support the illicit marketing of illegally acquired objects. It is also wrong for the objects to be sold on the open market and removed, probably forever, from the country of origin. At times, museums

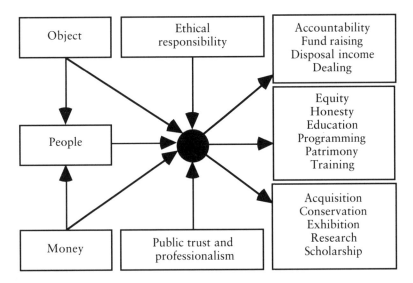

Figure 2.4 Museum practices and ethics

decide to purchase the objects believing that to be the lesser of the wrongs and the one that preserves the objects for future generations.

The ethical issues associated with acquisition of cultural property are complex. The "rescue argument" (Messenger 1989: 3) that gives valid claim to persons rescuing objects from possible destruction or loss has two sides if applied equitably. Assuming a museum rescues a valued example of cultural property to prevent it from being sold on the open market, then it is equally possible for any person to rescue objects for any seemingly valid reason. The ethical issues relate not only to right or wrong, but to values and utility as well (Messenger 1989: 4).

WHY IS THERE NOT A LIST OF RULES TO BE USED AS ETHICAL PRINCIPLES?

A common concern with the study of ethics is that it seems to propose answers without stating the questions. This idea is reinforced by the practice of using situations or anecdotes to demonstrate ethical canons rather than direct application of principles to practice. Ethics is concerned with values – not just what is, but what ought to be. Ethical theories explain how things ought to be and provide justification for actions by explaining the principles involved.

One of the strategies of analyzing ethics is the case study method. Although discussion is a time-tested means for formulating ethical thought, the case study approach evolved through the law system. The "case law" concept is attributed to Christopher Columbus Langdell, dean of the Harvard law school in 1870 (Beauchamp 1989). With the case study methodology came the "casebook" composed of legal cases selected, edited, and arranged to reveal the terms, rules, and principles of law. The theory was that training in the case method sharpened skills of legal reasoning – in both analysis and synthesis. When the case method decreased in popularity during the first part of this century, it left an established method for teaching the nature of principles. This premise and method have been applied to both business and ethics.

A primary disadvantage of the case method of information sharing is the unavailability of a single answer to the dilemma being discussed. Many students of ethics are more interested in the rules that govern professional activities than in the principles of correct action. Although having knowledge about the major ethical theories is a part of the learning process, it is reasoning and logical discussion that impart the nature of ethics.

Immanuel Kant assigned the foundations of morality to the human capacity to make rational choices. He noted that impulse is subjective and private, but ethical principles are objective and applicable to everyone.

Most museum workers endorse the need for a code of ethics within the museum field that will establish basic standards of conduct and values for decision making by which they can act and be evaluated. Also endorsed is the belief that ethical action must be more than applied logic or common sense – it must be founded on acquired knowledge, established museum practices, and a recognition of museological responsibility. Furthermore, a code of professional ethics must address a broad agenda that will allow for growth and change.

Undoubtedly there are differing ethical concerns within specific elements of the museum staff. However, there is a set of relatively similar museological needs and expectations common to all museum personnel. To meet that need, it is appropriate to recognize and endorse the overlying ethical principles that guide the thinking process whether consciously or subconsciously and to formulate a holistic code of ethics.

QUESTIONS FOR FURTHER CONSIDERATION

1   Does the museum community have an ethical responsibility to provide training for staff relating to museum ethics?
2   Are museum personnel responsible for their own professional growth?
3   Should the museum staff be involved in explaining the expectations of museum ethics to members of the board of trustees?
4   Should museum staff members take an interest in the professional development of those with whom they work?
5   Should museum staff be expected to adjust to the changing requirements of the museum community?
6   Is active participation in museum-related professional organizations a means of gaining valuable information for evaluating ethical practices?
7   Is there an ethical responsibility for all persons working in or with a museum to abide by the same code of ethics?
8   When the law allows actions that are contrary to museum ethics, how is it possible to convince people to comply with the ethics?
9   Should every museum worker take an active role on promoting museum professionalism?
10   Should museums and museum workers be reprimanded for violating ethical standards?

ETHICAL SITUATION FOR DISCUSSION

Situation

Assume you are employed by a museum. On a particular day you enter into discussion with the curator of history who mentions that she is interested in old radios. She notes that because of her position and the fact that the museum has several old model radios in the history collection, she does not collect radios but enjoys repairing them. As your discussion develops, you remember that you have an old radio that once belonged to your grandfather. It does not work but because of the sentimental value you have kept it for many years. You mention the radio to the curator who, as a friend and colleague, says why not let her take a look at it and maybe she can make it play.

A few days later you bring the radio to the museum in the box in which it has been stored for years. During your lunch hour, the curator of history happens by your office and you tell her you have the radio and would she mind taking a look at it. Based on a quick inspection, the history curator says that not only can the radio be fixed, but that it will be an easy repair job taking only a few minutes. However, she says that she has no time right then and would prefer to take the radio to her office where she can work on it later. You agree to the suggestion and are very pleased with the idea that the old radio will actually produce sound.

The next day the curator of history returns with the radio under her arm. She pronounces it is repaired and asks you to plug it into the electrical outlet. Immediately you have music and you are delighted. You say thanks and offer to pay but the curator say no thanks, it was fun, and besides what are friends for.

That night as you leave your office you pick up the radio and realize that the box you brought it in is not there but it does not matter as the radio will not go back into storage. It can now be placed in an important location for all to see. So you put the newly repaired, brown plastic radio with its big gold dial under your arm and stride happily out of the museum.

Concerns

- Have you ever found yourself in a position like either of these curators?
- What should "The person who does the right thing" do in this case?
- Is this an ethical issue or a legal one?
- Are you benefiting personally from this transaction that occurred in the museum, even though it did not happen during regular work hours?
- Can this activity be considered to be in the best interest of the museum?
- Might there be a perception of impropriety?

Comments

Ethics is about correct conduct and actual or perceived misconduct. Often the appearance of wrong-doing is as damaging as the act itself. An uninformed observer might view the removal of a "vintage" radio as the use of museum (public) property for personal purposes. Reason recommends against the appearance of wrong-doing.

Unless authorized by the museum governing body, use of museum facilities, equipment, and/or materials ought to be limited to museum or profession-related activities and should not be, or give the appearance of being, for personal purposes.

Loyalty to colleagues and to the employing museum is an important professional responsibility, but the ultimate loyalty must be to fundamental ethical principles and to the profession as a whole.

(ICOM 1990: 31)

FURTHER READING

Callahan, Joan (ed.), *Ethical Issues in Professional Life*, Oxford: Oxford University Press, 1988, chapters 1 and 2.

Finnis, John, *Fundamentals of Ethics*, Washington DC: Georgetown University Press, 1983, chapter 1.

Garnett, A. Campbell, *Ethics: A Critical Introduction*, New York: The Ronald Press Company, 1960, chapter 4.

Goldman, Alan H., *The Moral Foundations of Professional Ethics*, Totowa, NJ: Rowman and Littlefield, 1980.

Guy, Mary, *Ethical Decision Making in Everyday Work Situations*, New York and London: Quorum Books, 1990.

International Council of Museums, *Code of Professional Ethics* (revised), Paris: ICOM, 1990.

Kultgen, John, *Ethics and Professionalism*, Philadelphia: University of Pennsylvania Press, 1988, chapter 10.

MacIntyre, Alasdair, *A Short History of Ethics*, New York: Macmillan, 1966.

McDowell, Banks, *Ethical Conduct and the Professional's Dilemma*, New York and London: Quorum Books, 1991, chapters 1, 2, 3, 8, 10, and 12.

Messenger, Phyllis (ed.), *The Ethics of Collecting Cultural Property*, Albuquerque, NM: University of New Mexico Press, 1989.

Mount, Eric, Jr., *Professional Ethics in Context*, Louisville, KY: Westminster/John Knox Press, 1990, chapters 1–3.

Taylor, Paul, *Principles of Ethics*, Belmont, CA: Dickenson, 1975, chapters 1, 2, 4, and 5.

Wheelwright, Philip, *A Critical Introduction to Ethics*, New York: The Odyssey Press, Inc., 1959, chapters 1 and 2.

3

Ethics and museums

Ethical responsibility is personal responsibility. A group cannot act ethically until its members, as individuals, choose to do so. When individuals act ethically, together they produce a group action that is ethical.

(Guy 1990: 155)

Human beings exist not merely as individuals, but as members of a greater organism that assumes some level of control and responsibility for those within its boundaries. This organism may be called by many names: community, society, state, or nation. The word "nation" often implies a unique, self-contained entity normally based on political union. There is also an inference of linguistic and racial commonality. In reality, most nations are composed of several nationalities using numerous languages. While the word "community" also has a number of ambiguities, there is no suggestion of racial or linguistic sameness.

Human activities can be divided into two categories: individual and social (Bowne 1892). As the society forms laws, rules, and conditions of co-existence, the individual is normally subordinate to these regulations for proper conduct. Persons in an organized community entrust that entity with authority greater than that of the individual members. This collaborative organism may be called the museum community and to function it must have some form of underlying structure. Ideals and ethics are the base for that structure and the means for recognizing the highest common good.

DOES MUSEUM ETHICS ALSO SERVE THE PUBLIC?

If the museum community determines the rights of its profession with reference to the greater social order, then it is equally appropriate to determine the rights of society in reference to the museum profession – *quid pro quo*. Ethics is a basic part of the equation, and a code of ethics is a means of communicating those rights and expectations.

Museums and their activities are an important part of global socio-cultural activities, and they will have greater prominence in the future. Museums can

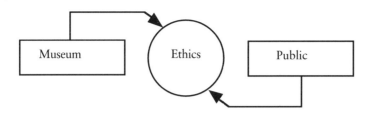

Figure 3.1 Museum ethics and the public

have an impact on both humankind and the ecosystem in positive ways. The means by which this challenge is met will depend on the ethical attitudes and practices of all museum personnel. Each member of the museum community has an opportunity to participate in establishing museum standards to serve as the base for the museum profession.

People working in museums have positions and titles. They may be registrars, curators, security personnel, collection managers, educators, administrators, trustees, or volunteers. With each position there are associated duties and privileges. People occupying these positions are expected to do certain jobs. When each person does their job efficiently and correctly, the institution is able to make the system function properly. Cooperation is based on knowledge of the system, that is, knowing what is expected of each person, and that each is participating with the same level of professionalism. To assist in this process, the museum has a mission statement, code of ethics, collections policy, and operating procedures. These documents help employees in knowing the expectations of the system and their role in the institution.

Chaos exists when there are no rules to resolve conflicts of interest. To avoid chaos, order and organization are necessary. An integral part of every professional organization is a code of ethics.

IS DECISION MAKING AN ETHICAL CONCERN?

"Responsibilities tend to be broad . . . obligations . . . tend to be narrow and clearly defined" (Lewis 1991: 23). In positions of responsibility it is impossible not to make decisions. For museum employees, many decisions involve an ethical issue. Acquisition of objects, the care of collections, exhibitions, censorship, interaction with colleagues, personal collecting, deaccessioning, loans, and many other everyday activities of the museum staff relate directly to ethical standards. In fact, the basic concept of museums is one of public trust, and upholding that trust is an ethical concern, as well as, in some cases, a legal responsibility.

There is no way to avoid making judgments. However, rational decision making is based on the assumption that others from the profession, faced with the same situation, would make the same choice (decision). As rational decisions reflect accepted practice, they normally uphold established ethical standards. This is to assume that rational decision making is the opposite of impulse actions that are subjective and personal in nature (Sommers 1986).

An important part of rational action is imagining alternative actions, not just reviewing the current conditions (Mount 1990). People tend to have a "first action" that is impulsive – a reaction, followed by a more thoughtful assessment. The time of the second part of the response is often after the fact and described as "hindsight." In analyzing a situation ethically, it is necessary to go beyond the impulsive response and to view the events from different perspectives. Often the first analysis is a validation of the anticipated rather than the actual.

The idea of systematic investigation is a part of the process of ethical conduct. It is both a responsibility and an obligation of those endorsing a code of professional ethics. Such calculated conduct ought to apply to actions in more significant relationships, that is the museum profession, being considered from the standpoint of ethics.

DO OTHER PROFESSIONAL GROUPS HAVE CODES OF ETHICS?

In the first half of the twentieth century, more than three hundred businesses and professional groups in the United States adopted codes of ethics (Titus 1947). That number continues to increase owing, in part, to a growing ethical consciousness. The increasing number of organizations with codes of ethics makes it clear that professional ethics cannot be ignored. This point demonstrates the need for a basic understanding of ethical theory to serve as a guide in dealing with the issues that arise. It is also apparent that codes must be constantly scrutinized in anticipation of change. Ethical standards should be adjusted to achieve more adequately the objectives of the profession.

The term "museum profession" is used to signify a group of people who, because of their special training, are qualified to perform a particular type of work or service with greater skill than the average person (Patterson 1949). Besides the required academic and technical training, an additional factor is a part of the professional equation. That component is service. The museum professional should be more concerned about promoting public service (social welfare) than personal economic gains. The acceptance of the service motive as distinct from the profit motive is characteristic of the museum profession.

> A museum is a non-profit making, permanent institution in the service of society and of its development, and open to the public which acquires, conserves, researches, communicates and exhibits, for the purposes of study, education and enjoyment, material evidence of people and their environment.
>
> (ICOM 1990: 3)

To maintain a high degree of efficiency in museum work where technical skill and knowledge of current programmatic and research advancements are an imperative, continuous study is required. For this reason, it is preferable to exclude from the museum profession those persons who do not demonstrate a commitment to the ideals of service or who disregard the established code of ethics. Professional standards are maintained only when it is possible for those outside the profession to distinguish between those who are competent to perform the necessary work and those who are not. This separation is also important from the standpoint of legal as well as fiduciary responsibility. In some cases, the ethical expectations of the profession are reinforced by legal enactment. An example of this supplementation relates to self-dealing. If a museum worker gains personal benefit through knowledge acquired as a member of the museum staff or by arranging to obtain objects from a particular source, legal action may be taken. The ideals of public commitment and public trust are paramount.

Every profession has its own particular problems or concerns regarding the conduct of its members. The code of ethics is used to define the "primary group" relationship. As the group becomes larger or the distances between persons in the profession increases, there is a need for more formal rules of conduct. The museum profession can be described as a "secondary group," in that the relationship of the members is based on commonality of purpose. The contact is specific in purpose and formal, rather than personal and informal as is often the case in the primary group.

WHY STUDY MUSEUM ETHICS?

There are at least two reasons for studying museum ethics. The first relates to the profession in that ethical practice is dictated by those who are peers in the museum community. The ethical practices museum workers are asked to support and maintain are from the profession. Those who wish to be a part of the museum profession are expected to accept the established ethical code and conform to its standards. Museums and museum workers normally endorse the ethics of the profession, though they may wish to do otherwise, and they usually conduct their business according to the accepted standards. Because the profession is constantly changing, there is a continuing need for review and re-evaluation of ethical practices. The review process does not imply the profession has been wrong in the past, rather that change, more information, and improved practices may alter previously accepted principles.

The second reason to study museum ethics is the need to understand and expand accepted museum practices. The more informed and better educated the museum workforce, the greater their potential as contributors to the museum community. Knowledge stimulates critical thinking, and thoughtful reflection often leads to conclusions and applications different from those of the general museum community. Better understanding of ethical issues will also give the individual a basis for self-judgment and professional self-respect. Without an advanced level of understanding, the traditions of the past provide the only ethical guidelines.

> A knowledge of ethical theory has enormous practical benefits. It can free us from prejudice and dogmatism. It sets forth comprehensive systems from which to orient our individual judgments. It carves up the moral landscape so that we can sort out the issues to think more clearly and confidently about problems. It helps us clarify in our minds just how our principles and values relate to one another, and, most of all, it gives us some guidance in how we should live.
>
> (Pojman 1990: x)

The idea of "ethics" is often associated with the notion of right and wrong. When applied to personal actions in a life situation, that association may be acceptable. When directed toward a group of people – a profession – then the assumptions of application become more difficult to fix and endorse. Most professions establish "norms" by which adherents to that profession are expected to act or perform their associated duties. A norm then becomes a rule that prescribes what is to be done or what is to be avoided (Banner 1968). In the case of the museum profession, ethics establishes the standard for acts or actions that are acceptable, that is, good or correct within museological boundaries.

Museums are about objects and all the ramifications associated with objects – they are also about people. Museum ethics is about how people and objects are treated.

Ethics may be considered a branch of philosophy that deals with how humankind ought to live or act and that it is concerned with the idea of the Good (with a capital "G") or with the concepts of right and wrong. On the basis of this idea, ethics should be important to each person regardless of his or her profession or occupation.

One of the difficulties encountered in considering ethics is its philosophical base, and philosophy is thought to be esoteric. The Greeks pursued the love of knowledge and wisdom, and placed intellectual achievement on the highest level of earthly accomplishment. In the Eastern world, mystics emphasized the nature of human existence and philosophical oneness as a basic condition of being and personal interaction with the universe. Both professed a view of awareness that was held to be intellectual and experiential.

Philosophy is defined as meaning:

> 1. the love of wisdom or knowledge. 2. a study of the processes governing thought and conduct; theory and investigation of the principles or laws that regulate the universe and underlie all knowledge and reality; included in the study are aesthetics, ethics, logic, metaphysics, etc. 3. the general principles or laws of a field of knowledge, activity, etc., as, the philosophy of economics. 4. (a) a particular system of principles for the conduct of life; (b) a treatise covering such a system. 5) a study of human morals, character, and behavior.
>
> (McKechnie 1977: 1347)

As the demands on the museum community increase and the available resources become less abundant, the need for ethical guidance increases. In the way of giving guidance, ethics defines answers. Ethics offers directions for conduct as demonstrated by the following examples from the ICOM *Code of Professional Ethics*: "The museum should take every opportunity to develop its role as an educational resource used by all sections of the population or specialized group that the museum is intended to serve" (1990: 26). "Museums should assume a position of leadership in the effort to halt the continuing degradation of the world's natural history, archaeological, ethnographic, historic, and artistic resources" (ICOM 1990: 28).

IS ETHICAL THEORY IMPORTANT FOR UNDERSTANDING ETHICS?

Usually, it is not the practical aspect of ethics that is studied but the theoretical that is given attention. As a theory is a general body of assumptions, practicality is not a primary outcome. Ethical theorists generally focus on establishing the status of ethics by analyzing the personal decision making processes. This theorization is founded on the idea that diverse principles can be combined or defined to become one inclusive principle of ethical judgment.

The belief in the universality of ethics has a number of detractors. Some contend there are no common ethical concerns that cross political boundaries and cultural affiliations: that one nation or group of people has a different ethical foundation than another proves little. There are also many other differences between one people and another. In some cultures the people believe that scholars should do no manual labor or that taking a photograph of someone steals their soul. Based on this thinking, it is not presumed that manual labor is unimportant or that photographs are dangerous to a person's health. Instead, it is assumed that some cultures are less well informed or less concerned about such matters than others.

Because some group practices are relative to a particular culture, there is no reason to believe that all must be. It is equally illogical to presume that all persons within a particular culture will act or respond in the same way. By fostering the ideals of ethical practices for museum workers, it is possible to motivate others to endorse the same beliefs. By providing information about ethical issues that relate to the museum community, it may be assumed that the general knowledge base will be increased and that related practice will follow. The process of developing a code of ethics has no ends or means (value), if the process does not ultimately result in good for those in the profession.

WHY DOES THE MUSEUM PROFESSION NEED A CODE OF ETHICS?

For a profession to have a code of ethics, it is necessary for there to be certain ethical conditions that are common to all persons subscribing to that profession.

There are two very basic and logical reasons for having a code of ethics. The first is immediate and described as the pursuit phase of the ethics process. This is the step of defining ethical standards and assigning them to the activities of the museum. The second is the ultimate phase that defines the outcome or results of the code. This phase is the application of an established code to the everyday practices of the museum. Each step is important.

It is also possible to describe the establishment of a code of ethics as having three parts:

1   to recognize the ethical objective,
2   to describe the ethical objective, and
3   to achieve the ethical objective.

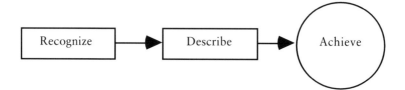

Figure 3.2   Establishing a code of ethics

The idea of ethical recognition is a relatively simple one. There are some things that are right (good) and some that are wrong (bad). Rational action must have some end or objective beyond itself. Assuming there is no logic for irrational actions, especially if an irrational act is negative or pointless, such acts must be considered unethical and counterproductive. Following this idea, a rational action must lie in some good or correctness. Those laws or rules that are irrational or selectively applied are either ignored, altered, or expunged. Laws, rules, duties, and actions that are rational and good warrant equal application. It is through equitable application that rational actions gain authority. Ethics is realized in the same way.

The study of ethics is of paramount importance. It is of more importance to the museum community at the end of the twentieth century than at any previous time. "Ethics has a distinct action-guiding, or so-called normative, aspect, and, as such, belongs to the group of practical institutions that includes religion, law, and etiquette" (Pojman 1990: 3). The social role of ethics or perhaps ethical deviation for the sake of social acceptability manifests itself in many ways. Acceptable and unacceptable social acts vary dramatically as defined by culture.

It is a fact that ethical concepts change as social life changes (MacIntyre 1966). In this way the concepts and measures of ethical right and wrong are a moving point of the social horizon. Consequently, it is impossible to separate ethical ideas and social life. "One key way in which we may identify one form of social life as distinct from another is by identifying differences in moral concepts" (MacIntyre 1966: 1).

There are few universal statements that apply to every person in every society. There are several universal statements that apply to most adults in most cultures. In all cultures/societies, there is a presumption of honesty/truth. Communication is a form of truth verification. Honesty/truth establishes a level of trust and without trust, communication is impossible. As there is a critical period for first language acquisition, there may very likely be a corresponding time for developing the concept of truth.

This is not to say that people do not lie. Lying is a social imposed or allowed condition, but without the assumption of honest use of words, the ability of people to function in a verbal-oriented social environment would not be possible. Information exchange between two or more persons is based on the trust that the words being used are the correct (right) ones to express the ideas appropriate to the situation. Without that trust, the belief that certain words will be understood to mean a certain circumstance, need, or wish, there is no reason to communicate. Once basic trust has been established, information exchange is possible and a base for other truths is instituted. Some may argue that there are numerous examples of dishonesty perpetuated by the word of world leaders. However, it is the results that are at times false and not the communication (words). Were the words not understood, a message, true or false, could not be transmitted.

There are many matters that are described in terms of an objective right and wrong – most are little more than social conventions or beliefs. Knowledge, technology, economic progress, or political stability (order) are not automatic generators of ethical progress. Normally these factors create conflicts with existent ethical standards because traditional ideas are not adequately inclusive to address the new conditions. "[T]he difficulties and disagreements . . . are mainly due to a very simple cause: namely to the attempt to answer questions, without first discovering precisely *what* question it is which you desire to answer" (Moore 1902: vii).

Completing form A before form B is not an ethical issue in itself. The sequences of duties are normally described by institutional procedures. However, completing the forms accurately and honestly, keeping the related information confidential, and carefully accessing the object for conservation or other special care requirements, should fall within the standards defined by an institutional code of ethics.

"Not all attempts to state clearly the basic and general standards for acting and judging are ethical theory" (McInerney and Rainbolt 1994: 5). It is not the purpose of a code of ethics to compile a list of facts and to give directions for their compliance; nor does a code of ethics give personal advice or instructions (Moore 1902). Ethics defines conduct relating to standards of acceptability within a society. In the case of museum ethics, that society is the museum community.

As an example of the impact of change, the political acknowledgment of national patrimony, the reassessment of cultural colonialism, and the recognition of international accountability caused a need for an ethical statement on museum activities relating to illicit trafficking in cultural or natural objects. This situation is basic to ethical practices in that a code of ethics recognizes the existing situation and describes what ought to be. Without this "reason" there is no logic of ethical formulation or alteration.

IS ETHICS A FORM OF "COMMON SENSE?"

Most people believe their judgment to be "right." They believe what they are taught to believe, that is, their thinking is the expression of the cultural tradition from which they come. However, if all people make correct (right) judgments and the decisions are self-serving, then conflict arises. Indiscriminate acts based on emotional reactions cause a clash of one set of expectations or standards with another. To maintain social order, laws serve as guides to acceptable practice and establish a baseline against which society can judge its members. Compliance with the laws of the community should not be dependent on monetary, social, or intellectual standing. In many ways the same must be said of ethical practices, if these activities are merely an extension of the social environment.

Two additional factors must exist for effective ethical application:

1 documentation of acceptable ethical practices as they relate to the institution, organization, or group and
2 self-analysis and mutual criticism.

Compliance with an established code of ethics has minimum validity unless based on self-analysis and the shared responsibility of review and criticism from within the institution, organization, or group. It is this process that allows and supports reformulation of ethical conduct based on the needs of those involved in the associated activities.

"Groups and organizations tend to formulate and alter ethical practices based on what has been described as the utility principle" (Garnett 1960: 58). Pursuing that attitude, ethical norms are established that the particular group believes will have a favorable impact on its membership and those with whom they interact. This attitude of utility is balanced with the trust factor that places the good of the whole above the wishes of the individual. Trust is an abstract concept that is often confused with legality. Acts that are legally correct may not engender trust. Appearance, attitude, and accountability are parts of the trust factor with the initiating concern the anticipated consequence for others.

Ethics is a part of many daily activities. Most people describe their actions as the "right thing to do" under predetermined conditions. As a simple example, it is normal practice to treat another person fairly as long as they do the same. The idea of the reciprocal arrangement is thought to be "playing fair." As long as the prevailing social and economic conditions remain stable, the ethical reaction is unchanged. This response is normally spontaneous as an expression of mutual understanding. The same is true within the museum environment. Mutual respect, cooperation, and honesty are normal attitudes of professional interaction.

IS ETHICAL UNIVERSALISM POSSIBLE FOR THE MUSEUM PROFESSION?

Although the museum ethics tradition in various parts of the world differs in many details, the view of ethical responsibility is essentially the same. It is a view that is based on service and commitment – on an intellectual experience of reality – and an understanding that this experience has several basic characteristics that are independent of the museum's geographical, historical, and/or cultural background. A museum person in Ecuador and Nigeria may stress different aspects of ethics and a person in China may interpret his or her ethical responsibility in terms that are different from those used in the Netherlands, but the basic elements of the code of ethics used in all these locations are the same.

The system called ethical universalism forwards the idea that ethical right and wrong is basically the same for all people. The theory allows that people may think differently about right and wrong acts or actions, but it submits that when a person does a wrong act when a right act is the accepted norm, then that person is mistaken (Holmes 1992).

In contrast to universalism, relativism, as already stated, concludes that ethical right and wrong may vary from person to person or from group to group. The issue between the two theories is not about correct ethical judgment but about the influences on the decision making process. Specifically, universalism holds that correct basic standards are the same for all people. This concept allows a universal code of ethics for all museums and museum workers. Relativism maintains that not all ethical judgments are consistent but may vary according to individual or cultural conditions or circumstances. Following the relativism idea, a universal code of ethics for museums and museum workers is impossible.

Universalism and relativism are theories of ethical behavior. They are not about correct ethical judgment but rather the ideas behind those actions. Each has a positive and negative side. Assuming relativism is the accepted pattern of ethical judgment, then no nation, people, institution, or individual is more correct than any other. Any people or person can point to another people or person and find some custom or practice to be wrong by the accepted standards they profess. However, there would be no objective standard or measure by which they could prove their practices to be superior. According to this thinking, each person can do as they please about almost anything as no one can prove their method or practice is superior. No common practice is possible – except in theory.

Universalism contends that ethical right and wrong are fundamentally the same for all people, and that all respect the same basic truths. However, problems arise in attempting to validate this theory. If universalism is the true method for accessing ethical judgment, then in theory there can be universal standards by which one people or nation can be shown to be superior to another.

In reality it would appear that either relativism or universalism could serve as a platform for imposing one set of ethical standards on another. As the concept of relativism does not preclude disapproval of practices by one people of another, then there is no reason to assume that social pressure will not cause eventual intervention. Universalism declares commonality of right and wrong but offers no model for standardizing the judgmental process. This allows for the imposition of one standard on all persons, regardless of cultural or personal preference.

This is another case where the notion of morality adds complexity to the issue, as morals reflect religious beliefs. However, it may be said that all religions are fundamentally the same. That is, they are founded on the belief of a greater power that resides outside humanity. It is the manifestations of religion that vary, causing diverse thinking about morality. Moral issues aside, it is relatively

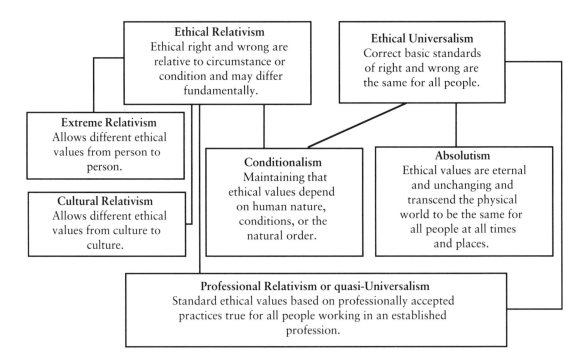

Figure 3.3 The relationship of ethical relativism and ethical universalism

simple to defend or condemn any number of basic ethical assumptions following either relativist or universalist thinking. However, assuming the issues being considered are professionally oriented, as within the museum profession, the thinking is far less complicated.

Applying the relativism theory to a practical situation may give some insight. If each member of the museum staff decided to acquire, accession, catalog, and house objects according to a personal standard, there would be no order to the museum's collections. By extension, if there is no viable provenance, there is no usable collection and consequently no valid museum. This dilemma can be resolved by assuming there is a professional relativism or a quasi-universalism based on professional practices. This concept may be described as objectivism in that it advocates that right and wrong are determined by standards external to the person judging. The established practices of the museum profession ought to determine the right and wrong for all people working in museums based on certain common truths.

An ethical theory supporting this approach is contextualism. This idea "contends that you simply cannot know what is actually right much of the time, so you must make the best judgments you can from a perspective of limited knowledge and understanding" (Holmes 1992: 221).

HOW DOES MUSEUM ETHICS WORK IN DAILY ACTIVITIES?

It is commonly recognized that museum ethics applies only to those within the museum profession/community, including those persons participating in museum-related activities. The individual collector, connoisseur, or for-profit gallery owner are not bound by the ethical practices of the museum profession. If so, museum ethics obviously does not and cannot exist apart from the museum profession (or those persons committed to perpetuating the highest standards of practice within the museum community). Further, if the museum profession leads to the recognition of ethical standards that approve or disapprove the same actions, then that ethical practice is universalistic though it is conditional to human nature and situation.

Among every people in every part of the world there are some things that are not done. In most lands, stealing and lying are acts ethical people do not do, no matter what the circumstance or the consequence. It is possible to discuss which actions are odious to which society, but generally speaking, doing the "right" thing is a strong motivation for most people. The difficulty arises when the correct action is unclear or undefined. In many instances, the actions of people are regulated by laws, but laws are based on facts. If a certain act or action is done, a predictable result occurs (X = Y). When a driver ignores a red light and enters the intersection, that act endangers the life and property of others entering the same intersection, assuming they have the right of way (green light). The law, at least in this example, seems relatively clear and easy to understand. If a person does X, then Y will result. Society has determined that Y is an unacceptable situation, therefore there are laws to restrict the doing of X. If a person continues to act contrary to laws, regulatory action is taken by society.

The contemporary museum community tends to be benevolent toward those within the profession who act unethically owing to ignorance. Errors in decision making, inappropriate actions, and questionable conduct may result first in constructive criticism and eventually in avoidance. A prime example of this kind of reaction relates to loans. A museum staff known to be careless with loan objects will often find itself in a position where they are unable to arrange loans. Other institutions are unwilling to expose their collections to the careless or irresponsible handling. Most museums expect a certain standard of care and, when that level is not achieved, a responsive attitude is evoked.

WHAT DOES ETHICAL AWARENESS MEAN TO THE MUSEUM COMMUNITY?

Social change has had an impact on moral attitudes and caused a change in ethical behavior. Multi-cultural acceptance has manifested itself as a part of the new ethical orientation of museums. Concern for right action, right representation, and equal and fair treatment for all has altered the thinking, planning, programming, and orientation of many museums. The changes manifest themselves in many ways, but one of the most important is the change in museum community attitude in formulating a more clearly defined code of professional ethics.

Obviously, multi-cultural acceptance is not a new way of thinking. However, it is finding greater acceptance across a broader range of the world's population. Perhaps what is more important, it is the prescribed socially accepted order of the time. This thinking has had a direct impact on the museum community.

"Social changes have not only made certain types of conduct, once socially accepted, problematic, but have also rendered problematic the concepts which have defined the moral framework of an earlier world" (MacIntyre 1966: 5). Times change and social evolution is a fact. To draw a parallel with the museum community, a reference can be made to the different emphases of each of the American Association of Museums codes of ethics of 1925, 1978, and 1993/94. Each had a different focus to meet the needs of the incumbent museum workforce. The early code addressed the individual; the later code gave greater attention to the object; and the latest code formulates principles of social responsibility.

With no code of ethics to guide the activities of a museum, a good person may be a poor employee. With guidance from a well-formulated code of professional ethics, a good person and a good employee can be one and the same.

Almost all explanations of ethical rightness or wrongness vary enormously. Each situation is likely to invoke the intellectual concepts of justice, freedom, equality, rights, duties, and obligations, or the principle of maximizing benefits. There are compelling, often very personal considerations, like fairness and equal opportunity. There may even be a conflict between the principles of democracy and meritocracy. There is the question of when should benefits be available to everyone and when should ability, potential, and achievement influence the distribution of benefits and opportunities. These issues manifest themselves in museum exhibits, education programs, and special events. They may deal with language, accessibility, educational level, cost of admission, or something as simple as the type size for labels.

There are also practical matters that may involve rules and how they are applied and interpreted. The obvious museum application of this principle is in dealing with donors or board members. How much contribution has to be made to allow an exception to the rules? When does a museum allow special privileges to one person or group of persons that is not available to everyone? Concerns of this kind can be addressed by having a carefully considered code of ethics.

HOW DOES MUSEUM ETHICS ADDRESS PERSONAL BIAS?

The biases of the museum workers may involve numerous ethical considerations. As an example, the curator, educator, exhibits manager, or director may select the theme of an exhibit, the material to be exhibited, and the interpretation of the material. At issue is the fact-value problem: can the curator or exhibits designer separate the "facts" of a particular exhibit from the value-laden perspectives that are inherent in individual assumptions or preference?

"The museum should seek to ensure that information in displays and exhibitions is honest and objective and does not perpetuate myths or stereotypes" (ICOM 1990: 26). Unfortunately, for interpretation, programming, education, and a number of other museological activities, the problem of assumptions, bias, stereotypes, and myths becomes more critical when these are commonly held. These attitudes are taken for granted and become the unconscious basis for decision making. As ethics is about choice, the process of decision making is not always easy, since choosing is not an objective process but a matter of point of view.

"What is the relationship between facts and values and between descriptive statements and prescriptive judgments?" (Pojman 1990: 137). For example: The photograph in an exhibit is of two people standing under a tree (descriptive statement). They represent a typical couple from the western region of the country at the beginning of the last century (prescriptive judgment). The fact statements attest to a truth that is validated by the images in the photograph. The value judgment is an assessment or appraisal of the images based on assumption or personal belief. Granted that belief may be influenced by education but the statements do not verify that foundation. The two parts of the interpretation do not reinforce each other, that is, they are not mutually validating.

Accumulated facts may support or contradict personal assumptions owing to differences that reside in interpretation of information more than in the information itself. A means for evaluating facts, ideas, and different opinions is the process of ethical reflection (Brown 1990). This method of review or assessment involves discussion beginning with the accumulation of viewpoints and analysis of their similarities and differences. In this way a number of shared values can be determined and a basis for decision making established.

QUESTIONS FOR FURTHER CONSIDERATION

1 Should museum workers respect the public their museum serves?
2 Should museum workers place commitment to their museum before that of personal activities, family, friends, other employment opportunities, or the public?
3 Should each museum employee feel his or her work is worthwhile or important to the overall achievements of their museum?
4 Should museum employment be considered a "job" or a professional commitment?
5 Is it ethically important for museum workers to meet deadlines and target dates in completing their assigned tasks?
6 Should every museum worker seek ways to enhance the public service element of their museum?
7 Is it ethically correct for a museum worker's commitment to professional standards and ethics to be limited to a basic endorsement of general principles?
8 Should the ethical practices of each museum worker contribute to the public service element of his or her museum?
9 Can the ethical actions of a museum worker positively influence those persons with whom they work or does excessive attention to good ethical practices alienate others?
10 Does the rhetoric of museum ethics exceed the reality of ethical practices in most museums?

ETHICAL SITUATIONS FOR DISCUSSION

Scenario One

Situation

A recently graduated museology student accepted a museum position knowing the ethics policy of the institution was contrary to his personal convictions. As a member of the museum's staff, he was required to endorse the ethics policy of the institution. However, from the first day of his employment, he criticized the museum for its attitudes about certain issues. When he was asked why he took the job knowing he did not agree with the ethics policy, he said it was because the job paid better than working at other museums.

Concerns

- Was it ethical for him to take the job?
- Should he try to change the ethics policies of the museum to agree with his personal convictions?
- Is loyalty to the hiring institution a part of the ethical equation?

Comments

> Loyalty to colleagues and to the employing museum is an important professional responsibility, but the ultimate loyalty must be to fundamental ethical principles and to the profession as a whole.
>
> (ICOM 1990: 31)

> members of the profession may properly object to proposals or practices which may have a damaging effect on a museum or museums, or the profession.
>
> (ICOM 1990: 34)

The right of all members of the museum profession must be balanced against their responsibilities. However, in all cases personal preference, opinion, or desire should not supersede professional standards.

Scenario Two

Situation

One day the curator of anthropology in a large museum happens into the ethnology storage area when the ethnology collection manager has gone. On a shelf behind the holding table is a particularly striking piece of pottery. The design is simple, monochromatic, geometric, and very pleasing. It reminds the curator of the Casas Grande material in the anthropology collection and particularly of two pieces that are to be included in a forthcoming paper.

Without thinking about it too much, except a quick rationale that the pot is not being studied or exhibited at the moment, the curator moves the piece to his office. The curator tells himself that he will inform the curator of ethnology of his interest in the piece and ask that he be allowed to study it for a few days. However, the curator gets busy and forgets to mention the pot to anyone.

Two or three weeks later as the curator is working on the Casas Grande paper, he realizes the pot from the ethnology collection does not really relate to the research. The curator reminds himself that he must remember to tell the ethnology curator that he has the piece. In the meantime and unknown to him, the ethnology curator is working on a paper about the same piece of ceramics. In fact, the design is the center of her investigation. She has determined that the simple monochrome pattern is very special and warrants further study. To gain additional information she has sent 500 letters to institutions and individuals describing the design and asking for information about similar pieces of pottery. As the calls and correspondence begin to come in about similar designs, there are several questions about the exact nature of the surface of the pot and the angle/slant and curve of the design. Of course, this information is very important to the curator and she wants to have the pot where she can refer to it immediately.

The curator of ethnology goes to the collection storage area to get the piece and finds it gone from its assigned location. She questions the people working in the collection but no one knows where the pot has been placed. A careful search of the collection reveals nothing. The clay vessel is missing. In the meantime the deadline for submission of the research paper is drawing near. The curator must have the pot to finish her paper. A thorough search of the collection is initiated but there is no sign that the pot has been relocated or removed for any reason. It is simply gone.

At last the deadline for the paper passes and the curator of ethnology misses an important opportunity to present her research. It will be at least a year before the chance comes again and because she was unable to deliver the paper according to her commitment, that organization may not invite her to present again. This would be a great professional loss.

A few weeks later, the curator of ethnology happens to visit the curator of anthropology's office. There on the shelf is the missing pot. The curator of ethnology cannot believe her eyes. Why is the pot here, she demands to know? Why was it removed from the storage area? What right did the curator of anthropology have to remove something from someone else's collection area and why, if it was so important to his research, did he not inform someone he had taken the pot?

The curator of anthropology explains his actions by saying he did not know that the pot was a part of the curator of ethnology's research. If he had known, he would not have borrowed the pot. As far as he knew, no one was using the clay piece for ongoing research. He reasons that, after all, it was not as if someone had actually taken the artifact. He just borrowed it for a while and forgot to return it. If the curator of ethnology wants to take it now, she is welcome to do so. He says he is sorry for any confusion.

Concerns

- Is there an ethical issue in this scenario or is it a question of following rules and procedures?

- If you put yourself in the place of the curator of ethnology, what would you say to the curator of anthropology?
- Is this a discretionary situation that reflects questionable decision making?
- Is there a greater good involved in the issues or is the concern related to self-achievement, social indifference, and egoism?
- How might the situation have been avoided?

Comments

This situation can be considered from the perspective of consistency. If the arbitrary removal of material from an assigned area is acceptable practice for one person, then it must be considered acceptable for all persons. If this is allowed, then the basic notion of collection control, inventory, cannot be accomplished with any level of dependability.

> Relationships between members of the museum profession should always be courteous, both in public and in private.
>
> (ICOM 1990: 34)

FURTHER READING

Brown, Marvin T., *Working Ethics*, San Francisco and Oxford: Jossey-Bass Publications, 1990, chapters 1, 2, 3, and 11.

Caplan, Albert and Callahan, Daniel, *Ethics in Hard Times*, New York and London: Plenum Press, 1981, chapters 1 and 5.

Goldman, Alan H., *The Moral Foundations of Professional Ethics*, Totowa, NJ: Rowman and Littlefield, 1980, chapter 5.

Guy, Mary E., *Ethical Decision Making in Everyday Work Situations*, New York and London: Quorum Books, 1990, chapters 1, 2, 4, 5, and 7.

Rosenthal, David and Shehadi Fadlou (eds), *Applied Ethics and Ethical Theory*, Salt Lake City: University of Utah Press, 1988, chapters 1 and 4.

Tsanoff, Radoslav, *Ethics* (revised edn), New York: Harper & Brothers, 1955, chapter 5.

van Mensch, Peter, *Professionalising the Muses: the Museum Profession in Motion*, Amsterdam: AHA Books, 1989, chapter 7.

4

Ethics and duty

*The dilemma is inescapable: either we act in every case as we happen,
at the moment of choosing, to like . . . or else we can in some cases
guide our choice of action by appealing to a principle.*

(Wheelwright 1959: 91)

WHAT IS THE RELATIONSHIP OF ETHICS AND DUTY?

In most codes of ethics, the obligation (duty) to perform or omit certain acts is
made quite clear and is indicated by implication in the rest (McDowell 1991).
There are certain duties that most persons in the museum profession understand
and accomplish on a regular basis. These duties may be divided into three levels
or categories. They are:

1 **General duties**: activities performed daily such as accessioning in an
approved manner, housing collections in an acceptable and safe method, and
interacting with colleagues and the public.
2 **Special duties**: activities performed occasionally that involve protection of
objects, personal integrity, or professional standards beyond those associated
with the daily activities of the workplace.
3 **Extraordinary duties**: activities that are critical to the well-being or safety of
objects, visitors, institution, or profession.

Acts or actions are normally guided by two elements: one that objectively states
the necessary actions that ought to happen (duty), and the second that motivates
the subjective decision making process (conscious). The first process makes the
action a duty, and the second makes the duty into a motive (Gowans 1987).
Some claim that a duty must be fulfilled according to the rules regardless of the
consequences. Others believe that duty must be tempered by the resident conditions at the time the action is performed. The difficulty arises when determining
when and how to administer subjective reasoning.

The relationship of duty and ethics is clear. When a person acts without thought
of the eventual impact of that act, there is no sense of duty or responsibility. If,

instead, the decision to act is guided by a principle concerned with what ought to be done in a given situation, then that person has a sense of duty or responsibility. This sense of duty defines the right, honorable, or correct action to be taken regardless of impulse or personal inclination. "People who do right merely because it pleases them are not yet intrinsically moral [ethical]. For had it pleased them they would have done wrong" (Sommers 1986: 8).

IS A CODE OF ETHICS A TOOL TO MAKE PEOPLE DO THEIR JOBS?

The idea of duty is most often associated with law or honor. The relationship between duty and law is obvious. If there is a law, there is a duty to observe it. The duty to observe the law is based on the knowledge that failure to do so can result in some form of regulatory action. However, ethics binds without the imposition of external force. Ethics provides the standards by which individuals can evaluate their own conduct and the conduct of others. It serves as the base for rational decision making and assignation of duty.

It is not uncommon for museum staff, trustees, and volunteers to view ethics as a challenge to their personal integrity. They know themselves to be honest and hard-working. They do their work because it is their duty and because they enjoy it, not because of a code of ethics. Most are conscientious workers laboring under the belief that museum work is an honorable and meaningful vocation and that it is populated by honest and ethical people. Doing right or wrong is viewed as a personal decision, not one that is dictated by some externally imposed document. There are those that believe the need for a viable code of ethics is because people have lost confidence in the ability of others to know right and wrong. They believe that this condition is the result of a disintegration of traditional values and complicated by the extremes of a contemporary society. Others realize that an ethical foundation guides and protects the museum worker, the visitor, and the collections.

Intellectual investigation often is assigned to two areas of study. One area deals with practical matters – where things come from, how they are made, and how they interact. The study of these problems seeks to organize or classify things according to their distinctive and essential properties. It is called "science" and it attempts to formulate general laws that define and describe the relationship of things. The second area of study deals with the pursuit of wisdom. It is the study of ideas. The name applied to this activity is "philosophy." Many of the concerns associated with philosophy lack the clarity of those found in the scientific world. Absolute determinations are seldom a part of this area of study. However, a basic understanding of ethical theory will aid in formulating and perpetuating a practice of ethical behavior.

IS THERE AN ETHICAL THEORY THAT ADDRESSES THE ISSUE OF DUTY?

"Traditionally, two major types of ethical systems have dominated the field: one in which the locus of value is the act or kinds of acts, the other in which the locus of value is the outcome or result of the act"(Pojman 1990: 73). The first of these two systems is called deontological or "duty" based and the second is teleological or "end" or "goal" based.

According to the teleological theory, a teleologist is a person whose ethical decision making focuses on maximizing non-moral responses such as pleasure, happiness, welfare, and the amelioration of suffering. When these actions are "right," they increase happiness and diminish misery. They have the opposite effect when "wrong."

It is normal to want to do the right thing. The difficulty in achieving this goal is knowing what makes a right act right. How does a person know right from wrong or vice versa? To function within the museum community, it is not possible to carry a guide of "rights" and "wrongs" that can be consulted every time a question arises. Basic rules can be formulated and written to guide certain repetitive acts or actions. For instance, "Be at work at 08.00 in the morning," is a rule of the institution, not an ethical issue. It is a pre-established guide to the beginning of the work day and defines a part of the normal work responsibility. A rule of this kind is not abstract. There is no right or wrong decision making involved with the statement. Right action can be accomplished by simple compliance with the directive. It makes a simple statement and does not allow for interpretation.

An ethical issue may be considered if the question is asked, "Why should the museum worker be at work at 08.00 in the morning?" Or, "Why should I work?" However, there is a tendency to consider ethical issues in such abstract or philosophical terms that they appear to be irrelevant to daily activities. Is it important to ask, "Why be at work?" if it is understood that the determined start of the work day is at a pre-established hour? Probably not, though the issue of time abuse is considered to be behavior contrary to ethical standards in public related service (Lewis 1991).

IS THERE A DIFFERENCE BETWEEN "RESPONSIBILITY" AND "OBLIGATION?"

Responsibilities and obligations as different types of duties may emanate from different sources and impact different entities according to the relationships that exist between the individual and others. Responsibilities are self-imposed. Obligations are externally imposed. Both play a role in defining and determining the level and kind of interaction between people.

To understand the responsibilities associated with the museum profession and consequently the significance of a code of ethics, it is important to distinguish

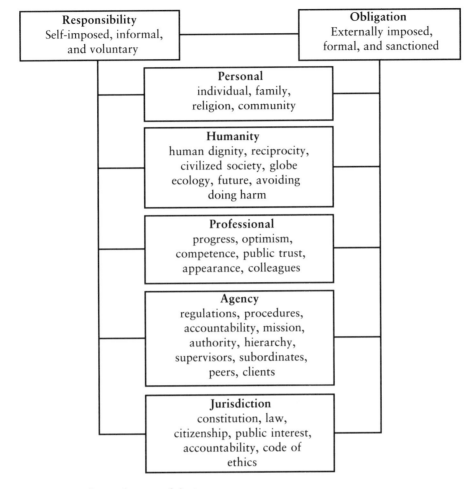

Figure 4.1 Roles and types of duties
Source: Adapted from Lewis 1991: 23

between the consulting profession and the scholarly profession. The museum profession falls into the latter category with teachers, journalists, and scientific researchers. Members of the consulting profession (such as lawyers, doctors, engineers, accountants, and architects) have traditionally practiced for a fee and have served individual clients on a professional basis. In contrast, a scholarly profession serves many clients (groups) at the same time and works for a salary rather than a fee (Bayles 1981).

There are other contrasting features between the consulting and scholarly professions. Consulting professionals provide an essential service that has an impact on the personal lives of their clients – justice, health, safety, wealth, and comfort. Scholarly professionals provide a supplemental service that alters the "quality of life" for a group of people. The consulting professionals have a monopoly on the services they offer and require a license or legal certification to practice. Scholarly professionals normally attain their positions based on scholastic or technical achievement. They maintain their standing through some form of accreditation by peers. In most countries the privilege to practice is conferred on consulting professionals. This privilege may require a test or examination to determine the individual's qualifications. In all professions there is a common element of anticipated trust.

> Every profession considers itself the proper body to set the terms in which some aspect of society, life, or nature is to be thought of, and to define the general lines, or even the details, of public policy considering it.
>
> (Hughes 1988: 31)

ARE THERE ABSOLUTE RULES THAT DETERMINE ETHICAL DUTY?

Duty is closely aligned with the basic theory of ethics. The study of duty-based ethics refers to the deontological system. Immanuel Kant (1724–1804) formulated a system of duty-based ethics including the concept that ethical action is a matter of following absolute rules without exception. Kant approached the recognition of a moral (ethical) precept from an initial assertion that nothing is unconditionally good – except good will. Health, wealth, and intellect are good only in so far as they are used well. Deontological ethics is defined as, "the view of obligation as immediately perceived and therefore independent of any reasons which may be offered in support of one duty as against another" (Banner 1968: 165).

According to Kant, "the Moral [ethical] worth of an action is not derived from the purposes it seeks to achieve, but from its being in accordance with a policy – or maxim – that respects the moral law" (Van Wyk 1989: 80). This notion may be stated as "duty for duty's sake," to differentiate from the concept of duty for the purpose of fulfilling another requirement.

Kant believed that with reason a consistent set of moral principles can be formulated. "Always act in such a way that you also can will that the maxim of your action should become a universal law" (Kant 1993: v). This concept is described as the one supreme principle for the field of morals (ethics), including the philosophy of law (politics) as well as the moral requirements for maintaining personal integrity and determining duty to others. This approach to ethical responsibility is what Kant called "categorical imperative" – unconditional moral law. "The categorical imperative is the way to apply the universalizability test" (Pojman 1990) to an act or principle. Kant theorized that it was the person's duty to obey the imperative and not to be concerned with the consequences. On the basis of Kantian theory and rule-deontology, moral law (ethical duty) must be unvarying. Once a categorical imperative has been discerned, there can be no exceptions.

To further explain this concept considers the following question, "Is there some law or principle to which this [particular] action conforms, to which all other action also can conform?" (Van Wyk 1989: 81). This approach reflects the mathematical base of Western philosophy as demonstrated by the following equation:

$$P \text{ (Principle)} = A \text{ (Action)}$$
$$A \text{ (Action)} = AA \text{ (All Action)}$$
$$P \text{ (Principle)} = AA \text{ (All Action)}$$

To describe this idea in museological terms, assume a curator accepts an object from a donor for the museum, and while transporting the object from the donor's home to the museum, the curator decides to keep the object for personal use. In ethically evaluating this act, consider the question already stated, "Is there some law or principle [ethic] to which this action conforms, to which all other actions also can conform?" The law is theft and the principle [ethic] is a promise of correct action – two elements of the act are incorrect.

> In the interests of the public as well as the profession, members of the museum profession should observe accepted standards and laws, uphold the dignity and honor of their profession and accept its self-imposed disciplines.
>
> (ICOM 1990: 33)

If all curators were allowed to act in this way, curatorial integrity would signify nothing. Under these circumstances, nothing would be treated as a promise of trust, and no curator could make an honest commitment. If this is true, then curators could make false promises or commitments whenever it was convenient. To justify the act of taking the gift for personal use, the curator would have to endorse the practice of giving false information and stealing as a universal concept and in this way to act against reason. If it is against reason to endorse this action, then it is contrary to the same principle for a person to grant themselves permission to do what is impossible to grant everyone else.

IS THE ETHICAL ESSENCE OF THE CATEGORICAL IMPERATIVE CONSISTENCY?

The categorical imperative is a command form without defining the expected outcome. Action should be taken because reason discloses it to be the intrinsically right thing to do. As an example: "Tell the truth."

To demonstrate this ethical concept, assume you are a curator of anthropology. Suppose a "pot hunter" (used as a derogatory term for an unauthorized and often unqualified scavenger of archaeological sites) asked you the location of a particularly significant Paleoindian site. Rather than give the person the requested information, you lie because you do not want this person to do harm to the archaeology. You give the pot-hunter wrong directions. The person follows your directions, but unknown to you, the pot-hunter discovers a deposit of early pottery at the exact location you told him to look. The pot-hunter is successful as a result of your lie, and you are responsible because you lied. Had you told the truth, you could not have been held responsible because telling the truth is the moral (ethical) thing to do. Kant contends that the moral (ethical) value of an action is based not on the purposes it seeks to achieve, but from its being in accordance with a policy or maxim that respects the moral (ethical) law.

A museological application of the M (Maxim) = P (Principle) (Pojman 1990: 97) equation is as follows:

> **M (Maxim):** Whenever I want an artifact for my museum's collection from another culture that cannot be obtained legally, I should steal it. (By applying the universalizability test to the Maxim, the Principle is defined.)

> **P (Principle):** Whenever anyone wants an artifact for their museum collection from another culture that cannot be obtained legally, they should steal it.

Assuming the principle is one that the museum profession can endorse as a general rule for curatorial conduct, the Maxim may stand. If, however, the Principle is unacceptable as a general rule, the Maxim must be rejected as unacceptable to the profession. Endorsing the type of curatorial action presented in the example would be to the detriment of the museum profession and museums. Such an attitude would invalidate the concept of fiduciary responsibility in that the curator would be stealing from one people (donor) to enhance the enjoyment of another people (himself or herself). While the enjoyment of the latter group might be great, it is comparatively equal to the displeasure of the former. If the unrestricted stealing of cultural material is allowed or universalized, museum collections would constantly be suspected and distrusted. Museums would lose credibility and the whole reason for stealing in the first place would be meaningless.

> Museums should recognize the relationship between the marketplace and the initial and often destructive taking of an object for the commercial market, and must recognize that it is highly unethical for a museum to support in any way, whether directly or indirectly, that illicit market.
>
> (ICOM 1990: 27)

A second museological application of the M (Maxim) = P (Principle) theory is:

> **M (Maxim):** Whenever I find an object I want for my museum's collection, I determine the availability of a valid legal title and the museum's ability to give the object proper care and use.

> **P (Principle):** Whenever anyone wants an object for the museum's collections, they should determine the availability of a valid legal title and the museum's ability to give the object proper care and use.

To access the applicability of the theory, the following test may be applied.

1 Maxim formulated
2 Ends-Test (Does the Maxim involve violating the dignity of rational beings?)
3 Categorical Imperative (Can the Maxim be universalized?)
4 Successful moral principles survive both tests (Pojman 1990: 104).

IF AN ETHICAL ISSUE IS UNIVERSALIZED, IS IT UNIVERSALLY APPLICABLE?

This ethical concept, in its most basic form, supports the idea of an international code of ethics to provide guidance for all museums. However, care must be taken not to define a code of ethical conduct for one nation or one people with the expectation of imposing external standards of ethical behavior on another land or people. According to Kantian theory, once the moral law (ethic or rule) has been established, there can be no exceptions (Pojman 1990).

Kant's theory is based on reason and the duty to obey commonly held ethical requirements. The concept supports the idea that duty need not always make the person happy, nevertheless every reasonable person is required to follow the underlying principles of ethical actions. Kant proposed that everyone was familiar with the things they should do and equally aware of those actions they should not do. By using reason, they ought to make the right choice (decision).

One further equation of museological application should be considered. The Principle (P) plus the Circumstance (C) equals Outcome (O).

> **Principle (P):** It is relevant to our museum's mission to collect objects related to the history of this region. The object being offered is related directly to the history of the area.
>
> **Circumstance (C):** The person offering the object has no valid title to the material.
>
> **Outcome (O):** The museum should not accept the object without a valid title regardless of how important it is to the collection.

In contrast to the categorical imperative is the "hypothetical imperative." In this theory the first part of the equation, the expected action or act, begins with the word "if" to be fulfilled by the outcome of the second part of the equation: that is, "If you want A, then do B." As an example: If you want an effective museum board (part A), select them carefully, educate them thoroughly, and

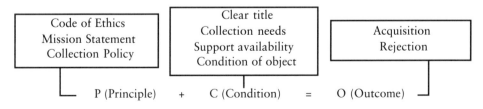

Figure 4.2 Example of P + C = O equation

give them meaningful duties (part B). This concept is pragmatic in orientation and easier for most contemporary museologists to endorse. The notion of input equating to outcome is basic to most thinking as with the idea of "A fair day's work earns a fair day's pay."

DOES THE THEORY OF DUTY ETHICS HAVE DIFFERENT FORMS?

There are two forms of deontological theories: act- and rule-deontological systems (Pojman 1990). The two systems are also described as particularist and generalist. Act deontology considers each act as a unique ethical occasion and that deciding right and wrong in each situation is determined by consulting individual conscience or intuition or by making a choice apart from any rule. The two key words in this methodology are "decide" and "intuition" as the act-deontological system is further divided into two types: intuitionist and decisionist. Intuition is defined as, "the immediate knowing or learning of something without the conscious use of reasoning; instantaneous apprehension" (McKechnie 1977: 964). Intuitionists believe that the conscience must be consulted in every situation to discover the ethically right thing to do.

The second type of act-deontological system is decisionism. Decisionism is sometimes called existentialism, a concept rooted in the writing of Søren Kierkegaard (1813–55) and furthered by the work of the French philosopher/ writer Jean-Paul Sartre (1905–80). Decisionists believe there is no morally right answer until the agent chooses for himself or herself what is right or wrong. Nothing is in itself right or wrong, but choosing makes it so. However, most people allow their everyday lives and actions to proceed at the "intuitive level." They instinctively respond to situations without giving careful thought to the conditions they encounter. At more critical times, they carefully determine which intuitions and loyalties are to be preserved and fostered.

Current thinking supports the following theory of intuitionism: intuition is a normative statement sincerely made and believed in some ordinary sense (Brandt 1979). A "normative statement" is considered to be the application of an accepted general principle. An example is that it is wrong to steal because the act of stealing is contrary to the already accepted general principle that stealing is wrong. While this appears simplistic, it is important to realize that individual commitment of such normative statements may and usually does differ from situation to situation and from person to person.

Considered in this way, the expected results of intuitionism can be no more than common sense. In many situations common sense has valid application but it cannot be the basis for a professional approach to museum work or an international code of ethics. When decision making goes beyond the common-sense level, it is based on previously acquired knowledge and can no longer be considered intuitive.

It is reasonable to assume that ethical consistency within an institution or a group of institutions is understandable. The challenge to ethical standards arises when establishing a code of ethics that has universal application. Consistency of actions is one of the better ways of resolving conflicts of interest in a just, reasonable, and broad-based manner. If everyone and everything is treated equally and can anticipate that treatment, then conflict ought to be minimized. Even the most general aspects of the museum community are in a constant process of flux – with a viable code of ethics, change has a course to follow.

IS ETHICS INTENDED TO REPLACE ALL OTHER EXISTING RULES?

The rules that prevail in most groups, professions, or societies are beneficial in some ways. The intent of a code of ethics is to determine which rules are beneficial in terms of their results and which are not. Those that do not provide the best outcome or consequence should be altered or replaced. The ultimate value in this system is happiness, that is, correctness or consistent outcome.

"Utilitarianism . . . is a universal teleological system that calls for the maximization of goodness in society – for the greatest goodness for the greatest number" (Pojman 1990: 74). Utilitarianism is divided into two forms: act utilitarianism and rule utilitarianism. Act utilitarianism is "the view that a right action is an action that produces at least as good results as any other that an individual might choose" (Van Wyk 1989: 102). It has a tendency to focus on the future and not on the past, and in this case, the future is immediate rather than long-term. In utilitarianism, personal and public ethics are described in terms of the "empirical psychology of the basic affections of pleasure and pain" (Banner 1968: 96). By contrast, with Kant's ethics, the claims of morality are founded on the laws of reason (ethics).

As an example of act utilitarianism: Assume you are the director of a museum and, as in most museums, your institution has a policy against loaning objects to individuals. One day a member of the museum's board of trustees comes to the director's office to say that she and her husband are entertaining some important people in their home and they want to borrow a few paintings to add a touch of cultured elegance to the evening. The board member says she knows there is a policy against loaning to individuals but this is important and it would make her very happy to have a few paintings for the evening. No one will have to know about the loan. She adds that the exhibits staff can bring the paintings to her house and hang them. They will include the artwork on their insurance for the evening, and they will be hung in the room used for entertaining away from the dining room. She explains that their home is climate controlled at least as adequately as the museum. Of course, the museum director knows that she and her husband are very responsible individuals and have been long-time supporters of the museum.

The board member will have a great deal of pleasure if allowed to borrow the paintings. If refused, she will be unhappy and be displeased with both the museum and the director.

The request is against the rules of the museum, but the paintings will not be harmed and no one will know about the loan. What is the issue? If the director ignores the mission of the museum and decides to loan the paintings based on the idea that loaning to the board member will generate the most happiness, pleasure, or good, what will be the results of this situation? This predicament demonstrates the problem associated with an ethical concept that confirms "happiness" as a primary outcome. It is difficult to explain how a person concerned with personal happiness can be directed to uphold general happiness.

The act utilitarian can always find justification to loan objects to individuals and consequently the museum's collections will be used for the happiness of a few people and not to benefit the public. Secrecy does not excuse the incorrectness of a wrong act or justify disregarding ethical practice. Museum ethics should reinforce guidelines that maintain the ideals of public responsibility, fairness, equal treatment, and consistency.

In contrast to act utilitarianism, those endorsing rule utilitarianism interact according to rules that increase happiness and decrease unhappiness. As noted, act utilitarianism is the theory that the rightness and wrongness of an action are to be judged by the consequences of the action while rule utilitarianism is the view that the rightness or wrongness of an action are to be judged by the consequences of a rule. The following anecdote (Sommers 1986: 108) describes the difference between act and rule utilitarianism. "The batter swings, the ball flies past, the umpire yells 'Strike three!' The disappointed batter pleads with the umpire, 'Can't I have four strikes this once'?" If you are the umpire compelled by act utilitarianism, what will you do? If you are an advocate of rule utilitarianism, what will be your call? The difference should be obvious. The act utilitarian may agree to the request for a fourth strike while the rule utilitarian will explain that to allow the batter to take a fourth strike will require allowing everyone to take four swings at the ball and that allowance is contrary to the rules of baseball.

As another example: Assume a person comes to the museum with an object he wishes to donate. The person states he has used this object all his professional life and that he purchased it in 1921. He explains how important this object is to him, and that now he is retired, he wants it to be in the museum. As he hands you the object, you remark that it is in excellent condition to have been used for so many years. Tears came to the man's eyes as he explains how he has taken care of the object as an important tool of his profession. You carefully remove the object from its leather case and turn it over to find "Copyright 1976" stamped on the back.

If you tell the man you cannot accept his gift because it is not as he said and that it is against the museum's policy (rule) to accept such objects, he will experience great personal unhappiness and pain. If you accept the gift and make the man happy, you disregard the policies of the museum by incurring an obligation that will have an impact on future curators who will be unhappy with an inappropriate object.

What should be done? Should the director disregard the truth and break the rule of honesty, as well as the rules of the museum, by accepting the object though it is of no value to the collection? Or, should the director make the person happy by accepting the gift knowing that future curators will be unhappy to occupy their time providing care for an object that is meaningless to the collection and should never have been acquired?

HOW ARE VALUES A PART OF THE ETHICAL PROCESS?

Values are a part of all aspects of a person's life. Decision making requires making choices between values. The easiest decisions are between good and bad values. In those situations the choices are obvious and the decision is simple. The good value will make people happy, bring important collections to the museum, and provide the funding and personnel to offer and sustain effective exhibitions and programming. The bad value makes a segment of the museum public angry. It minimizes the museum's role in the community, and alienates donors. Between these options, the decision is easy.

However, the values associated with most decisions are not so easily classified (good versus evil). It is usually a question of deciding between competing good values, and it is a situation such as this that causes a dilemma. The good of the museum versus the good of the individual, or the good of the general constituency versus the good of a special interest group. To add to the quandary, the decision also must consider the long-term good versus the short-term benefits. Fads, trends, money, popularity, special interests, personal preference, and public pressure are concerns that have an impact on many decisions. None by itself is wrong.

Maximizing one value often requires diminishing others. For example, providing the maximum care for collections may cause a reduction in the attention given to exhibitions and educational programming. Similarly, allowing the importance of friendship on the job may interfere with other meaningful values such as efficiency or equity. Properly and thoughtfully applied, a code of ethics ought to maximize the important values and minimize those of lesser importance (Guy 1990).

A value judgment is a subjective concept. It is that part of the ethical spectrum that allows various shades of the black and white. Normally values are described in opposing terms – good or bad; better or worse; desirable or undesirable; right or wrong, etc. These are judgments that may be described as true or false, and because of this judgmental nature there is a *prima facie* imperative, that is, because circumstances may indicate a higher priority for other measures. Value judgments should not be confused with existential judgments that indicate factual situations. If they are value judgments, then they must be subjective.

The theory relating to values is more easily understood if divided into "means" and "ends." A means value, also called an instrumental value, is a value that serves as a means for bringing into existence an intrinsic value. An end value or intrinsic value is a value that is self-contained and is not required to serve any other value to maintain its identity. Problems arise when the distinction between the two forms of value, intrinsic and instrumental, become confused. It has been proposed that the way to determine intrinsic value is to ask the question of whether the concept, ideal, emotion, or object can stand on its own out of context. If it can, it has intrinsic value; if not, it has instrumental value (Lamont 1981).

HOW DOES ETHICS RELATE TO DECISION MAKING?

The process of ethical decision making manifests itself in several forms. Many decisions focus on one area – interaction with others. Extreme examples of interaction are easy to determine. Decisions in the form of value judgments and discretionary actions become less obvious and less clearly defined. "All decisions except those, if any, that are completely arbitrary are to some extent decisions of principle" (Hare 1952: 65).

The following is a guideline for making ethical decisions (Guy 1990):

1 Define the problem.
2 Acknowledge the context in which the problem arose in order to identify all stakeholders involved.
3 Identify the values that are at stake:
    (a) caring   (f) loyalty
    (b) honesty   (g) fairness
    (c) accountability   (h) integrity
    (d) promise keeping   (i) respect for others
    (e) pursuit of excellence   (j) responsible citizenship.
4 Select the values that must be maximized.
5 Choose the alternative that maximizes the essential values and minimizes as few as possible.
6 Assure that the consequences of the decision will be ethical in regard to both its short-term and its long-term consequences.
7 Implement the decision.

An act may be judged wrong, not because of its consequences, but because the consequences of everyone doing the same thing would be harmful. As an example: If one person takes a flash picture in a gallery where there is a sign saying NO FLASH PHOTOGRAPHS, it can be argued there will be minimal negative impact on the artifacts. However, if everyone is allowed to take flash photographs, the ultra-violet rays emitted by the flash undoubtedly will harm the objects in the gallery.

> There are some kinds of acts that have little or no effect if any one person (or two, or three) does them but have very considerable effects

if everyone (or even just a large number) does them. Rule utilitarianism is designed to take care of such situations.

(Sommers 1986: 110)

Rules should be designed to insure the greatest good for the largest number of people regardless of the immediate displeasure or unhappiness of a few.

It is important to understand that rule utilitarianism, for the most part, is circumstantially applicable. That is, if the circumstances are the same, the application of the rule ought to be the same. To make the situation more difficult, circumstantially relevant criteria will vary according to a number of external factors. For instance: A tall person with red hair and glasses wearing a green shirt is taking photographs with a Nikon camera. None of the descriptive information is relevant to the fact that the individual is taking a flash photo in a gallery marked NO FLASH PHOTOGRAPHS. If this person is allowed to take flash pictures, then everyone should be allowed to take flash pictures – not only tall people with red hair and glasses wearing a green shirt and using a Nikon camera. The effect of taking the flash pictures is the same, the outcome is the same, and the value level is the same.

However, if the photographer is a reporter for the local newspaper and has the permission of the museum director to take photographs with limited lighting for a future news release about the exhibit, the circumstances are act specific. In this case there is a defined and desirable value that is an acceptable circumstance to allow an exception to the rule.

Obviously the pitfall of this thinking is who and what determines which circumstance is a viable exception and how broadly that exception will be applied and with what regularity. As soon as an exception is made to a rule, it is necessary to define the limits of the rule governing exceptions.

In the strict sense of rule utilitarianism, there can be no exceptions to the rule. This dilemma is one of the most difficult for the museum community. When rules are applied inflexibly, opportunities may be lost. However, if every situation constitutes a valid exception, then rules have no value and decision making is arbitrary. To avoid the pitfall of rules that require regular exceptions, careful consideration should go into establishing rules (ethics) and policies.

IS ETHICS ABOUT RIGHT BEHAVIOR?

"Ethics seeks to establish principles of right behavior that may serve as action guides for individuals and groups" (Pojman 1990: 2). Ethics is the theory of right conduct, and in applying the idea of duty to the museum profession, a code of ethics ought to define the museum professional's relationship with others. The others may be individuals, groups, or larger entities, and they may change in priority depending on the mission and role of the museum. However, most of the following elements ought to be included in all missions (McDowell 1991):

1 **Professional duty to public (constituency)**
   (Re: ICOM *Code of Professional Ethics*, 1 Definitions, 1.2 Museum; II Institutional Ethics, sub-sections 2.6, 2.7, 2.8, and 3.5; III Professional Conduct, Section 7, Personal Responsibility to the Public, sub-sections 7.1, 7.2, and 7.3.)

2 **Professional duty to employing institution**
   (Re: ICOM *Code of Professional Ethics*, Section 3. Acquisitions to Museum Collections, sub-sections 3.1, 3.2, 3.3, 3.4, and 3.7; Section 4, Disposal of Collections, sub-sections 4.1, 4.3, and 4.4; Section 6, sub-sections 6.1, 6.2, 6.3, 6.4, and 6.8.)

3 **Professional duty to other museum professionals**
   (Re: ICOM *Code of Professional Ethics*, 1 Definitions, 1.1 The International Council of Museums, sub-section (c); III Professional Conduct, 5 General Principles, sub-section 5.1, and 5.2; III Professional Conduct, Section 8, Personal Responsibility to Colleagues and the Profession, sub-sections 8.1 and 8.2.)

4 **Professional duty to persons in other professional groups**
   (Re: ICOM *Code of Professional Ethics*, III Professional Conduct, Section 4, Disposal of Collections, sub-sections 4.2; Section 8 Personal Responsibility to Colleagues and the Profession, sub-sections 8.3, 8.5, and 8.6.)

5 **Professional duty to the museum profession**
   (Re: ICOM *Code of Professional Ethics*, III Professional Conduct, Section 5, General Principles, sub-section 5.1, 5.2, and 5.3; III Professional Conduct, Section 7, Personal Responsibility to the Public, sub-section 7.1, 7.2, and 7.3; Section 8, Personal Responsibility to Colleagues and the Profession, sub-sections 8.2, 8.5, and 8.6.)

6 **Professional duty to society (in general)**
   (Re: ICOM *Code of Professional Ethics*, I Preamble, Section 1, Definitions, sub-section 1.2, Museum; II Institutional Ethics, Section 2, Basic Principles for Museum Governance, sub-sections 2.6 and 2.7.)

Out of context, duty ethics appears to be an abstract idea resulting from considering the "good" of a duty or obligation apart from the associated conditions or objects. It is also unwise to regard ethics, in any form, as valid or invalid simply because there are no obvious (immediately discernible) positive or negative results. The positive or correct nature of an ethical action is not always describable as the opposite of negative or incorrect action, just as apparently correct actions may be totally unethical and irresponsible. Value judgments based on ethical principles are an integral part of the daily activities of every museum.

QUESTIONS FOR FURTHER CONSIDERATION

1 Should museum workers feel personally responsible for maintaining a high level of performance to assist their museum in meeting its public responsibility?
2 Should museum workers allow their feelings about particular persons or projects to influence their professional behavior?
3 Are conflicting (real or assumed) concerns in the museum, the profession, visitors, and support organizations allowed, encouraged, or suppressed by ethical principles?
4 In inter-staff discussions, should museum workers take a position based on principles or concentrate on the demands of the immediate situation?
5 Should museum workers seek input on sensitive issues?
6 Should museum workers undertake assigned tasks with the same enthusiasm as those they identify and favor?
7 Is doing a good job an important part of ethical practice?
8 Should museum workers seek and undertake tasks that will contribute to the general goals of their museum or concentrate on their area of responsibility?
9 Should museum workers treat all persons within their museum (staff, volunteers, and visitors) equally, respecting their rights and preferences as long as they do not disrupt the role, responsibility, or standards of the museum?
10 Is the idea of a "work ethic" something about which most museum workers ought to be concerned?

ETHICAL SITUATIONS FOR DISCUSSION

Scenario one

Situation

Assume you are working in the ethnology collection and, for some reason unknown to you, the rack holding part of the Native American pottery collection begins to sway. Your first reaction is to grab the case to give it stability as it appears to be on the point of collapse. Just as you get a grip on the case, one of the most prized pieces of pottery tumbles from the shelf. It is almost within your reach but to catch it you will have to release your hold on the case. You have less than a second to decide. Do you catch the prize pot and take a chance the rack will fall, perhaps breaking many pieces of pottery? Or do you continue to stabilize the rack, knowing that the prize pot will crash to the floor and be destroyed? What would you do?

Concerns

• Is this an ethical issue?
• Does decision making of this kind relate to ethics or is it an intuitive response to a situation?

- Can a situation such as this be considered in museum rules, policies, or procedures?

Comments

Consider the principle of the greater good. Does holding the rack and making the greater number of pots safe outweigh the value (aesthetic/intrinsic) of the one piece of pottery? Will the greater loss be sustained by the destruction of one piece or all those on the rack?

Scenario two

Situation

The museum board is faced with a major problem. The investment income has decreased due to low interest rates, and it appears there are insufficient funds to meet the annual budget. The problem is compounded by the fact that a number of important projects are underway and, if they are not completed, the board will have to inform donors and supporters of the museum's financial situation. The overall effect could be very bad for the fund raising campaign planned for the following year.

The president of the board visits with the museum director before a special meeting of the board finance committee. The president feels strongly about the need for additional money to meet the projected expenditures but has no plan for generating additional funding. The director proposes a number of possible fund raising activities but none will produce the amount of revenue needed.

During the finance committee meeting, one member suggests selling a few pieces of the collection to meet the budget shortfall. There are a number of objects, paintings especially, that are not of particularly high quality but will bring a reasonable price if sold. An auction can be held and the money put into the museum's general fund to complete the projects already approved by the board.

Several members of the committee agree with the idea and ask that it be put in the form of a motion so a vote can be taken. The director asks the committee to consider other options before they make the decision, but the general feeling is that this is the best solution to the budgetary problem and it may be a way to fund a major building project they have been considering for several years.

Concerns

- Is this an ethical issue or simply a financial matter that falls within the assigned duties of the governing body?
- Does this situation call to question the "stewardship" duties of the museum board?

- Should the director take a stronger stand against the deaccession and sale of museum objects to meet a budgetary shortfall?
- Might there be legal ramifications from a situation of this kind?

Comments

> The governing body holds the ultimate financial responsibility for the museum and for the protecting and nurturing of its various assets: the collections and related documentation, the premises, facilities and equipment, the financial assets, and the staff.
>
> (ICOM 1990: 25)

> Any moneys received by a governing body from the disposal of specimens or works of art should be applied solely for the purchase of additions to the museum collections.
>
> (ICOM 1990: 30)

Once the collection becomes a ready and available financial resource, it will soon be depleted and the primary asset of the museum will no longer be available for the public. In most museums, the collections are given by and for the public, and the stewardship responsibility is one of primary importance for the museum and those persons holding positions of accountability for museum assets.

FURTHER READING

Baier, Kurt, *The Moral Point of View*, Ithaca, NY: Cornell University Press, 1958.

Brink, David, *Moral Realism and the Foundations of Ethics*, Cambridge: Cambridge University Press, 1989, chapters 7 and 8.

Broad, C. D., *Five Types of Ethical Theory*, London: Routledge & Kegan Paul, 1930.

Fagothey, Austin, *Right and Reason: Ethics in Theory and Practice*, Saint Louis, MO: The C. V. Mosby Company, 1972, chapter 12.

Feldman, Fred, *Introductory Ethics*, Englewood Cliffs, NJ: Prentice-Hall, 1978, chapters 7 and 8.

Gowans, Christopher, (ed.) *Moral Dilemmas*, New York and Oxford: Oxford University Press, 1987, chapters 1, 3, and 4.

Kant, Immanuel, *Grounding for the Metaphysics of Morals*, translated by James Ellington, 3rd edn, Indianapolis: Hackett Publishing Company, Inc., 1993.

Lewis, Carol W., *The Ethics Challenge in Public Service*, San Francisco and Oxford: Jossey-Bass Publishers, 1991, chapters 5, 9, and 10.

McDowell, Banks, *Ethical Conduct and the Professional's Dilemma*, New York and London: Quorum Books, 1991, chapter 3.

Pojman, Louis, *Ethics: Discovering Right and Wrong*, Belmont, CA: Wadsworth Publishing Company, 1990, chapter 6.

Raphael, D. D., *Moral Philosophy*, Oxford: Oxford University Press, 1981, chapter 6.

Solomon, Robert, *Ethics and Excellence: Cooperation and Integrity in Business*, New York and Oxford: Oxford University Press, 1992, chapter 25.

Sommers, Christina, *Right and Wrong: Basic Readings in Ethics*, New York: Harcourt Brace Jovanovich Publishers, 1986, chapter 1.

Wheelwright, Philip, *A Critical Introduction to Ethics* (3rd edn), New York: The Odyssey Press, Inc., 1959, chapters 5, 9, 10, and 11.

5

Ethics and truth

The regard for truth implies in the first place that we ought to abstain from lying, that is, a willful misrepresentation of facts, by word or deed, with the intention of producing a false belief. Closely connected with this duty is that of good faith or fidelity to promises, which requires that we should make facts correspond with our emphatic assertions as to our conduct in the future. Within certain limits these duties seem to be universally recognized, though the censure passed on the transgressor varies extremely in degree.
(Westermarck 1908: 72, vol. 2)

WHAT IS "TRUTH" FROM THE MUSEOLOGICAL PERSPECTIVE?

The search for truth (or accuracy in decision making and action) is a difficult and continuous task. The process is further complicated by the changing conditions that influence decision making. Values, relating to the idea of truth of judgment, are often flexible in that everyday conditions and special interests alter or modify the importance placed on decision making measures.

The idea of truth is very difficult to explain as an intellectual phenomenon. Truth as a concept fills a certain logical need. It verifies an act, idea, or statement by relating it to a greater or more accepted source. As an example: Prolonged exposure to ultra-violet light rays is harmful to paper objects. This is a qualified true statement. The qualifications may include a number of controls that limit or ameliorate the UV influence, but it is accepted to be a true statement. Why – because everyone is an expert on ultra-violet light rays? No, because the statement corresponds with established information on the subject of paper conservation. It is this association that gives truth to the statement. In this way, truth relates to knowledge.

The idea of the "correspondence-notion" of truth (Joachim 1906), has been widely discussed and debated. It proposes that a statement or act is true if it represents the real order of events and facts as a source of knowledge. Therefore, truth is most commonly used to mean correspondence with facts or with actual occurrences. In some cases, a determination of truth "sets a standard" that has application to other similar situations. That is to say, that when a judgment is made about a particular statement or action, that judgment is held to be true in similar activities. However, it is likely the determination of "truth" refers to a particular act or statement associated with a specific set of circumstances.

The difference between the truth and falsity of a particular act or activity *may not* exist apart from the museological practices in which these values are initiated. This is not to say that truth is true on some occasions and not others, but that practical conditions may define the limitations of a particular act while directing it toward a museological "common good." This process has been called "passing for true." In that a statement conveys the truth when, "it passes from a source to a receiver, successfully soliciting belief, penetrating practical reasoning, and thus to an infinitely variable degree modifying the subjective representation of options and necessities for belief and choice" (Allen 1993: 4). This notion equates truth with the value "good."

Many scholars advocate the theory that truth is relative to communal practices as they evolve in particular cultures (Holmes 1992). They submit there is no standard of truth that applies to everyone. This is not an argument against a universal code of ethics, in fact, it reinforces the possibility of such a code, as truth and ethics can be installed for a specific group (the museum profession). It also underscores the need for constant reassessment of accepted "truths," requiring them to be re-validated based on practical factors or evidence.

IS TRUTH A PRIMARY PART OF PROFESSIONAL ETHICS?

If truth is condition specific when the activities pass beyond the normal restrictions of society, then a code of ethics is a vital part of that process. In this way, truth supports the idea of sameness while falsity notes a difference. A code of ethics establishes standards for a museum and fixes the criteria for sameness of purpose and practice. However, due to the relative nature of truth, those standards ought to be flexible to allow for change and independence to consider local convention. The requirement of independence allows for external influence, including professional development and international input.

It is commonly believed that people follow the path of least resistance, and that they act in a manner that is the least likely to solicit a negative response. In that way, right (honest) or wrong (dishonest) actions reflect the anticipated reaction rather than objective analysis. This situation becomes more complicated when the act is based on assumed conformity. Normal human activity may be in response to two kinds of motives. First are those activities done as a means to an end, even though they may not be enjoyable or satisfying in themselves. The second are those dictated by obligation. These activities are completed even when there is no enjoyment and no desired outcome (Sommers 1986).

To put this in museological perspective, consider the circumstances associated with a relative or friend asking for information about a museum acquisition. A worker in a museum has special knowledge about collections and their value. A friend asks for information about a particular object recently acquired by the museum because there is a similar object available for purchase but the identification of the piece is unclear. The friend wants to buy the object but needs to be reassured of the value. The museum employee has access to the collection records. It will be easy to review the curator's analysis of the particular object, and to give the information to the person. The museum worker does not want to do it, but feels an obligation. The person is a long-time acquaintance and if the museum employee does not cooperate, friendly relations could be damaged.

The sense of personal obligation is strong. In some parts of the world personal obligation supersedes all other activities. However, the trust assigned to each museum worker does not allow personal feelings and commitments (obligations) to supplant professional responsibility. The idea of this duty is a part of the ICOM *Code of Professional Ethics*: "Members of the museum profession must protect all confidential information relating to the source of material owned by or loaned to the museum" (ICOM 1990: 33).

ARE TRUE AND FALSE RELATIVE TERMS REFLECTING INDIVIDUAL OPINION?

> We may judge something to be true for many different kinds of reasons, e.g., because it has been empirically certified, or well corroborated, or because it is the best explanation, or the simplest and most conservative inductive projection of the data.
>
> (Ellis 1990: 11)

The idea of true and false is not limited to words, but must extend to actions. The reason for this is that most acts convey meaning at some level, and if they are true, that is, that they correspond to what actually exists, they are ethically correct (Patterson 1949). It may be assumed that when a statement or act does not agree with actual fact, it is false.

As an example: A person is assigned the task of completing an inventory of a collection of archaeological material. However, the person does not feel well and, after randomly checking several objects, decides everything is as it should be. When the supervisor returns, the person reports that everything is correct. The falseness of the act is compounded by the falseness of the statement. Objective truth is not dependent on the attitude of the person knowing the truth, and belief or opinion should not be confused with reality.

People usually want to know the truth and they want to be thought of as being honest. Trustworthiness is the primary element in personal integrity. To act in an untruthful manner is a betrayal of trust. Such deceptions undermine the public nature of museums and create an attitude of suspicion that have a negative impact on all museological activities. Public confidence in a museum (or all museums) is impaired when duplicity is discovered.

For consistent ethical measures (values) to be integrated into the total decision making program of a museum, they must be institutionalized. "Structured perceptions provide operational definitions of reality and are used by employees to interpret their situation and act within that definition of the situation" (Guy 1990: 98). Values of primary importance include accountability, honesty, pursuit of excellence, loyalty, and personal integrity.

> Man [humanity] has not only a right to be but a right to know, not only
> a right to life but a right to truth. He [or she] demands respect for his
> [or her] own intellect and must show similar respect for his [or her]
> neighbor's intellect by putting right order in the communications
> between his [or her] own mind and the minds of others. He [or she]
> who speaks is obliged to speak the truth.
>
> (Fagothey 1972: 233)

The nature of speech as a means of communication and the function of communication in society requires an assumed respect for truth. In the museum profession, the foundation for truth, that is, correct action, is formulated in the code of ethics and refined in institutional policies and procedures. These documents define the functions of museum-related activities within the museum community. They also delineate the "ethical duty to maintain, and if possible enhance, all aspects of the museum, its collections and its services" (ICOM 1990: 24).

WHO IS TO DETERMINE WHAT IS TRUE OR FALSE?

In a public environment there are many guidelines and the responsibility of deciding correct or incorrect action is seldom an individual act. However, each person has a responsibility to deal with daily activities in a truthful manner. The attitudes that govern adherence to truth are reason and desire, and they manifest themselves in the process of choice. It is the individual who is ultimately responsible for deciding right or wrong in most cases. However, an established code of ethics aids in defining the reasons for honest (truthful) decision making. It is the desire to comply with the expectations of the profession that activates reasoned thinking.

> Truth may mean conformity to fact or reality or the agreement between
> one's thought and objective conditions. Truthfulness is the agreement
> of one's word with one's thought; it involves the intention and the
> responsibility of the person.
>
> (Titus 1947: 280)

An action, either right or wrong, may be the result of, or motivated by, ethical thinking. When considering how it is possible to know right from wrong, the answer may be as different or similar as the person pondering the question.

However, if the inquiry concerns belief in the rightness of a particular act or action, there is a tendency to rely on promotion of the common good as an inclusive reason. "The ideal order would be that action should spring from a right principle of action and should then be guided by perfect knowledge to the best results" (Bowne 1892: 31).

Ethics is described as an academic pursuit in the "investigation and affirmation of truth" (Finnis 1983: 4). There is a temptation to reduce the importance of ethics by "envisaging ethics as a deduction from metaphysical or general anthropology (the descriptive knowledge of human nature), or as an intuition of non-natural properties of agents and action" (Finnis 1983: 4). It may be possible to eliminate the truth-seeking character of ethics by viewing it as the expression of practical attitudes or feelings, to be conveyed to others for motives of self-expression or a pre-determined outcome. "Moral judgments are given in order to guide actions – to answer questions of the form 'What shall I do?'" (Pojman 1990: 148).

DOES TRUTH CONSIDER ISSUES AS THEY ARE OR AS THEY OUGHT TO BE?

Truth relates to epistemic valuation, the idea of knowledge or the act of knowing. It is about secure views based on shared values, including the concept of uniform conditions, circumstances, or statements. A code of ethics viewed as a normative guide to the "best practices" for the profession gives validity to its existence and purpose. For most museum workers, there is no doubt about the basic ethical responsibilities of the museum profession. Difficulties generally arise when determining exactly what activities are included under the ethics code or to which problems they apply.

If a code of ethics is considered as setting forth principles of correct action rather than rules for approved action, the ideas may be more acceptable and the universality more achievable. This approach embraces the "is/ought" theory in a simplified and practical form.

"Ethics is concerned with values – not what is, but what ought to be" (Banner, 1968: 3). The "is" application defines the response to a particular situation based on a related situation/response. The "ought" perspective is to consider the situation and guide a reaction based on the principles involved.

- An "is" (rule) situation and response:
  1 Museums preserve objects of cultural significance.
  2 This flag is an object of cultural significance.
  3 Therefore, take this flag to a museum.

- An "ought" (principle) situation and response:
  1 Museums ought to preserve objects of cultural significance.
  2 This flag is an object of cultural significance.
  3 Therefore, a museum ought to preserve this flag.

Although (or perhaps because) ethical discourse has given a great deal of attention to the "is/ought" theory, more modern thinking assumes that it is not possible to decide what "ought" to be done from what "is" being done. This supposition recognizes the fallacy of assuming that "just because something is, it should be" (Brown 1990: 19). What an organization does cannot be the only factor to take into consideration when determining what that organization ought to do. This seems to be a contradiction to the idea of the evolving nature of museum ethics. However, in the case of the museum profession, "best" practices from within the professional workforce are important factors for validating ethical expectations. While addressing immediate needs, past practices do not always provide the level of knowledge, understanding, or vision to know what ought to be done.

Many examples of this point of view can be found in the museum profession:

- The fact that pressure-sensitive tape was commonly used in museums does not mean it ought to continue to be used. Why? Because evidence shows that many kinds of material are damaged by the adhesives used on pressure-sensitive tapes. (Note: It is not the use or non-use of the pressure-sensitive tape that reflects ethical concern, it is the overall care of the collections that is the issue. The tape is a part of that process.)

- That casual maintenance of accessions records is a common practice does not mean it ought to be continued. Why? Because facts show that carefully organized and maintained accessions records are necessary if the museum is to provide proper care for the collections and meet its fiduciary responsibility.

- The fact that it was common practice for museums to admit only the affluent members of society does not mean that such exclusivity ought to continue. Why? Because museums are "institutions in the service of society and of its development, and open to the public which acquires, conserves, researches, communicates and exhibits, for purposes of study, education and enjoyment, material evidence of people and their environment" (ICOM 1989: 3).

It is often the case that a person attempts to explain or justify their actions by describing what "is" rather than verifying what ought to be done based on their value judgment and assumptions.

IS TRUTH A QUESTION OF VALUE?

Truth is a commonly held value that is recognized and endorsed by most people. The underlying motive of truth is respect. Persons void of either self-respect or respect for others have no compulsion about being untruthful. Knowledge is basic to truth. The only truth without knowledge is the admission of ignorance.

"Truth . . . is a foundational value" (Fried 1978: 62) in that it precedes choice. In the decision making process value judgments and truth judgments may be interchangeable concepts in that both seek a "good" or "honest" result. When dealing with value judgments, decision making is a process of evaluation that determines which alternative is most closely related to the interests of the individual or group. A value may be defined as something desired or desirable based on relative need or circumstance. It appears to be a result of interaction between a person and a situation – an attempt to determine truth.

Values may be individual or social, and they may be of various types – economic, professional, or aesthetic. Ethical values include the ideas of "goodness" and "truth." When dealing with decision making, it is normal to make selections based on values, that is, to consider which option will provide the greater good. "[T]he purpose of ethics is not to make people ethical; it is to help people make better decisions" (Brown 1990: xi), and decision making is the core of ethical conduct. It would be relatively easy to act ethically if all decisions were true (good) or false (bad). Unfortunately, almost every critical issue has differing levels of correctness or incorrectness. The most significant aspect of all ethical thinking is to determine when, how, and to what degree a particular issue must be addressed and in what way.

When making decisions, the first factor to consider is the presence of value. To describe an action as having value is to decide that it is in some sense true (good) or honest (correct). It is then possible to assess the relative good of the act, action, or statement. On a relational basis, one act should be better, that is, more honest (correct) than another. This determination is comparative and requires the assigning of values. Also a part of the value equation is the possibility of alternatives. For a particular problem, they are x, y, and z as possible solutions. By carefully analyzing the situation, solution z is determined to be the better (most honest) of the three possibilities.

> Ethical decision making is the process of identifying a problem, generating alternatives, and choosing among them so that the alternatives selected maximize the most important ethical values while also achieving the intended goal.
>
> (Guy 1990: 39)

DO PERSONAL VALUES MANIFEST THEMSELVES AS PART OF A CODE OF ETHICS?

The individual museum worker is an element of a particular social order or profession. For many, the museum profession is their primary means of support. For most, it is also a source of personal pride, self-development, personal expression, and a primary part of daily existence. For those people, the endorsement of a professional code of ethics is a matter of understanding, that is, cognition.

A modified form of the theory of this process of understanding is as follows (Lamont 1981):

1   The individual system of values has its source in the individual.

2 The individual is part of the larger order of humans and by the association the bounds of development are established.

3 The human race exists only in the form of communities which may be described as social orders large or small.

4 The individual is dependent on parents and interaction with the social order in which they exist.

5 As the individual matures, the extant social order is either embraced or rejected to be replaced with another.

6 In whatever social order the individual elects to live, there are rules to promote the common good.

7 The individual accepts the rules that are a condition of membership.

8 The individual alters or adjusts personal values to endorse or in some cases justify compliance with social (i.e. group) rules.

It may be said that individuals have a compulsive tendency to imitate and assimilate the social order in which they find themselves either by design or default. Assuming this is true, a code of ethics promulgated and endorsed by the world museum community should override previously held political, cultural, and individual ethics (or lack of ethics). It is the desire to be a part of the greater community of museums that causes individuals to abandon certain ethical practices in favor of those of the profession.

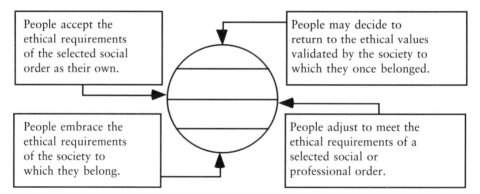

Figure 5.1 The hypothesis of ethics adaptation

A person has the capability to be both objective and subjective when assigning values. However, greater guidance supports a more objective, consistent, and predictable approach to value judgments. Values common to the profession are likely more productive, that is, more easily chosen and less likely to cause a negative result, than those selected for personal reasons. Professionally shared value judgments tend to bring decision making toward a common standard and support the concept of truth as "good."

IS TRUTH ALWAYS BASED ON FACTUAL KNOWLEDGE?

To determine truth based on corresponding fact is a reasonable process when it can be applied, that is, when the circumstances provide the appropriate factual reference. Some truths, particularly those relating to individual beliefs based on historic or cultural values, are difficult to validate or invalidate based on factual knowledge. Traditionally held beliefs often supplant facts and alter the process of determining truth.

Assume a person has been taught to believe a certain idea is true. The ideas or attitudes may relate to any number or kind of acts or actions – a certain food is a delicacy, a certain color is more pleasing, or a certain form is more beautiful. For these attitudes (beliefs) there is no factual foundation to validate the truth. Beliefs of this kind do not challenge the notion of good (truth), or impact (falsify) the beliefs of others, rather they reinforce cultural identity of the group in which they reside.

Beliefs become problematic when they are held as truth, and false knowledge is fabricated to validate their truthfulness. Situations of this kind may include attitudes of group, race, or gender superiority, historic interpretation (or mis-interpretation), ecological misuse, and race or gender stereotypes. Belief-based misconceptions of this kind are very important to museum ethics, particularly as they relate to collections, exhibits, and educational programming. The issues are made more complicated in that within a culture's specific environment, some of these attitudes are held to be unequivocally true and are totally ingrained in the intellectual foundation of the people.

Owing in part to the growing cultural diversity of most parts of the world, museums must often address issues that challenge the traditional beliefs of some element of the visiting public. Depending on the nature of the belief, exhibits may serve as a platform for information to acquaint others with the nature of the associated cultural attitude, or they may describe the non-universal nature of beliefs that are determined to be "false" according to corresponding world values.

Some have contended that truth must be objective. However, most agree that world values change, altering the measuring devices for truth. In recognition of this fluidity, the ICOM *Code of Professional Ethics* (1990: 26) requires displays, exhibits, and special activities to be "honest and objective and . . . not [to] perpetuate myths or stereotypes," placing the greater responsibility on the museum worker to make those determinations.

Museum exhibitions provide information that the public is asked to trust. Personal opinion (beliefs), lack of knowledge, or prejudice may cause a member of the museum community to give data that are incorrect. The information ought to be directed toward a wholly responsible and predetermined outcome.

To relate this idea to the museum profession or at least a museum code of ethics, consider "all moral [ethical] codes are rooted in practices that are them- selves rooted in traditions or forms of life" (Pojman 1990: 119).

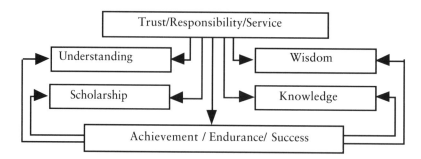

Figure 5.2 Directed responsibility

DO VALUE JUDGMENTS HAVE A CORRESPONDING ETHICAL OBLIGATION?

When a person claims the right to make judgments and establish a truth, that person has an obligation to seek the most correct value appropriate to the situation. The idea of obligatory activity extends to every aspect of the museum profession. The right to professional status assumes the obligation to recognize and endorse the expectations of the profession, that is, to acquire the appropriate knowledge and attitude.

> Work may be done merely for the material profit that it brings. It is then a [person's] job and nothing more. It may also engage his [or her] trained gifts and capacities; it may be his [or her] special expert share in the social enterprise, so motivated and so recognized. It is then his [or her] profession. Or a [person's] work may pervade his [or her] entire life and personality, set the tone and direction of his [or her] thought and feeling, so that he [or she] sees it as his [or her] self-expression. It is then in truth his [or her] vocation.
>
> (Tsanoff 1955: 278)

In theory the higher a person is in the institutional hierarchy, the greater the ethical responsibility. Those at the institutional base enjoy a latitude unacceptable at higher levels. "Some of the most common ethical dilemmas emanate from

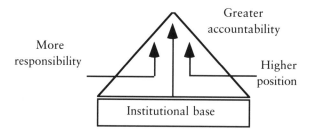

Figure 5.3 Hierarchy of ethical obligation

hierarchical relationships that produce a clash between administrative routines and professional, personal, or democratic values" (Guy 1990: xvi).

Ethics serves as a guidance device and aids in formulating institutional and professional order. However, any act or action founded on professional expertise, on standards of ethical conduct, and by experience rooted in museum history and traditions, may be described as a professional obligation. Consequently, all persons directly involved in museum matters, whether custodian, curator, or trustee, have an ethical obligation to the museum community and the public.

IS THERE A DIFFERENCE BETWEEN PRINCIPLE- AND RULE-BASED CODES OF ETHICS?

Most people in most parts of the world understand the idea of rules. In general their lives are lived from birth to death according to rules. They are said to "know how to play by the rules." There is a difference between principles and rules. A principle states a reason for thinking or acting in a certain way, but does not require a particular decision. A rule requires a response based on the facts or information given. It is an all-or-nothing concept – right or wrong. Each has a validity depending on circumstance. The difficulty with a principle-based code of ethics is that it lacks specific instructions on how to deal with particular situations. It is easier to comply with rules than to recognize and address the spirit of the code. The exercising of ethical judgment is a part of the professional responsibility. It relates to the idea of truth, accurate decision making, and sound reasoning.

Ethical reasoning is a form of analysis drawn from the idea of ethical imperatives. It describes the action that ought to be the result of the two conditional potentialities – situation and condition. This is an example of a quasi-imperative: " . . . ethical statements are prescriptions (quasi-imperatives), which can be of any content (no truth is at stake) providing only that the prescriber is willing to do the prescribed action himself in like circumstances" (Finnis 1983: 28). The equation describing this process may be written in the following way:

$$\text{Situation} + \text{Condition} = \text{Results}$$

This sequence explains that in given situations with like conditions the results always are, or should be, the same. This is a theory that reflects a generalized notion about what people ought to do under certain kinds of circumstances. It is a projection acknowledging that similar kinds of situations recur and social or professional survival may depend on people acting in similar ways in like situations (Bahm 1974).

A practical application of this reasoning is as follows: if person a deals with a problem while experiencing the same situation and conditions as person b, they should generate the same x results. The equation might read:

$$a + \text{situation} + \text{condition} = x \text{ (results)}$$
$$b + \text{situation} + \text{condition} = x \text{ (results)}$$
$$a + \text{situation} + \text{condition} = b + \text{situation} + \text{condition}$$

In this way it is possible to establish principles or ethics that apply across the museum workforce for those in a particular position, that is, curator, registrar, collection manager, etc. If the equation is correct in principle, then all curators, registrars, and collection managers ought to be expected to act in the same way in a similar situation. This rationale challenges the idea that moral right-ness and wrongness vary from society to society and that there are no universal standards.

If it can be determined that situation x has a certain feature z and by comparison establishes that situation y is exactly as x, then by extension situation x should also have feature z. Consequently, it may be rationalized that if person x acts in an ethical manner and the result is a professionally endorsed system of collection management and care, then if person y acts in the same ethical manner and treats the collection in the same way, then the result can also be assumed to be worthy of professional endorsement. This is a simple application of the ethic/fact/truth theory, and roughly the concept of museum and academic accreditation.

ARE THERE COMMON TRUTHS IN THE WORLDWIDE MUSEUM COMMUNITY?

Physical law has an absolute nature. That certain physical alterations occur is beyond question. The cause may be analyzed and the remedy discussed, but alteration of the original state of an object due to the influence of natural or human-made causes is inevitable. As a counter to this phenomenon, the museum community formulated the practice of preventive conservation and conservation. Their existence would seem to support the truth of a common concern for the condition of museum objects. Actual practice may vary and the level of expertise may be relative to the training and facilities available to the conservator, but the awareness and existence cannot be denied.

Regardless of location, condition, society, nation, or culture, there are certain truths common to all museums. These truths are described as "ascertainable facts in which universally accepted standards are available" (Titus 1947: 225). The most obvious are those that deal with the physical nature of the collections. Some of these truths are as follows:

1   Deterioration from ultra-violet light is cumulative and irreversible.
2   Museum collections are by material designation organic, inorganic, or superorganic. (The latter category includes high-tech materials.)
3   Sulfur dioxide (SO_2), generated from the combustion of fossil fuels, is a major factor in the deterioration of paper, cotton, leather, and some types of stone.
4   Metal objects are generally immune to light and heat, but may be damaged by high levels of humidity (compounded by heat).
5   Air-borne dust is a problem for collections.
6   Insect infestation can cause major damage to collections.
7   High temperatures can cause wood objects to crack or separate at joints.

8   The small dark spots that appear on drawings and prints are normally a form of mold growth as the result of the object being stored in a damp environment.

9   Calcium carbonate ($CaCO_3$) is an unstable compound that can cause damage to ceramics and bronze sculpture.

10 Soluble salts can cause a form of decay that affects limestone and sandstone.

Few can argue that these conditions or attributes are true for most, if not all, places in the world. That is not to say that they are considered in the same way, or treated in the same way, but they exist and impact upon collections in basically the same way. By following this line of reasoning it is apparent there are other values that must be more or less universal: "there are some moral [ethical] rules that all societies will have in common, because those rules are necessary for society to exist" (Rachels 1993: 26).

HOW IS IT POSSIBLE TO DECIDE IF SOMETHING IS TRUE OR FALSE?

Truth is validated in three ways:

1   **tradition**: that is, the assumption that past truths remain true until determined to be untrue,
2   **proof**: a simple demonstration or example to corroborate a pronouncement, and
3   **investigation**: in the form of fair inquiry into a subject to verify its factuality (truth).

An example of a traditional truth is: "White objects reflect light and black objects absorb light." An example of proof to confirm a true statement: "This object has been repaired" (show repaired area). An example of investigation-based truth is: "Two objects from different locations having the same stylistic elements, same coloration, same construction method, same general shape, and dating from the same general time were probably made by the same culture."

ARE OTHER WORDS ASSOCIATED WITH ETHICS AS DIFFICULT TO DEFINE AS TRUTH?

It may be reasonable to assume that determining the exact meaning or intent of each word will make the ethical nature of an issue clear or at least more clear. In reality, it seems that attempting to evaluate each ethical principle word by word complicates the thinking process and results in lack of understanding rather than the opposite.

The words "good" and "bad" can be viewed as relative terms that must be defined in context before their meaning can be understood. Assuming this is factual, then ethical relativism is the only remaining option and there can be no universal imperatives. Consequently, good will or good or truth can have no intrinsic value. Also, if there are no imperatives, then good is simply a value judgment. If ethical judgments are a form of value judgments centered in the idea of achieving good, and ethical judgment entails an imperative, then good must have a logical form. "Although moral [ethical] judgments do not have truth-value, they do have a logical form" (Pojman 1990: 149). Ethical judgments are viewed as a guide to actions in the sense that the perpetrator accepts a decision (judgment) to do a certain act and not doing that act implies that the perpetrator rejects the judgment.

Assume a person is working in a museum doing their best to be an ethical museum professional. They conduct themselves in a manner that is exemplary. They take the greatest care to avoid doing wrong at their job yet there remains a large part of their life that is for the most part discretionary. In this case discretionary means that space between extreme right and extreme wrong. It is the gray area that fits neither the ethically correct nor the ethically incorrect. "In filling this discretionary space we make a life which is characteristically our own" (Fried 1978: 167).

What the person does during this time is not defined by museological rules or principles. If no judgment can be made about this intimate and discretionary part of a person's existence, then there is evidence that ethical theory values are subjective, at least in part. That is, if a person acts one way during a controlled situation, and differently when removed from the situation, then ethical values relate only to the controlled situation and consequently they are subjective. In the virtue-based system, ethical consciousness manifests itself in the person not the act and is not subjective.

It is possible to draw a connecting line between discretionary space (decision making) and roles (jobs). There are certain obligations attached to roles. The role, whether related to job or profession, impacts on the way the discretionary decision making space is filled. Being a "professional museum person" defines the role and establishes the obligation inherent in that role with regard to objects, the profession, and the community served. That obligation restricts discretionary options. "Once one has assumed the role, it binds with the obligations of right and wrong" (Fried 1978: 168). A truth is the outcome of an ethical commitment.

QUESTIONS FOR FURTHER CONSIDERATION

1 Should the concern for factual truth be of primary importance to every museum worker?
2 Should museum workers be concerned that almost any culturally specific identifying factor used in an exhibition may be viewed as stereotyping?
3 Should every museum worker be concerned about conflict of interest issues?

4 Is there one truth that is common to all people in all parts of the world?
5 Do museum workers have an ethical responsibility to be aware of the laws that govern or regulate the political activities of persons employed by not-for-profit institutions?
6 Should personal beliefs influence museum workers' involvement with organizational programs and practices?
7 Does loyalty to the institution and museum colleagues override the obligation to the public?
8 Should the ethics of the museum community be different from personal ethics?
9 If most people understand the concept of rules, and rules are often outside the cultural framework, cannot museum ethics be common to all people?
10 Is the idea of truth different today from what it was fifty years ago?

ETHICAL SITUATION FOR DISCUSSION

Situation

The director of a museum has a problem. The museum has a respectable Oriental art collection, and it is part of the duty of the curator of Oriental art to review and recommend works of art for acquisition. On this occasion, an exceptional *emaki*, a narrative picture scroll produced in Japan during the thirteenth century, was offered for sale to the museum by a local art dealer. The curator of fine art voiced his liking for the piece and recommended it for purchase. The acquisition committee endorsed the recommendation and agreed to buy the scroll.

Some months later an expert on *emaki* sees the piece and declares it to be a nineteenth-century reproduction. The expert's absolute certainty of the authentication causes the curator to question his earlier thinking. After some thought, the curator decides that the "expert" is probably correct.

Rather than discuss the situation with the director, the curator talks with members of the museum staff and soon the word gets out into the community and to the local newspaper. Eventually, the curator is contacted by a reporter who asks if the piece is a copy. The curator, being an honest person and not wanting to tell a lie, answers the question in the affirmative. The next day the newspaper has the headline, "Museum Buys Fake Art." The article quotes the curator and questions not only the *emaki* but other recent acquisitions regarding their authenticity. The underlying theme of the article seems to question the fiscal responsibility of the museum and its board.

The director receives a message from the president of the museum board requesting an immediate meeting regarding the newspaper article. Before the director meets with the president, she decides to talk with the curator of Oriental art to get as much information about the situation as possible. The curator admits he now believes the *emaki* to be of recent vintage and not the important piece he originally thought. He says that when the reporter asked for his opinion, his personal integrity would not let him lie by saying either that the painting was genuine or that he did not know if it was authentic or not. He told the truth.

Over the next several days the director has numerous conversations with the museum board members concerning the actions of the curator. On their instructions the director informs the curator that when his contract expires in two months it will not be renewed. The director informs the curator that the termination is for ethical reasons.

The curator decides to petition the court for re-employment by the museum, and eventually the question is presented to a panel for arbitration.

Concerns

- Is this an ethical issue or should the museum director terminate the curator's employment because of the latter's incompetence as he lacks the ability to authenticate an object relating to his area of expertise?
- If the curator is fired for ethical reasons, what issues are involved in this situation?
- Is the curator right to be honest with the media and is the board wrong to punish him for his honesty?
- Is the curator wrong to have discussed the issue with the press without having spoken to the director of the museum?
- Are the curator's comments harmful to the museum?

Comments

> Any museum related activity by an individual may reflect on the institution or be attributed to it.
>
> (ICOM 1990: 31)

> Loyalty to colleagues and to the employing museum is an important professional responsibility, but the ultimate loyalty must be to fundamental ethical principles and to the profession as a whole.
>
> (ICOM 1990: 31)

When personal ethics supersede professional ethics, it is possible to overlook the responsibility of loyalty to the employing museum. The curator placed his personal commitment to truth before his obligation to protect the integrity of the museum. There is a potential for conflicts of interest between the individual acting as a professional or pretending to represent an institution and an individual acting on their own.

FURTHER READING

Allen, Barry, *Truth in Philosophy*, Cambridge, MA, and London: Harvard University Press, 1993, chapters 1, 2, and 8.

Aristotle, *Nicomachean Ethics*, Indianapolis: Hackett Publishing Company, Ltd., (translated and edited by T. Irvin, 1985).

Blum, Lawrence A., *Friendship, Altruism and Morality*, London: Routledge & Kegan Paul, 1980.

Foot, Philippa, *Virtues and Vices*, Oxford: Blackwell, 1978.

Gelven, Michael, *Truth and Existence: A Philosophical Inquiry*, University Park and London: The Pennsylvania State University Press, 1990, chapters 1–6, and 13.

Harlte, Anthony and Kekes, John, *Dimensions of Ethical Thought*, New York, Berne and London: Peter Lang, 1987, part v.

Johnson, Lawrence E., *Focusing on Truth*, London and New York: Routledge, 1992, chapter 8.

Landesman, Charles, *The Foundations of Knowledge*, Englewood Cliffs, NJ: Prentice-Hall, Inc., 1970, part 1.

Mayo, Bernard, *Ethics and the Moral Life*, London: Macmillan, 1958.

Pojman, Louis, *Ethics: Discovering Right and Wrong*, Belmont, CA: Wadsworth Publishing Company, 1990, chapter 7.

Rachels, James, *The Elements of Moral Philosophy*, New York: McGraw-Hill, Inc., 2nd edn, 1993, chapter 12.

Sommers, Christina, *Right and Wrong: Basic Readings in Ethics*, New York: Harcourt Brace Jovanovich, Publishers, 1986, chapter 4.

Tsanoff, Radoslav, *Ethics*, (revised edn) New York: Harper & Brothers, 1955, chapter 5.

Van Wyk, Robert, *Introduction to Ethics*, New York: St Martin's Press, 1990, chapter 10.

Wallace, James, *Virtues and Vices*, Ithaca, NY: Cornell University Press, 1978.

6

Ethics and the museum community

Our judgment is not bounded by what is, nor by what will be, nor even by what can be. For there is always also our view of what should be. The vision of our mind's eye extends to circumstances beyond the limits of the possible.

(Rescher 1987: 132)

Museum ethics deals with the interrelationship of people and the museum as a "non-profit making, permanent institution in the service of society and of its development, and open to the public which acquires, conserves, researches, communicates and exhibits, for purposes of study, education and enjoyment, material evidence of people and their environment" (ICOM 1990: 3). People provide the service as museum workers and receive the service as visitors. The museum is the central element.

Ethics addresses the connectedness of all aspects of museological activity and constitutes an open-ended contract with the public, including current and future generations. A viable code of ethics is essential for the survival of museums in all their diverse manifestations. It establishes the foundation for public trust, and describes the forms that the connecting activities will take.

HOW DOES A CODE OF ETHICS HAVE AN IMPACT ON THE MUSEUM COMMUNITY?

The well-being of museums depends on two very critical elements:

1 the ability to acquire the information (in various forms) needed to better serve society, and
2 the ability to use that information properly and productively.

These elements are directed both inward and outward, and both are embodied in a code of ethics and a part of the professional ideology. Museum workers have a right to a code of ethics to guide their work-related activities and to aid in the fulfillment of their professional life. The need for a code of ethics reflects the quintessential nature of museums – the core standard of values.

Figure 6.1   The relationship of museums and people

Museums and museum workers have no congenital code of ethics to guide their activities or assure their survival. There is no instinctive course of action or set of values to direct the itinerary of the profession. There is no natural sense of what will meet the needs of the profession or the community being served. Nor are there instinctive methods for addressing public service, collection care requirements, conservation needs, and inter-professional activities. Legal and ethical recognition and response must be learned by conscious effort. To go beyond the routine of daily activities and the restrictions of repetition, conceptual knowledge is required (Rand 1964).

The concept of "good" and "bad," from the ethical perspective, is arbitrary at its foundation. The information that establishes these values is, for the most part, acquired. Proper handling of objects and the awareness that "Museum employees and others in a close relationship with them must not accept gifts, favours, loans or other dispensations or things of value that may be offered to them in connection with their duties for the museum" (ICOM 1990: 31) are not common knowledge or intuitive considerations. They are expectations formed by a code of ethics to fix the limits of museological values and responsibilities. Because these values are delineated and kept by the museum profession, any breach between museum worker and the code of ethics should be viewed as unacceptable and unprofessional.

DOES MUSEUM ETHICS HAVE A UNIVERSAL NATURE?

The universal nature of ethics may be considered in two ways. One may be described as a realistic approach and the other a semantic approach. In general terms, the realistic approach presents explanatory information, such as: "Employment by a museum, whether publicly or privately supported, is a public trust involving great responsibility" (ICOM 1990: 30). These statements explain how museum personnel ought to act.

The semantic approach addresses meanings. In this conception, the universal nature of ethics is examined by the meaning of the terminology. An example of this approach is:

> It is an important responsibility of each governing body to assure that the museum complies fully with all legal obligations, whether in relation

91

to national, regional or local law, international law or treaty obligations, and to any legally binding trusts or conditions relating to any aspect of the museum collections or facilities.

(ICOM 1990: 27)

This approach is inclusive in that it broadly defines the duties of all museum workers.

Although the two approaches may complement each other and reinforce the idea of universality, each suggests a different universal aspect of ethics. Similarly, each may be given greater or lesser importance according to the interpretation of the terminology used. However, the ultimate goal or end value of a code of ethics is the furthering of the professional "life" of the museum community, and that process is to aid the museum worker in discovering which decision among many will produce the best results for a given task (duty).

The conditions of the modern museum community deny the possibility of isolationism. Cross-cultural exchange, multinational commerce, and worldwide telecommunication cause interdependence and shared values. The codified ethics of the museum profession outlines the duties of the worker to museological activities, the worker's colleagues, and to the public in matters concerning museology. The principles of the code reflect the actual professional standards of the best museum personnel.

The museum profession with a code of ethics is extremely useful, perhaps necessary, for the promotion of museums and museum personnel. The museum profession is more than an aggregate of people, it is a group advocating common principles of practice and similar ideals – it is a society cooperating for a common good.

IS EVOLUTIONARY ETHICS A FACTOR FOR THE MUSEUM COMMUNITY?

All ethical concerns evolve. They change according to social and professional requirements, however the theory of evolutionary ethics is a separate concept. This approach to ethics was stimulated by Darwinian thinking and came into being toward the end of the last century. Some theorists have applied this idea to the "cultural lag" that occurs when an institution or society fails to adapt to its environment (Pepper 1960). At the same time, pragmatic adaptation to social demands can cause museums to over-react and jeopardize long-range goals for short-term achievements. All museums, regardless of their public posture, gain security by uniting with an established and identifiable group or profession. A code of ethics is a part of that security mechanism. Group affiliation and identity are safeguards against impulsive action or reaction and a valid explanation for either change or resistance to change.

The nineteenth-century theory of evolutionary ethics included the Darwinian idea of "survival of the fittest" that is only selectively applicable to the museum community. The idea of fitness as a durability factor has some relevance to ethics and secondarily to museums. If the processes within the museum community are analyzed based on those that are chosen for adaptation and established as the standard, it may be argued that selectivity (survival) is a part of the acceptance equation. Those ethical principles that continue to serve the interests of the museum community must be assumed to be the "best" and most appropriate. Similarly, museums that adjust to the needs of the public, as well as the profession, may be considered, at least in relative terms, successful.

Another aspect of the evolution process that has only nominal application to the museum community is that of institutions or ethics going from "lower" to "higher" forms. Each institution may be fully developed ethically within its environment. It may have achieved the highest level of ethical recognition and responsibility allowed by external or internal limitations, and as those circumstances allow (or require), institutional and ethical standards evolve.

Each museum and museum worker can contribute to the development of the social environment. It is one of the most important ethical obligations of every museum to contribute to this evolutionary process. The ability to interact with other professionals gives museum workers ethical security as long as they endorse mutually recognized goals. It is within the power of the museum community to modify its standard of ethics and to keep it current.

One of the primary strengths of museums is the commonality of purpose. It is also a strength that there is a shared opinion about acting for the common good among those endorsing the museum profession. That is not to say that all members of the profession have or can achieve the level of activity considered to be in the universal interest. The willingness to act or participate is often not the issue – in some cases ethical development is repressed by lack of information, individual dynamics, or authoritarian direction. It is not the exact measure of every participant that gives credibility to the museum profession but the collective endorsement and recognition.

The boundaries of a museum's activities are often the real or perceived limits of the institution's obligation. When the view is worldwide, the institution tends to fulfill those expectations and seeks to meet the requirements of the profession. It is important that every person and every museum be all they can be. Survival is not an adequate reason for existence. New museums are being established at a phenomenal rate while older institutions are scrambling to provide collection care, public service, and heritage preservation. The easiest and often the most irresponsible thing to do is to gather a group of objects and name the conglomeration a museum.

IS ABIDING WITH PROFESSIONAL ETHICS SELF-SERVING?

It has been said that the virtuous person obeys the ethics of his or her own community, group, or profession. However, it is easy to recognize that an ethic based on individual conscience has numerous inadequacies because individual consciences differ (Russell 1955). To be functional, a code of ethics must have some criterion other than conscience by which to describe correct or desirable conduct.

If the museum profession as a community of persons is joined in a unifying effort to achieve a collective good, a reasonable set of criteria other than individual conscience must be promulgated. Without a code of ethics there can be said to be no ethical limits upon what one person may do within the museological context.

Although it is usual to speak of the "museum community" as an inclusive body of museum professionals, ethics resides in the individuals who make up that group. Apart from those people as individuals, there is no place for ethical practices to exist; that is, ultimately, ethics is a matter of individual consciousness. However, between the individual museum worker and the museum profession is a reciprocal arrangement in that neither can be fully corroborated without the other.

In the ideal situation, the ideal person will be completely integrated into the selected community (profession). This idea relates to the human ego and the theory of ethical egoism. It presumes that people are willing to promote their self-worth and self-interest to gain the desired degree of satisfaction or pleasure. Since most people prefer that which gives pleasure in some form and avoid that which gives displeasure in any form, then total immersion into the professional order and adherence to the established standards should be desirable. An ordered existence is generally associated with a level of personal satisfaction (pleasure).

In theory, museum workers should desire to maintain a standard of right action in their self-interest, therefore it is essential for them to know:

1   the accepted standard of right action,
2   the expectation of those establishing the standard of right action, and
3   the anticipated outcome of performing the right action.

A well-formed code of ethics provides these answers and creates a basis of common understanding for all museum workers.

The only reality for the museum profession is in the people who compose it – those providing and receiving services. The museum profession is not an end in itself but a means for interaction with people. Some have suggested there was no right or wrong way of validating museological duties before there was a formalized museum community. This notion presupposes that no act is wrong unless regulated by laws or rules. Following this line of thinking, museum personnel would be obliged to do only that which must be done, and they would be free to avoid that which ought to be done. The museum profession cannot enact laws of proper conduct, however it can exert peer pressure to approve good conduct and disapprove lesser levels of museological behavior.

HOW DOES ETHICS CORRESPOND WITH CURRENT MUSEUM NEEDS?

It is human nature to collect. Every person collects something either by intent or accident. Sea shells, rocks, photographs, match books, and special interest memorabilia collections abound. Each may be "near and dear" to the person doing the collecting, but seldom do they have validity or intellectual value outside the personal realm of the collector. However, the objectively determined merit of the collection appears to have little influence on the person or persons doing the collecting.

For museums, special norms should not apply, in the sense of lesser but greater standards as required to fulfill the expectations of public trust. Special norms may be applied if they are necessary to define the profession and if they are vital to its fulfilling its function. Museum workers have a dual obligation – to the profession and the public. Each has special requirements that may, at times, appear to conflict.

In the past, ethics was generally considered in theoretical and imperious terms. Today the perspective is more contextual and germane to correspond with the practicalities of the changing social order. However, the growing demands for more space, funding, and audience have caused some museums to allow survival needs to supersede ethical requirements. Due to this "real-life" situation, museum ethics is often thought to be a set of impositions and constraints intended to obstruct individual activities rather than a force to motivate positive behavior.

In most situations there is more than one possible solution for museological problems that can be justified based on ethical thinking. It is for this reason that conflicts arise and why professional or discipline-based codes of ethics are of special importance. There are at least two classes of actions:

> one is the set of actions which we may not want to do, but which we do anyway as a means to an end. . . . The other set of actions are those which we do, not because we want to, nor even because there is an end which we want to achieve, but because we feel ourselves under an obligation to do them.
>
> (Sommers 1986: 182)

The reasons for one act or action instead of another always depend on the prior existence of certain attitudes. As an example: that working hard makes a person a better employee is a reason for working hard only if that person wants to be a better employee. Or, that caring for the collection makes a person a better curator is a reason for caring for the collection only if that person wants to be a better curator.

IS THE IDEA OF OPERATING A MUSEUM LIKE A BUSINESS AN ETHICAL ISSUE?

It is not difficult to draw a correlation between museums and the business community. In this time of accountability, profit maximization, up-front costs, and "bottom line" mentality, more and more museums are being encouraged to adopt "business strategies." Unfortunately, the relationship usually aligns itself with funding objectives and management styles rather than fundamental practices. Whatever the reasoning, ethical principles are germane because the concept of profit maximization applies the utilitarian perspective under certain conditions.

Figure 6.2 Strategic relationship of business and museums

As an example: a stockbroker or investment banker has an obligation to protect the investments of others, and at the same time increase the value of those investments. The normal perception is – the greater the investment risk, the greater the potential gain. Profit maximization is a popular phrase in the business community. It is also an idea worthy of consideration by the museum community. The idea is directly related to the ways and means of public account-ability. By making the best use of the raw material of the museum, the greatest profit is achieved. In this case, the profit can be defined as public service. However, as the business community guards its investments, museums must take care of their primary assets – the collections. There should be no unnecessary risk or harm to the integrity of the institution.

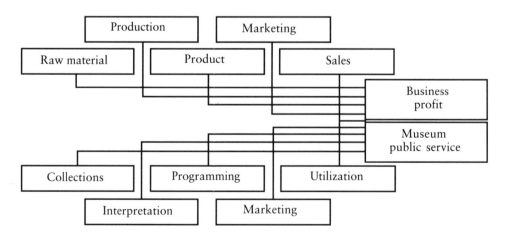

Figure 6.3 The process of maximization

WHO IS TO SAY WHAT IS RIGHT OR WRONG?

Every member of the museum profession is responsible for investigating, learning, and fulfilling the mission of responsibility associated with museums. Each person has to make decisions about the activities in which they are involved. "The universal character of reason accounts for the possession by different individuals of a common standard of truth" (Fuller 1947: 281).

In the museum community there are special, often unique, interpersonal relationships that are defined and sustained by professional practices. These associations may exist both inside and outside institutional boundaries (Goldman 1980). In addition, there are professional norms that supersede personal ethics and assumed relevant correctness. Intellectual property, personal privileges, and conflict of interest questions may fall into this category. The need for role differentiation is a valid concept as the museum profession has special requirements that exceed normally accepted ethical standards. At the same time, deference to national and international laws is required. The profession clearly notes that the authority of individuals to act according to their personal ethical perceptions is limited. The reason for this limitation is due to the cumulative impact of unilateral decisions on the institution and subsequently on the museum professional.

HOW DOES ETHICAL RELATIVISM RELATE TO THE MUSEUM COMMUNITY?

There are those persons in the museum profession who maintain that what is right or wrong action for one person may depend on where they live, what they believe, or what the society requires. The beliefs of the individual are considered a primary factor in ethical thinking. Ethical relativism is often subdivided into two forms. The first is described as social relativism and the second as individual relativism. Social relativism endorses the notion there is no standard of right and wrong that is not completely relative to the views of a particular society, and that standards of various societies are all equally valid or justified. Individual moral relativism may contend that all moral (ethical) judgments are a matter of personal taste.

Contemporary thinkers agree that neither ethnocentrism nor supernationalism is the ideal attitude for this period in the continuum of cultural evolution. The time has passed when the world should, or can, re-create itself in the image of a particular nation or people. However, mutual understanding and shared objectives are sometimes, perhaps too often, confused by the failure to realize that different places have different ethical values.

"Most individuals are plastic to the moulding force of the society into which they are born" (Sommers 1986: 133). The concept of rights and duties is a part of every society, and in most situations there is a duty associated with a right or privilege. In all cases where people deal with each other, the privilege of an action is only half the relationship that requires a balance of rights and duties. Regardless of the familial, organizational, or cultural affiliation, the general rule is reciprocity.

When a person claims a right without acknowledging the associated duty, it is not difficult to recognize the incorrectness (wrongness) of the act. Acquiring an object (right) without payment (duty) is understood as violating the system. A worker may falsely claim hours not worked, or a board member may expect benefits or privileges beyond those allowed. In both cases, the rights and the duties do not equate and eventually corrective action is required. The reciprocal process is recognized at all levels of the social scale. Although this appears to be a very elementary idea, it is a good beginning for an attitude of right action and positive social interaction.

Ethical ideals change in a number of ways, and often the changes are social or ethical adjustments that evolve slowly. The easiest example to describe this gradual change relates to the acquisition of new information. Often an existing practice or ethic is a response to limited knowledge, and this situation can be altered, either positively or negatively, by the opportunity to interact with different cultures or cultural thinking on a personal basis. Another adjustment is the form of knowledge exposure through the media. Other adjustments are the result of social modification based on the idea of the correctness of a person's actions.

> The concept of the normal is properly a variant of the concept of the good. It is that which society has approved. A normal action is one which falls well within the limits of expected behavior for a particular society.
>
> (Sommers 1986: 140)

The number of persons who deviate from the behavioral patterns a culture has institutionalized will be few because the majority of humankind is quick to take the shape that society bestows on them.

Ethical issues may be considered universal, although not all are viewed as having the same significance in all lands and by all people. However, the concern for correct action (right) is a commonly held aspiration. It is the definition of rightness that varies. Western thought tends to focus on results (outcome) rather than intent. This method of assessment allows for a relatively easy determination of the ethical rightness or wrongness of a particular act. If the outcome is good, the initiating act or action is thought to be right or correct. Negative or bad results are considered the consequence of wrong actions.

For honest assessment, ethics must be viewed as an inclusive process. The appropriateness of one act or action should not conflict with another. Equal application of ethical standards is an absolute requirement. Conditions that allow special circumstances to alter ethical judgment violate the foundational notion of self-worth and equity, as well as the standards of the profession. "The basic idea of duty must be simply that of acting in accord with general principles, principles which one can recognize as valid for anyone – and claiming no right that one does not admit as right for others too" (Garnett 1960: 198).

DO ETHICAL STANDARDS HAVE TO BE PREDICTABLE?

A professional code of ethics demonstrates the need for predictability, consistency, and stability through accepted practices and standards. It also provides a profession-wide document of empowerment to explain the fundamental premise of the museum profession. The code projects the social role of museums and establishes the museum profession outside the ethics and practices of other professional and non-professional organizations.

Sometimes the museum profession is difficult to understand, much less evaluate, apart from the social interaction associated with museum activities. "Inconsistency in an ethical statement or principle, or in a group of them, is a fatal defect" (Brandt 1966: 59). The assumption of ethical consistency and predictability within an institution or limited group of institutions is understandable. The challenge to ethical standards arises when attempting to establish a universal ethic – a standard for all museum workers to endorse. However, sapient thinking supports an ethical code that is universally applicable to similarly motivated people. This reasoning is the motive for ethical action and compliance with universally applicable ethical principles. The only requirement for this process is that the ethical nature of the act applies to all rational human beings (Garnett 1960). This methodology follows the principle of consistency.

Ten ethical principles that support the ideas of consistency and predictability for museum professionals, and that ought to be considered when preparing the code of ethics, are as follows:

1   Museum professionals ought to act responsibly, both legally and ethically, in all matters relating to the operation of the museum and wholly endorse the responsibilities and duties incumbent upon a position of public trust.
2   Museum professionals ought to address, with equity, the social consciousness and cultural needs of all members of the museum's constituency, and endeavor to maintain a positive presence in the community.
3   Museum professionals ought to acquire, maintain, study, document, and provide public access through exhibitions of objects appropriate to the museum's defined mission and provide for all acquired objects equally.
4   Museum professionals ought not to derive personal profit in any way from museum-related duties, activities, and/or information gained in the execution of museum work, nor ought any action to be knowingly allowed that will give the appearance of impropriety in dealing with museum-related interests.
5   Museum professionals ought to exercise extreme care in the selection of objects to be added to the museum's collections including: ethical and legal status, relation to mission, availability, need, condition, donor requirements, and the ability of the museum to preserve and utilize the objects.
6   Museum professionals ought not to acquire objects significant to the cultural heritage of other lands or people, and ought to give extreme attention to those objects already in the museum's collection that may have religious or sacred meaning to others.

7 Museum professionals ought not, except under special circumstances, to deaccession objects and never in a manner that will bring question or discredit to the museum regarding the care and maintenance of the collections.

8 Museum professionals ought to place honesty, integrity, and social consciousness foremost in defining the education, exhibition, interpretation, and special program content of the museum, being certain that no intentionally hurtful or demeaning attitudes or concepts are fostered.

9 Museum professionals ought to provide both opportunity and support for the intellectual growth and education of all members of the museum's staff, including board members, curators, technical and support personnel, and volunteers.

10 Museum professionals ought to act in a supportive manner to the world community of museums by providing loans, information, technical assistance, or other aid as appropriate to the means and mission of the museum, and by endorsing and sustaining a comprehensive code of professional ethics.

IS A CODE OF ETHICS ABOUT IDEALS AND EXCELLENCE?

Ethical actions require going beyond the minimum requirements and acting responsibly with regard to the well-being of the society served by the museum, the museum profession as an organization, and the objects placed in the care of the museum community. Museums do not make decisions, people do. A code of ethics helps in the decision making process, but the responsibility rests with each person.

Decision making is guided by a number of factors, including survival and physical well-being. Also, it is possible for decisions to extend beyond the limitations of immediate needs to address more exultant aspirations. In this way, people can seek a life (or employment) that is meaningful as well as secure and pleasant. The quest for the "ideal" is a part of the decision making process that is excellence oriented. "As such, they motivate rather than constrain, urge rather than demand" (Rescher 1987: 135).

However, as with ethics, ideals can conflict. Values are assigned to ideals as part of the decision making process. These values are determined by the anticipated outcome of the action and the influence it exerts on the humans or objects involved – the unachievable perfection. It is pursuit of the ideal that causes exhibitions, programs, services, collection care, and many of the other activities within the museum profession to evolve and improve. This concept supports the idea of a code of ethics that describes the ideals of museological practice.

Ethical ideals exceed the expectations of normal practice. They go beyond what must be done to achieve minimal results to specify what ought to be done to gain maximal outcome. In this way, they combine the "best practices" of the museum profession with the requirements of the participating public. Ethical ideals are not a substitute for professional norms – they amplify them.

Ideals also may reflect personal priorities that go beyond accepted norms. It is possible to imagine two members of a museum staff being at odds while each is pursuing the highest professional ideals associated with his or her particular discipline. An education program coordinator may seek to exceed the normal practices (an ideal) associated with programming and in so doing place museum artifacts in danger. A curator may seek the highest level of collection care (an ideal) and in the process deny the public access to the artifacts. Both are valid objectives and, in the properly functioning museum environment, both can be accommodated through careful planning and coordination.

The contextualization of ideals grounds them in the practicalities of the work-place. To regard something as ideal separates or isolates that element and sets it apart from other similar or related elements. The condition of idealization in most cases is ultimately untenable and consequently "an abstract notion." However, as ideals do not exist in a vacuum, the pursuit of one ideal may have an impact on either the normal or ideal condition of another act, action, situation, or element. The interactive, that is the co-existent or integrated nature of the museum community, limits the possibilities of achieving the ideal. In this way, pursuit of "the ideal" fosters the concept of excellence and stimulates the evolution of ethics.

> The fact that our ideals and values limit one another in actual operation has important consequences. It means that while ideals can – nay should – be cultivated, they never deserve total dedication and absolute priority, because this would mean an unacceptable sacrifice of other ideals.
>
> (Rescher 1987: 127)

HOW DOES THE MUSEUM COMMUNITY LEARN ETHICAL CORRECTNESS?

The validity and significance of a universal code of ethics are furthered by the theory of justice that advocates:

> the most important natural duty is that to support and to further just institutions. This duty has two parts: first, we are to comply with and to do our share in just institutions when they exist and apply to us; and second, we are to assist in the establishment of just arrangements when they do not exist.
>
> (Rawls 1971: 334)

This concept continues by assuming that, "if the basic structure of society is just, or as just as it is reasonable to expect in the circumstances, everyone has a natural duty to do what is required of him [or her]" (Rawls 1971: 334).

With the defining of principles for institutions (or society), the decision making process is simplified for the individual. In addition, individuals expect and accept the benefits of a just institution (or society), thereby establishing an obligation (or desire) to comply with the conditions (rules) of that society. By voluntarily accepting the benefits, the individual incurs a responsibility to support and to further just institutions.

In application, this means that when a person (paid or non-paid) voluntarily accepts the benefits of a museum, that person has a duty to follow the rules of that institution (code of ethics). This is true, even if those rules are not in complete accord with the person's sense of right or good. The person must understand that the rules are based on knowledge, that is, information gained through association with the institution, and that they apply to all people equally.

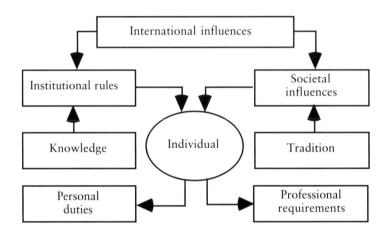

Figure 6.4   Reasoning for individual duty/requirements

Any personal duty or professional responsibility taken by itself may be influenced to a greater or lesser degree by outside causes, ideologies, or social expectations. Considered holistically, institutional rules coupled with the associated benefits have a primary impact on the individual decision making process and the resulting values. By receiving and transmitting knowledge, the museum worker can learn the requirements and expectations of the profession and the public it serves. It is the common bond between museum professionals and the museum community and society.

DOES EVERY MUSEUM WORKER ACKNOWLEDGE A UNIVERSAL CODE OF ETHICS?

One of the primary reasons used to deny the possibility of a universal code of ethics is that people embrace different moral beliefs. This attitude reflects the commingling of morals and ethics, and the use of religious grounding as a base for ethics. From this perspective, the probability of mutually endorsed ethical standards is unlikely, although not impossible. A secondary part of the reason for challenging the likelihood of international ethics relates to intuition. A natural extension of moral training is an automatic response or reaction said to be based on intuition. In this case, the act or action is not truly intuitive but a learned response based on prior knowledge often relating to religious instruction.

The attitude that assumes different cultures have different moral values ignores the fact that professional ethics does not relate to intuitive acts. Instead, ethics consists of learned activities and intellectually founded, sometimes abstract, concepts. Once the code is established, distribution and training are the means for insuring implementation. In this way, learned ethical responses become automatic, replacing previously held attitudes.

The first prerequisite for a code of ethics with universal possibilities is the availability of that code to be known (learned). The second is having a clear understanding of "good" or "right." If everyone knew which course of action to take in every case, there would be no need for a code of ethics (McInerney and Rainbolt 1994). Circulating a written code of ethics addresses the first requirement assuming it is made available in the appropriate languages. The second issue is more complicated. Not only is it impossible for people to endorse a code they do not have, it is equally impossible to endorse and apply that which they do not understand.

If it is assumed that all ethical standards are not self-evident, then they must be described and explained. (If they are self-evident, they are intuitive and no formalized code would be necessary.) The process of explanation must include both acceptable, that is "good" or "correct," practices and the reasons that "define as the whole truth about that which is at the same time common to all such judgments and peculiar to them" (Moore 1902: 1).

The idea of right action is a part of every museum regardless of its location or conviction, and the concern about how to achieve correctness is an inherent part of every museum worker's personal itinerary. Aristotle asked, "Do we deliberate about everything, and is everything a possible subject of deliberation, or is deliberation impossible about some things?" (Aristotle 1980: 55). He answered his own question by saying: "We deliberate about things that are in our power and can be done. We deliberate not about ends but about means" (Aristotle 1980: 56). To give this statement a museum application, consider that the profession does not deliberate about whether it ought to be ethical but about how to be ethical. Aristotle further states "[that] having set the end [we] consider how and by what means it is to be attained" (Aristotle 1980: 56).

QUESTIONS FOR FURTHER CONSIDERATION

1 If an act is unethical when people know about it, is it just as unethical when it is done in secret?
2 Are there reasons to consider the museum profession as an inseparable part of the museum worker's identity?

3 Is it reasonable to assume that most human activities, including being a good curator or exhibits designer, are motivated by selfishness?

4 Do the demands of self-satisfaction supersede the requirements of professional ethics?

5 What role does the human conscience play in ethical standards?

6 What are the ethical principles that have international (universal) importance?

7 Is it important to have a universal code of ethics that applies to all museum workers?

8 Should a universal museum ethics be a closed system, that is, should it only depend on itself for regeneration and replacement?

9 Why should inconsistency in an ethical principle be considered a fatal defect?

10 Do all aspects of a code of ethics have to be accepted to the same degree by all people to assume the code has universal value?

ETHICAL SITUATION FOR DISCUSSION

Situation

Suppose there are two museums in the same town – Museum One and Museum Two. Museum One is careful in its acquisitions, maintains its collections in excellent condition, has great exhibits, and provides exceptional programs for the publicly financed school in the community. Because of these outstanding qualities, the majority of the city and community financial support goes to Museum One, leaving Museum Two poorly funded. In an effort to improve the conditions of Museum Two, the director discreetly informs the local press that a number of the works on exhibit at Museum One are copies. The word "forgeries" is included in a story that appears in the local newspaper. The director of Museum One is quoted as saying that there is apparently some misunderstanding and that no reproductions are included in the exhibit, but the report sounds defensive.

A short time later, the director of Museum One receives a call from a donor questioning the care being given objects in the museum's collection. The donor indicates that he has heard that the museum keeps the anthropology collection in cardboard boxes. The donor also says that he knows for a fact that the museum has never exhibited two silver spoons he and his sister donated. He speculates they have been lost. In an effort to be totally honest with the donor, the director explains that archaeological material is often transported from the excavation site in boxes before being sorted and housed in metal storage units. The director also explains that the museum has numerous objects in the collection and that it is not possible to exhibit everything.

When the donor requests the return of the spoons, the director states that it is not the policy of the museum to return donated objects. However, he offers to show the man through the museum's collection storage area so he can see the high degree of care given to the collections. The donor has no interest in a guided tour. He makes it clear he will call the president of the museum's board to get the spoons returned.

When the board meets, each of its members has a different story to tell relating to some impropriety attributed to the museum. The director is at a loss. He knows the museum staff maintained the highest ethical standards but it appears they are doing everything wrong.

At about the same time, the director of Museum Two announces the discovery of a fantastic dinosaur egg. Unlike other fossilized eggs, this one is white and shell-like, and when held to a light, a perfectly formed embryo can be seen. The discovery receives extensive coverage in the local newspaper, and due to the notoriety, attendance at Museum Two quadruples. Almost every school child in the area goes to see the dinosaur egg. This increased attendance is accompanied by financial support from local individuals and businesses.

In reality, the egg is made of plastic. It is a prop to get people into the museum. The director reasons that it is no different from a "give away" advertising campaign at a supermarket or department store. Once the people come to see the prize, they stay to see the rest of the museum. He plans to have the egg discolor by gradually airbrushing it with paint until it can be removed from exhibit for safe keeping in the museum's vault. If necessary, there can be another fantastic discovery in six to twelve months to keep the people coming back to the museum.

Museum One is ethical, careful, professional, and unpopular. Museum Two is totally unethical and unprofessional but very popular. Museum One gradually loses all its support and the director resigns under pressure from the board. Museum Two gains tremendous local support including a number of significant grants to expand its facilities and to fund further paleontological fieldwork. The director of Museum Two is given a large increase in salary.

Concerns

- Suppose the director of Museum One realizes that Museum Two is perpetrating a hoax and decides to do the same. In that case both museums will violate accepted museum ethics. However, each will profit and neither will be worse or better than the other. Is this a reasonable course of action? What will be the result of this approach?
- Why should people be ethical?
- Why should a museum worker act according to the ethical standards set forth by the museum profession if others do not?
- Is the director of Museum One ethically correct even though it cost him his job or should he have responded in an equally unethical manner?

Comments

One issue in this scenario is the ongoing relationship between museums. Each violation of the ethical standards of the museum community weakens the rationale for adherence to a code of ethics and moves the entire membership toward a chaotic condition. All museum workers will benefit if each is motivated by a sense that it is right to uphold the ethical standards of the profession and wrong to abandon them. This attitude reflects the interdependence of members of the museum community and the fact that common interests provide the basis for a common set of professional actions. Consequently, it is in museum workers' self-interest to perpetuate the ethical practices prescribed by the museum profession.

FURTHER READING

Callahan, Joan C. (ed.), *Ethical Issues in Professional Life*, New York and Oxford: Oxford University Press, 1988, chapter 2.

Dewey, Robert, Gramlich, Francis, and Loftsgordon, Donald (eds), *Problems of Ethics*, New York: The Macmillan Company, 1961, chapter 1, section B, chapter 2, section B, chapter 3, section B.

Pepper, Stephen C., *Ethics*, New York: Appleton-Century-Crofts, Inc., 1960, chapters 4, 5, and 10.

Pojman, Louis, *Ethics: Discovering Right and Wrong*, Belmont, CA: Wadsworth Publishing Company, 1990, chapters 3 and 9.

Rand, Ayn, *The Virtue of Selfishness*, New York: The New American Library, 1964, chapters 1 and 7.

Rawls, John, *A Theory of Justice*, Cambridge, MA: The Belknap Press of Harvard University Press, 1971, chapter 6.

Russell, Bertrand, *Human Society in Ethics and Politics*, New York: Simon & Schuster, 1955, chapter 3.

Sommers, Christina, *Right and Wrong: Basic Readings in Ethics*, Harcourt Brace Jovanovich, Publishers, 1986, chapter 4.

Taylor, Paul, *Principles of Ethics: An Introduction*, Belmont, CA: Dickenson Publishing Company, Inc., 1975, chapter 3.

Tsanoff, Radoslav, *Ethics* (revised edn), New York: Harper & Brothers, 1955, chapter 10.

Wheelwright, Philip, *A Critical Introduction to Ethics* (3rd edn), New York: The Odyssey Press, Inc., 1959, chapter 10.

7

Ethics as a code

A code of ethics sets forth standards that a profession deems essential in order to uphold the integrity of the profession.

(Malaro 1990: 37)

Some dictionaries associate the word "museum" with the idea of "relic," "vestige," and "souvenir." Considering the popular use of these words, it may be possible to dismiss museums as repositories of notable relics of the past. Many have questioned the importance of museums and predicted an end to their usefulness. Some persons view commercialization as the only viable answer to the question of museum survival. They recommend a more business-like attitude that is modeled around the entrepreneurial strategies of fiscal management and accountability.

In fact, a number of elements must come together to support and maintain the museums of the world if they are to continue. The exact nature of those elements may vary from nation to nation, but one conspicuous component must exist in all. That component is a commitment to service as a part of professional responsibility, and the attitude of professionalism must be founded on a code of ethics and perpetuated by an understanding of the associated ethical theory. The absence of a sound theoretical base is a weakness that becomes apparent in the process of formulating and administering a code of ethics.

As the world is being altered by a variety of other society-modifying activities, global attention is focused on the cultural and scientific heritage of the world community. Museums can serve a primary role in stimulating a new sociological awareness by encouraging more coherent thinking and a broader vision of humankind and the environment. The responsibility is great. However, a thoughtfully formulated code of ethics will assure practical consideration of the museum's mission and the needs of the profession.

> The professional ideology maintains that every genuine profession has an ethic. An occupation's code conveys the impression that this is true for it and hence that it is a profession. Second, the code formulates what leaders of the profession would have the public think its operative ethic is. This is intended to instill trust in its actual practices.
>
> (Kultgen 1988: 212)

A code of ethics, no matter how well stated, does not guarantee the future of an institution or profession, nor does it provide insurance against all wrong-doing. However, the failure of a museum staff to act ethically will undoubtedly hasten the decline of an institution. Properly understood and applied, a code of ethics ought to be a set of constructive directives intended to define and guide professional activities. A successful code of ethics ought to benefit practitioners and reliant parties (Sheldahl 1979).

The unity of the museum profession may be defined by two different but related features:

1 the extent to which all the different institutions (museums) are dominated by a single set of related values (code of ethics), and
2 the extent to which individuals in the museum profession conform to those values (ethics).

WHY HAVE A CODE OF ETHICS?

A code of ethics cannot stop unethical behavior in a museum. It is a part of a total attitude that requires a commitment by all members of the staff. It also requires interaction, training, retraining, and dedication. Ethical behavior on the job is not a separate part of a person's life. An ethical person is a unit of value in an ethical system. Unless each person endorses a sense of personal duty, no community of such persons (profession) can have value or ethical merit. Every person must have a sense of personal obligation as well as a responsibility for others to assure ethical achievement.

A code of ethics has a number of functions, but two of the most important address the issues of guidance and protection. The first relates to guidance of museum professionals in fulfilling their responsibilities, and the second emphasizes protection of the museum constituencies from substandard services. The application of these functions differs in that guidance is offered as a rule of proper conduct, whereas protection of constituents is expected practice (Sheldahl 1979). Along with guidance and protection, there is a third element needed to formulate a code of ethics – classification or definition.

As an example, the ICOM *Code of Professional Ethics* (1990) is divided into sections that correspond with these elements.

Classification	"Preamble"
	Section 1 "Definitions"
Guidance	Section 2 "Basic Principles for Museum Governance"
	Section 3 "Acquisitions of Museum Collections"
	Section 4 "Disposal of Collections"
Protection	Section 5 "General Principles"
	Section 6 "Personal Responsibility to the Collections"
	Section 7 "Personal Responsibility to the Public"
	Section 8 "Personal Responsibility to Colleagues and the Profession"

Some aspects of the three elements are included in all parts of a code of ethics. Nevertheless, there is a stronger commitment to the protection element than to classification and guidance. This relationship re-emphasizes the service orientation of the museum community.

The idea of ethics is not abstract although some elements of ethical theory have a theoretical nucleus. Ethics is a real part of the daily activities of every museum professional. To understand ethics, it is necessary to comprehend the purpose it fulfills – what it is for. Most "things" have a reason for existing. Ethics is a practical process of melding the driving forces of a functioning museum worker to produce more benefit than damage to the public and the collection.

The museum profession is set apart from other occupations not merely by the level of knowledge and special training, but also by a commitment to a code of ethics that defines a responsibility to the public interest (client). The client may differ, but this duty is an implicit element in the idea of professionalism.

"Every time a person chooses between alternatives, the choice is based on assumptions that lie at the heart of a moral [ethical] code. The code is grounded in values that provide the framework for principled reasoning and ethical decisions" (Guy 1990: 3). One of the difficulties encountered in ethical decision making and in the teaching of ethics is that there is no one correct answer to most problems. In some situations several answers may be correct. The dilemma usually begins with an unclear interpretation of the problem to be decided. Often the issue being addressed is not the cause of the problem, merely one of the symptoms.

There are at least two options or alternative responses to every problem. Seldom are the choices clearly defined as "right" or "wrong." It is the ability to select the most appropriate response that requires skill and understanding. A code of ethics cannot guarantee right choices – it can aid in making consistent, thoughtful decisions based on established standards.

ARE VALUES AND ETHICS THE SAME THING?

Values are the foundation for the ideals that are called ethics.

A code of ethics is about these core values as they apply to work in a people-utilizing activity. As a code aids in ethical decision making, the core values assist in analyzing the options that will determine the most appropriate of the decision options available.

> Employment by a museum, whether publicly or privately supported, is a public trust involving great responsibility. In all activities museum employees must act with integrity and in accordance with the most stringent ethical principles as well as highest standards of objectivity.
>
> (ICOM 1990: 30)

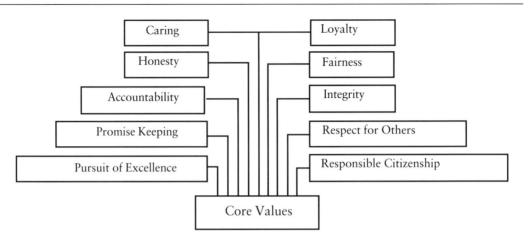

Figure 7.1 Ten essential values central to relations between people
Source: Adapted from Guy 1990: 14

1 A code of ethics fixes the limits of professional conduct. It defines expected conduct and training for new members and describes acceptable practices for the general membership.

> Professional museum workers include all the personnel of museums or institutions qualified as museums in accordance with the definition in Article 2 paragraph 1 (as detailed under paragraph 1.2), having received specialized training, or possessing an equivalent practical experience, in any field relevant to the management and operations of a museum, and privately or self-employed person practicing in one of the museological professions and who respect the ICOM *Code of Professional Ethics.*
>
> (ICOM 1990: 24)

2 A code of ethics accentuates professional responsibility for the purpose of minimizing external supervision and regulation.

> In the interests of the public as well as the profession, members of the museum profession should observe accepted standards and laws, uphold the dignity and honor of their profession and accept its self-imposed disciplines. They should do their part to safeguard the public against illegal or unethical professional conduct, and should use appropriate opportunities to inform and educate the public in the aims, purposes and aspirations of the profession in order to develop a better public understanding of the purposes and responsibilities of museums and the profession.
>
> (ICOM 1990: 33)

3 A code of ethics delineates the importance of developing higher standards of conduct for all members of the profession.

> Members of the museum profession require appropriate academic, technical and professional training in order to fulfill their important

role in relation to the operation of the museum and the care for the heritage, and the governing body should recognize the need for, and value of, a properly qualified and trained staff, and offer adequate opportunities for further training and re-training in order to maintain an adequate and effective workforce.

(ICOM 1990: 25–6)

4 The code of ethics identifies courtesies and the exchange of services between the members of the profession.

Members of the museum profession have an obligation, subject to due acknowledgment, to share their knowledge and experience with their colleagues and with scholars and students in relevant fields. They should show their appreciation and respect to those from whom they have learned and should present without thought of personal gain such advancements in techniques and experience which may be of benefit to others.

(ICOM 1990: 34)

5 The code of ethics verifies the service orientation of the profession and reinforces the primary function as advancement of the public interest.

The museum profession should understand two guiding principles: first, that museums are the object of a public trust whose value to the community is in direct proportion to the quality of service rendered; and, secondly, that intellectual ability and professional knowledge are not, in themselves, sufficient, but must be inspired by a high standard of ethical conduct.

(ICOM 1990: 34)

In theory the museum work force recognizes its ethical duty to care for collections and maintain them for future generations. To achieve this goal, a forward thinking (proactive) program of public service and collection management must be a part of the operational policy of every museum. A balance must be reached that will accommodate both preservation and utilization of collections. To meet the changing needs of the museum community, a well-formulated code of ethics will provide guidance and direction.

WHO SHOULD BE INVOLVED IN DEVELOPING A CODE OF ETHICS?

Ethical museum practices that emanate from those working in museums will be dynamic and evolve in response to developments and orientations.

From the perspective of ethical theory, the importance of internal unity within the great diversity of institutions (museums) is an indication of the role played by museological practice in the developing of ethical standards. This recognition should explain that museum ethics is not an arbitrary or imposed set of rules, but an expression of the attitudes derived from the profession. Museum ethics is based on accumulated knowledge, accepted practice, honest assessment of and response to individual and group requirements, and perpetuation of the profession. It is this consensus that gives the code of ethics validity and establishes it as "Good" for the group. In this way, the practice becomes the standard. It is this unanimity that allows critical inquiry and maintains the code of ethics as a dynamic document. It may be changed by the group for the good of the group.

"[A code of ethics] communicates ideas that promote the professional project of the particular occupational group" (Kultgen 1988: 212). The person opting to become a member of the museum profession enters into this specialized environment and must follow the existing code of ethics and the associated judgments. Whether or not the individual personally endorses every part of the code of ethics, most find themselves striving to follow the pre-established standards.

In the preliminary planning of a code of ethics, it is advisable not to consider the specific end objective or the success or failure of achieving a particular result. It is preferable to focus on the intellectual motivation for establishing the code. However, it is absolutely imperative that a code of ethics is conceived and written in a manner that addresses real issues rather than philosophical questions. A workable code of ethics must consider the reality of museum work as well as the ideals of museological activities.

A defined code of ethics establishes a point of reference for those members of the profession seeking guidance and direction. Persons or institutions being asked to comply with a certain set of standards must believe that compliance is important, just, and equitable. Arbitrary application of standards results in indifference and disregard. All those subscribing to professional standards must be assured of fair and equitable treatment.

It can be assumed there is both a theoretical and practical component to museum ethics. While the theory may precede the practice in concept, the practice (action) dictates the theory (thought). Museum ethics evolve from the profession and are consequently practice-based. The theoretical element reviews accepted practices to determine which is the most appropriate for the general museum community.

IS A CODE OF ETHICS THE CODIFICATION OF POPULARLY ACCEPTED PRACTICES?

"The field of ethics is the field of conduct" (Everett 1918: 1). The uncritical acceptance of popular standards may undermine sound ethical practice.

It is not unusual for a profession to have a system of constraints on behavior different from legal ones. The demands of ethics are unyielding and museum professionalism is based on the idea of adherence to the highest standards of ethical practice. However, these demands are not all-consuming – they leave room for decision making. Museum professionals may be constrained but not restricted by ethics, once the limitations of their responsibilities are known.

To believe there are limits to ethical activities may seem questionable or contradictory. As a professional, the ethical obligations of a museum worker do not end at closing time. However, not all persons have the responsibility to adhere to the ethical practices of the museum profession, and to assume that level of accountability often leads to personal anxiety and professional difficulty. For instance, private collectors, gallery owners, and commercial vendors (antique dealers) have no duty to comply with museum ethics. They must adhere to the law as it applies to the buying, selling, and exchange of objects but not the ethics of the museum community. Museum volunteers and trustees ought to follow the ethics as far as they pertain to museological duties. In this situation, training and communication are the keys for recognition and adherence to ethical expectations.

All museum workers should avoid being agents of wrong ethical action and/or contributing to the unethical actions of others that will reflect negatively on the museum community.

IS A CODE OF ETHICS ABOUT PROFESSIONAL LIMITATIONS?

Rational knowledge may be defined as either material or formal (Kant 1785: 1). Material knowledge is concerned with some object, that is, something intelligible or perceptible by the mind (application). Formal knowledge is concerned only with understanding, reason, and universal rules of thought (theory). Formal thinking (philosophy) is called logic. Material philosophy deals not only with objects but also with the laws to which those objects are subject. These laws are either laws of nature or laws of freedom (Kant 1983: 1). The study of that aspect of material philosophy dealing with the laws of nature is called physics, and that focusing on the laws of freedom is called ethics. This definition (according to Kant) is important in that ethics is the study of the laws of freedom rather than the laws of limitations.

A code of ethics is a systematic collection of the standards governing the conduct of the members of a profession. Functional codes of ethics are usually drawn from two philosophical theories – deontological and teleological. The deontological theory states there are universal rules that serve as ethical guides, and that the idea of duty is independent of the idea of good. That attitude allows certain acts to have significance regardless of the level of good that comes from them. A teleological approach assumes that the worth of an action is determined by the outcome (consequences) of the action.

Beyond the dictionary definition, a code of ethics is only words and ideas. It becomes a way of museological practice when the museum profession embraces the ethical content and follows its guidance. The code can be so complicated and detailed that it becomes impossible to accommodate or so simplistic that it fails to provide either direction or support. To achieve reasonable compliance, a balance of purpose, direction, and inspiration ought to be maintained. Furthermore, a code ought to express the ideals of correct museum practice, define the highest philosophical expectations of the profession, describe acceptable museum practice, and outline the methods for maintaining professional standards. A code of ethics should present ethical issues in a rational structure formed on universal and impartial norms that disallow self-serving preferences and prejudices.

WHY SHOULD A CODE OF ETHICS BE REVISED?

If a code of ethics is dynamic, as it should be, then its real purpose is to aid in getting a museum from where it is (ethically) to where it wants to be. A code of ethics ought to assist in the process of discovering which activities are the most workable – museologically, intellectually, and responsibly.

To paraphrase a question attributed to Socrates: Is museum ethics determined to be right because the profession requires it, or does the profession require it because it is right? A code of ethics must be supported by reason. If a code requires a certain action for no understandable reason, it is correct to question it. If there is no satisfactory answer, then the profession ought to decide to alter that part of the code based on valid reasoning. In this way, a code of ethics is more than personal or institutional preference. Without a reasoned basis, all rules, standards, and ethics may be viewed as arbitrary and unworthy of attention. A true test of any ethical concept is to evaluate the reasons on which it is based.

A properly constructed code of ethics is more than an institutional document. It aids in defining the museum worker's duties to himself or herself for maintaining personal integrity, and the duties to others with whom the museum worker associates (professional relationships). However, a code of ethics is not a substitute for personal integrity, nor is it an instrument to alter the general behavior of the museum profession.

Some view a code of ethics as a restraint that impedes their ability to act as they wish. Others consider a well-formed code of ethics the basis of a properly functioning museum and a support for museum employees, volunteers, and visitors. Because a code of ethics addresses the changing and infinitely complicated world of museums and humanity, it is always subject to refinement. In the process of refinement, ethics involves a search for the most appropriate statement of correct actions in the museum setting.

Ethics has been described as a spiral process that elevates itself. The forces of changing technology and accepted practice result in a more clearly defined code of ethics. The code defines the profession and imposes greater expectations on acceptable practice. The ethical/professional process expands its influence by becoming more inclusive each time the cycle of practice validation is repeated. Each of these cycles more clearly defines the ethical core of the profession.

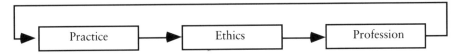

Figure 7.2   The ethical/professional process of renewal

WHY IS THERE A GREATER CONCERN FOR ETHICS TODAY THAN IN THE PAST?

There are several issues that have stimulated a growing concern for ethics and particularly professional ethics. In general, there is an unprecedented demand for ethical judgment and decisive action by persons in the museum profession. There is also a greater concern for public responsibility by those both in and entering the museum profession. This latter issue is of primary importance to those within the profession as unethical practices may jeopardize the standing of the group and depreciate the value of its services. In this way the code of ethics becomes a means of establishing a standard as a means of self-preservation.

A written code of ethics is an effective means of defining the expectations of the profession. It puts those expectations in a recognizable form that can be easily communicated to the membership and the public. A code also calls to attention that professional ethics are different from personal ones and that they require greater attention. This difference reflects the changing character of the museum profession – the complexities, demands, expectations, and ambiguities that present special problems that require ethical responses (Lewis 1991). Some of these special problems are outlined below.

1   There is a greater need for confidence in the actions of individuals than is expected of all people. That is, that those subscribing to the museum profession are expected to have higher ethical standards (relating to museum work) than those outside the profession, and that the standards are established by the whole of the profession rather individuals.

2   There is an assumption among national and international groups, organizations, and institutions that an established code of ethics vests a level of credibility in the subscribing individuals and institutions.

3   There is a need for validation of achievement and the belief that communicating the idea of establishing a code of ethics equates to truth.

4   "Ethical principles demand commitment and not merely nominal assent" (Garrett 1968: 6). Often ethical principles involve changes in the desires and impulses of those persons involved in adherence.

The first American Association of Museums code called the *Code of Ethics for Museum Workers* states:

> Museums, in the broadest sense, are institutions which hold their possessions in trust for mankind and for the future welfare of the

(human) race. Their value is in direct proportion to the service they render the emotional and intellectual life of the people. The life of a museum worker . . . is essentially one of service.

(AAM 1925: 1)

HOW IS A CODE OF ETHICS DEVELOPED?

A code of ethics is normally written in one of two styles and formats. One is a statement of philosophy that outlines the ethical canons to which the museum subscribes, and the second is a detailed description of the ethics and the application. The latter is normally preceded by a preamble that establishes the philosophical base for the code.

A code of ethics should encourage high standards of behavior by those in the profession and assist those persons in decision making. It also should increase public confidence in the profession by defining acceptable practices. For ease of understanding, a code of ethics may be divided into topic-related sections. In beginning to develop a code of ethics, it is helpful to determine the topics to be considered. By separating the material into related segments, the writing of a code of ethics becomes a more achievable project. Most of the topics are easily identified according to the specific requirements of the institution. Sections on governance, accessioning, deaccessioning, collection care, programming, and personnel are typically a part of the code of ethics. The ICOM *Code of Professional Ethics* (1990) is divided into eight sections:

1 Definitions
   1.1 The International Council of Museums
   1.2 Museum
   1.3 The Museum Profession
   1.4 Governing Body
2 Basic Principles for Museum Governance
   2.1 Minimum Standards for Museums
   2.2 Constitution
   2.3 Finance
   2.4 Premises
   2.5 Personnel
   2.6 Educational and Community Role of the Museum
   2.7 Public Access
   2.8 Displays, Exhibitions, and Special Activities
   2.9 Commercial Support and Sponsorship
   2.10 Museum Shops and Commercial Activities
   2.11 Legal Obligation
3 Acquisitions to Museum Collections
   3.1 Collecting Policies
   3.2 Acquisition of Illicit Material
   3.3 Field Study and Collecting

People dedicated to the ethical practices of a profession presume that others in that profession wish to act in an accepted manner. ("Accepted" meaning in accordance with the profession-established code of ethics.) Knowing that others within the profession will disapprove of an action or certain behavior causes most people to follow pre-established standards. One issue with every code of ethics is enforcement. As ethical standards are not laws with the power of governmental authority, enforcement is generally difficult. Compliance with most codes of ethics is voluntary and considered to be for the good of the group (organization, community, society, etc.). For extreme acts of unacceptable behavior, the normal means of censure (sanction) is exclusion from the group.

WHY SHOULD MUSEUM PROFESSIONALS ENDORSE A CODE OF ETHICS?

As a positive endorsement of ethical practice, it is common to regard with esteem those persons or institutions known to act according to the highest standards of the profession. In the museum community that esteem may manifest itself in the form of shared collections, research information, exhibits, or staff. Individuals and institutions known for their endorsement and practice of high ethical standards are "respected."

Communication of established professional practices is a primary mission of a code of ethics. The museum community cannot be expected to comply with established standards if those norms are not known. A code of ethics defines an "ethical obligation" for those subscribing to the profession. The sharing of a code of ethics reinforces the idea that people learn by an inductive process, that is, by having described the accepted forms of conduct endorsed by the profession.

The ICOM *Code of Professional Ethics* (1990) essentially is complete and can serve as a lead document for formulating an institutional code of ethics. The missing element is enforcement. Article 9, "Termination Of Membership," paragraph 1, section (d), of the ICOM *Statutes* states:

> The membership of an Individual or Institutional Member shall cease if any of the following circumstances applies: . . . (d) the Executive Council, acting on a recommendation of a National Committee or an International Committee or in exceptional circumstances on its own initiative, terminates the membership of a member for serious reasons relating to professional ethics or to actions which are substantially inconsistent with the objectives of ICOM.
>
> (ICOM 1990: 5)

In Article 15, "Regional Organizations," paragraph 7, section (c), of the ICOM *Statutes*, there is another statement relating to enforcement of the Code.

> A Regional Organization may be dissolved or suspended by the Executive Council, on the advice of the Advisory Committee, for . . .(c) actions that are serious violations of the *Statutes* or *Code of Professional Ethics* of ICOM.
>
> (ICOM 1990: 5)

However, these statements are in the *Statutes* and not an integrated part of the *Code of Professional Ethics* and the process of review for infractions is not defined.

WHAT ARE THE DIFFICULT ISSUES TO ADDRESS IN A CODE OF ETHICS?

One of the difficulties with museum ethics, as with most ethical issues, is determining what is "good" or "right" and appropriate for the museum profession. When there were only a few museums, most were familiar to one another, and it was easy to rely on personal judgment to assure ethical, or acceptable, conduct. As museums have proliferated and expectations have altered, it is the responsibility of the professional museum worker to design a code of ethics to complement accepted practice.

A clearly stated code of ethics should serve at least three very obvious functions:

1 as a reference of measure for other museums and museum personnel and those that come into contact with them,
2 as a benchmark to museums and professional museum workers when evaluating the effectiveness of their institutional policies, procedures, and practices, and
3 as a protection for museums and museum personnel if their institutional activities, programs, or conduct are questioned.

In addition to the general code of ethics for museums, there are codes for specialists in museum work areas such as conservators, curators, public relations officers, security personnel and registrars. This reality is reinforced by the statement that, "the movement to define standards of quality in museums and museum work has paralleled the growing need for public institutions of all kinds to be accountable for their actions, but it is also a natural step in the evolution of a profession" (Bloom and Powell 1984: 74).

> Ethics is a code or rule that applies to all equally. Ethical behavior or ethical decision making is where the mighty and the meek are subject to a fundamental code in which the rules of conduct are the same for everyone.
>
> (George 1988: 87)

In deciding right and wrong as related to the conduct of persons in the museum profession, there is another factor that should be considered. A code of ethics is a part of the museum community's reciprocal arrangement with the public it serves. The public supports museums through visitorship, direct and indirect funding, donations of objects, intellectual acknowledgment, and social perpetuation. In exchange, museums and museum personnel act in a certain way that provides assurances to the public that their investment will be protected and used in an acceptable way. The punishment for disregard of acceptable behavior is the loss of reciprocal services from the public (financial and political support and attendance). When the delinquency is adequately extreme, community judgment may be in the form of legal action.

At first view, the notion of reciprocity may be considered a variation of the "Golden Rule." The rule of "Do unto others as you would have them do unto you" embraces the notion of a reciprocal arrangement. However, with the museological code of ethics, the reciprocity is inclusive rather than exclusive. It includes all those in the profession rather than one person seeking to avoid retaliation. The principles of reciprocity and fairness in relationship (Westermarck 1917) with others in the profession are believed to be good for the group. When the practices or ethics fail to promote the values with which the profession is concerned, or when they are determined to be unfair to members of the group, they are allowed to fall into disuse (Garnett 1960).

The issues addressed so far have concentrated on the idea of establishing a code of ethics for the museum profession. The need for a code may be accepted even when not fully understood. However, total compliance with a partly understood code of ethics is sometimes difficult. Personal concerns, attitudes, and priorities complicate issues allowing for liberal interpretation of seemingly simple ethical concepts. Clearly defined ethical issues that allow for unqualified right or wrong answers usually are not difficult. It is that part of the ethical order that exists between the defined extremes that causes the problem: a situation that requires one to choose between two (seemingly) equally balanced alternatives. This middle ground allows for conflict between professional and personal ethics.

There are ethical conclusions that are accepted and applied without challenge. In society many of these commonly held attitudes have been transformed from ethical conduct into laws. A few issues relating to the museum community have made that transformation. As an example, in the United States there is the Native American Graves Protection and Repatriation Act of 1991 (Phelan 1994: 89). At the international level, there is the UNESCO Convention on the Means of Prohibiting and Preventing the Illicit Import, Export, and Transfer of Ownership of Cultural Property (Phelan 1994: 94).

Personal interest must be supplanted by the good of many. This statement is relevant to ethical consideration and should not be interpreted to be all-inclusive. Taken in the broadest context, the comment may suggest both positive and negative social and commercial notions. However, the idea of inclusive thinking as an ethical premise has good validity. When viewing a code of ethics, applicability is a point that must be considered. Institution-specific issues that address isolated ethical concerns tend to obfuscate rather than clarify both the purpose and intent of the code. Relevance to a particular museum is important but attention to museological concerns is imperative. It is also necessary to condense topics to definable issues. In that way a code of ethics can have an impact on individual as well as institutional attitudes and actions.

There are four fundamental problems with most professional standards (codes of ethics):

1 lack of understanding of the code by the general membership of the profession, therefore minimal endorsement,
2 no method for enforcement of the code,
3 code too general to provide sufficient direction, and
4 code out of date and the mechanism for revision is too cumbersome.

The value (good) of a code of ethics cannot be overstated. Each effort, no matter how flawed, becomes a reasonable foundation from which growth is possible. The recognition and application of professional ethics by every museum worker are primary steps toward promotion of a better self-image and the ability to contribute in a more meaningful way to the greater community of museums.

QUESTIONS FOR DISCUSSION

1 Is it important to have specialized codes of ethics to address discipline-specific concerns such as a code of ethics for registrars, curators, development officers, and museum shops?
2 Is the ethical decision making process more important in the museum community than in "for profit" business? Government? Medical or legal profession?
3 When an individual museum worker accepts the benefits of being a part of the museum profession, should that person expect to conduct himself or herself according to professional standards without question?
4 Should museum personnel know the amount of discretion they have in interpreting the rules of their museum and the impact of those rules on their employment?
5 Should museum personnel be aware of the method used to resolve conflicts between personal priorities and the standards and code of ethics established by their museum?
6 Is it reasonable for the museum profession to establish "best practice" standards for all museum workers worldwide?
7 Should non-compliance with museum ethics be grounds for dismissing museum personnel, volunteers, and trustees?
8 Are there special circumstances when a code of ethics should be disregarded or compromised?
9 Considering the various elements of the world cultural environment, is it possible to assume that all museum workers have a mutually shared concept of "stewardship" for the objects in museums?
10 To simplify matters, would it not be better to enact a number of international laws to regulate museums in all parts of the world?

ETHICAL SITUATION FOR DISCUSSION

Situation

The curator/director of a regional museum gets an unexpected call from the volunteer attendant at the front desk. The volunteer says there is a person with some objects to be donated to the museum, and she wants to talk to someone in charge.

The curator/director goes to the front entrance of the museum and finds an elderly woman holding a small suitcase. The woman introduces herself, saying she is 82 years old and that her best friend from the home for the elderly has died. The deceased woman had asked her to deliver the suitcase and its contents to the museum. The woman explains that her friend had talked for several months about giving the material to the museum but had simply failed to make the delivery.

The curator/director thanks the woman and tries to explain the museum's policy on donations and that every gift must be considered based on its importance and value to the museum. The woman says she knows nothing about such things. She is simply attempting to fulfill the wishes of her friend.

In a gesture of sympathy the curator/director opens the suitcase to evaluate the contents. Inside there are several personal letters to the deceased woman's daughter living in a distant city. There are photographs of unidentified people, a pair of reading glasses, and some drawings on notebook paper with captions saying, "I love you Grandma." Wrapped in a piece of tissue paper are a gold necklace and a diamond ring. Both have had considerable wear, and although they probably have monetary value, they are of little use to the museum.

The curator/director closes the case and tells the woman the gift cannot be accepted. The woman becomes agitated and confused, and says she must leave the case as it does not belong to her and that her friend said it was to go to the museum. As she makes this statement, she moves toward the door leaving the case on the reception desk. She says she has to go as there is someone waiting for her, and she leaves.

Concerns

- The curator/director does not know the name of the deceased friend, and only the family name of the woman who delivered the case, a name common to the community.
- The curator/director assumes the woman is in a home for senior citizens, but does not know the name of the home or where it is located.
- The curator/director has a suitcase of material that has no value to the museum, no contract of gift, and no way to authenticate either the ownership of the objects or the provenance of the material.

Comments

> Museums should not, except in very exceptional circumstances, acquire material that the museum is unlikely to be able to catalogue, conserve, store or exhibit, as appropriate, in a proper manner. Acquisitions outside the current stated policy of the museum should only be made in very exceptional circumstances, and then only after proper consideration by the governing body of the museum.
>
> (ICOM 1990: 27)

> Gifts, bequests and loans should only be accepted if they conform to the stated collecting and exhibition policies of the museums.
>
> (ICOM 1990: 28)

> By definition one of the key functions of almost every kind of museum is to acquire objects and keep them for posterity.
>
> (ICOM 1990: 29)

FURTHER READING

Guy, Mary, *Ethical Decision Making in Everyday Work Situations*, New York and London: Quorum Books, 1990.

Hare, R. M., The *Language of Morals*, Oxford: The Clarendon Press, 1962.

Heermance, Edgar, *Codes of Ethics: A Handbook*, Burlington, VT: Free Press Printing Company, 1924.

McDowell, Banks, *Ethical Conduct and the Professional's Dilemma*, New York and London: Quorum Books, 1991, chapters 1, 2, 3, 8, 10, and 12.

Mount, Eric, Jr., *Professional Ethics in Context: Institutions, Images and Empathy*, Louisville, KY: Westminster/John Knox Press, 1990, chapter 2.

Patterson, Charles, *Moral Standards: An Introduction to Ethics*, New York: The Ronald Press Company, 1949, chapters 16 and 19.

Rachels, James, "Can Ethics Provide Answers?" in: A. Caplan and D. Callaghan, *Ethics in Hard Times*, New York and London: Plenum Press, 1982, Chapter 1.

Rand, Ayn, *The Voice of Reason* (edited and with additional essays by Leonard Peikoff), New York: Meridian, 1990, chapter 4.

Rawls, John, *A Theory of Justice*, Cambridge, MA: The Belknap Press of Harvard University Press, 1971, chapters 2 and 6.

Taylor, Paul, *Principles of Ethics: An Introduction*, Belmont, CA: Dickenson Publishing Company, Inc., 1975, chapter 9.

Tsanoff, Radoslav, *Ethics*, New York: Harper & Brothers, 1955, chapter 14.

van Mensch (ed.), *Professionalising the Museums: The Museum Profession in Motion*, Amsterdam: AHA Books, 1989, chapters 1 and 7.

Part II
Ethical perspectives

Introduction to Part II

Kant asserted that everyone is familiar with ethical requirements relating to their conduct. The assumption being that everyone understands that there are things they ethically (morally) ought to do and other things that are unethical (immoral) and should not be done.

The traditional theories associated with ethics may seem restrictive or compartmentalized when compared with the complexities of contemporary society. Issues overlap. Concerns about environmental, social, financial, and intellectual issues seem to require complex ethical responses. However, it may be of value to consider that a code of ethics (or the ethical foundation of a museum) must be based on shared values rather than formalized theories. This concept reflects the idea of reciprocity. Shared values include: trust, respect, honesty, fairness, integrity, reliability, commitment, openness, and diversity (Bryce 1992). On these values, the museum can define the responsibilities of the trustees, administration, staff, and volunteers. It is these values that are formalized and explained by theories.

The identification of ethical norms that govern duties and responsibilities must be based on moral and social considerations, and project the character of public trust. Professional ethics for museums requires the articulation and internationalization of standards of behavior that reflect the museum community's origins and meet the current ethically justifiable expectations of that community. In some cases, the selection of the "right" course of action may not be as critical as the clear and public articulation of the course chosen. Honesty may not validate a particular attitude but it makes that attitude public and thereby allows choice. However, the key is internationalization (universalization) of standards of behavior. An institution may develop a plausible system of abstract concepts of duty and responsibility and, as long as it remains institutionally contained, no questions may arise. To withstand the test of the museum community, standards (ethics) must be placed in an international or universal context.

Issues of ethical significance come in all sizes and in all levels of museum work. However, it is the situation that seems the most insignificant which is most often overlooked or disregarded. Seemingly commonplace situations establish a pattern of ethical behavior (or the lack thereof) that is the foundation for an automatic response system. Although the scholarly approach to ethical issues may focus on points or conditions of absolutes, practical application includes professional standards and expectations. Sound museum ethics must be a part of all activities and cannot be reserved for only the "important" problems.

When an institution asks the public for trust, it passes the responsibility of trust to those granting the request. However, when an institution has a position of trust, as do museums, the responsibility for preserving that trust remains with the institution. It cannot be transferred by unilateral decision but is incumbent on the institution until it is removed by the public.

Ethics concerns not only the will to "do the right thing," but also the judgments and decisions associated with those actions. It is concerned with the tendencies of the person or institution. The major issues that challenge ethical activities in museums are those that involve either extremes in emotional issues or concerns that may be justified from different perspectives:

- Is a wrong act always wrong regardless of the outcome?
- Is an act that pleases the majority always justified?
- Is right and wrong a question of interpretation or perspective?

It is relatively easy to write hypothetical scenarios for theoretical ethical situations. By dealing with ethics theories in abstract, it is possible to demonstrate the basic concepts of right and wrong actions. Using allegories, it is possible to illustrate the need for ethical practices by considering situations in which ethical behavior is absent or unethical attitudes are present. However, it should not be assumed that there is only one way to respond to a particular situation, or that each theory of ethical behavior is fixed and inflexible. In truth, each situation may require the review of a number of principles to give ethical content to the final decision. It is this process of analysis that gives credibility to the decision making.

In the second part of this book, practicing museum professionals from various parts of the world present issues that are important to the museum community. Writers were requested to respond to a particular topic, but no directions or limitations were imposed. Each person brings to the subject his or her perspective, which reflects a particular sensitivity to ethical concerns. Chapters are introduced by a short statement and questions for further consideration.

8

Ethics and cultural identity

As the political nature of the world changes, the significance of museums as institutions of social and cultural identity has also changed. The importance of this role has not been lost on governments and political entities, nor have museums been ignored as instruments for projecting national identity. This condition exists to a greater or lesser degree in most places in the world as societies expand and contract to reflect changing demographics, economic and environmental conditions, and political disruption.

The relationship between nationalism and museums is a longstanding and often complicated issue associated with national unity and ethnic loyalty. Under current global conditions, the world's cultural and natural heritage is rapidly diminishing in scope and diversity as group identity is being homogenized owing to the blending action of technological advancements. At the same time, the diversity of the world's population is being recognized by inclusion of multi-cultural materials in museums.

There is an opportunity for museums to present and interpret a wide range of material previously viewed as curiosities from distant and unknown lands.

For many new and emerging nations, museums are addressing political and economic issues as well as cultural ones. Most museums have sought to avoid excessive partisanism or arbitrary value judgments when selecting, presenting, and interpreting objects. Others have been less scrupulous in these matters. Are the basic tenets of museum ethics compromised by the imposition of political or other externally generated priorities upon collecting, exhibiting, and programming?

QUESTIONS ABOUT ETHICS AND CULTURAL IDENTITY FOR FURTHER CONSIDERATION

1   When two countries in an armed conflict have agreed not to destroy each other's culturally significant property and one breaks that agreement, is the other country released from its promise? What theories of ethical behavior might be considered?

129

2   Is it unethical to remove archaeological objects from their country of origin even if there are no laws to protect them and no museums with adequate facilities to house them?

3   To be ethical, should every object, regardless of value, be returned to its place of origin, or would it be preferable to keep some objects and have the originating people aid in the interpretation?

4   Nationalistic pride is a powerful force that is often reflected in the history and attitudes of a people. It can equally influence both the oppressor and the oppressed. Both may pursue the right to claim or reclaim their heritage with equal vigor aided by an assertion of ethical correctness. Both may have the "power" of the people behind their efforts, but can both be ethically right?

5   Who has the ethical right to claim the cultural heritage of a people? Is it unethical for a museum to collect archaeological objects?

Community, country, and commonwealth

The ethical responsibility of museums

Silas Okita

INTRODUCTION

A number of developments in the museum movement during the last few decades have forced museums to pay greater attention to ethical issues. Of these developments, the ethical response to multiculturalism and globalization poses the greatest challenge. They, more than anything else, raise several basic ethical questions about the role of museums in preserving, presenting, and promoting cultural and national identity. Although belatedly, ICOM and a number of national museum associations now have codes of professional ethics, or other provisions that address ethical concerns. One of the aims of ICOM that constitutes an ethical responsibility is: "to advance knowledge and the understanding of the nature, functions and role of museums in the service of society and its development" (ICOM 1990: 4).

In pursuance of this goal, museums are assuming political and economic roles in addition to cultural ones. They are also responding to the needs of the whole society rather than to isolated segments. The idea of ecomuseums and community museums reflects this new trend. It is within this context that a positive response toward multiculturalism in the current museum movement can be appreciated.

Multiculturalism has attracted museum attention at both national and international levels, presenting different scenarios among both "developed" and "developing" countries, or in the relationships between former colonial powers and their colonies that are now independent nation states. Multiculturalism has been featured in the deliberations of ICOM. It is the theme of conferences, museum associations, professional meetings, and most significantly, recent museum publications.

Multiculturalism also has been helped and strengthened by the UNESCO *Convention on the Means of Prohibiting and Preventing the Illicit Import, Export, and Transfer of Ownership of Cultural Property*. The Convention has provided the political force that may be employed in articulating the requirements for restitution of cultural patrimony held by some museums. It is not only a threat to the existence of certain established museums, it also undermines the sense of national unity and integration in countries that have to address the issue of cultural pluralism.

This situation, coupled with increasing globalization, has made the ultra-narrow nationalistic spirit of nineteenth-century Europe, or that of the emerging independent nation states of Africa of the late 1950s and early 1960s, an anachronism. This change reflects the current economic, social, political strategies, and environmental problems that call for joint rather than individual solutions. In turn, it has created a major challenge and raised a number of fundamental ethical questions for museums in the 1990s. These questions must address the museum's role of preserving, presenting, and promoting the cultural identity of their communities, without unduly threatening their national identity, or undermining our common humanity. Whatever the ultimate response, whether through community museums, ecomuseums, or national museums, the profession is concerned with the basic role and ethical responsibility of museums in the service of society and of its development. In discharging this responsibility to humanity, museums may see their roles more in political, economic, or cultural terms, depending on place, time, and circumstance.

To examine the issues more closely, it is necessary to develop a historical perspective and examine the political role of museums in promoting nationalism and national identity. This will lead to consideration of museums and multi-culturalism, and museums and globalization. The cultural role of museums will be highlighted in the case of the former, and the role of museums in helping to create a better climate for economic cooperation, on a global level, will be considered in the latter. The aim is to search for a solution to basic human problems through fruitful cooperation and collaboration, rather than destructive competition and conquest. Given their primary responsibilities of collection, conservation, and communication, museums are the most appropriate institutions to discharge the ethical responsibility of assuring greater harmony among humanity on the one hand, and between humanity and nature on the other.

NATIONALISM: PRESERVING AND PROJECTING NATIONAL IDENTITY

The relationship between nationalism and museums has been a close and longstanding one. In Greek and Roman times, the public had the opportunity to view public displays of the spoils of war in honor of the gods and goddesses that had helped the rulers in their victories. In Europe, the nineteenth century was a time that engendered the spirit of nationalism. It was also the age of museum creation. In France, the same spirit that turned the former royal collection of the Louvre into an epitome of imperial glory and majesty forced the return of the art works looted from the rest of Europe. In London, the British Museum, a symbol of the imperial genius of Great Britain, remains a tantalizing experience for the nationals of the former colonies, who, also for reasons of nationalism, are eagerly awaiting the opportunity for the restitution of their treasures. In all parts of the world, the political role museums can play in promoting nationalism, through the preservation and projection of national identity, has led to the establishment of national museums.

Clearly, the political role of museums in promoting nationalism is significant. However, it should be equally clear that there are several problems associated with this role for museums. As an example, at the international level where the projection of nationalism by one country undermines that of another, there is bound to be a reaction. This is true in situations that involve conquest and expansion. For instance, the Louvre was an epitome of French imperial glory and majesty under Napoleon. The war plunder that enriched the Louvre also impoverished and undermined the sense of nationalism of those who suffered defeat. In the same way, certain art treasures held by former European colonial powers not only remind former colonies of a past but often lead to the articulation of demands for the restitution of such treasures, as symbols of regaining a lost glory. It is within this context that the political significance of the 1970 UNESCO *Convention on the Means of Prohibiting and Preventing the Illicit Import, Export, and Transfer of Ownership of Cultural Property* can be appreciated.

Preserving and projecting national identity presents problems also at the national level. In fact, the problems at this level are even more complex than the ones at the international level. For example, nation states such as the former Austro-Hungarian Empire and USSR, or others like India and Nigeria, have the "National Question" to resolve. The issue is national unity and integration versus ethnic loyalty and identity in an environment of cultural diversity and pluralism. In countries such as the United Kingdom and Canada, regionalism and separatism are very strong. It is necessary to contend with centralization on the one hand, and decentralization and devolution on the other. In other countries, including the United States of America, Australia, New Zealand, and South Africa (to some extent), all nation states that emerged largely owing to the immigrant factor, are confronted with the issue of a mainstream immigrant culture versus a minority indigenous culture. This situation in the United States is further complicated by the presence of African-Americans and Asian immigrants who, like Native Americans, represent minority groups with different historical factors accounting for the presence of the former group of minorities.

The issue of national identity is a complex one. It requires close observation and examination to appreciate some of the basic ethical issues involved in preserving and projecting national identity to enhance the sense of nationalism needed for nation building. To do this, a number of questions must be considered:

- What national identity is to be projected?
- Which social and cultural heritage is to be preserved?
- Whose identity and interests should the museum represent, preserve, and present?
- Which museums (national, local, community, or ethnic) better serve national identity?
- How far can museums afford to go in a political role?

- What aspects of heritage are to be glorified (the past that condemns the present or the present that demeans or ignores the past)?

The intention of raising these questions is not so much to provide answers but to show the range of the issues involved and the complexity of the problems. To be more specific, it may be helpful to examine two of these questions, which will serve to illustrate some of the main issues to be raised. The first of these concerns will address the definition of national identity. The second will deal with the issue of which heritage and whose identity and interest museums should represent, preserve, and present.

"Identity" has been defined as: the distinguishing character or personality of an individual. It is essentially a psychological phenomenon involving the perception, definition, and projection of self in relation to others. Although mainly psychological, there is also a cultural and political dimension. In terms of genesis and persistence, it emerges and thrives under situations of cultural diversity or pluralism. It exists where fear or threat of domination, assimilation, and repression, or a general sense of insecurity due to persecution, whether real or imaginary, is felt between nation states or among different ethnic groups within a multi-ethnic state. While such a fear may take the form of nationalism in the case of the former, it often expresses itself as ethnicity in the latter. In this sense, national, or ethnic identity, may be described as an ideological construct employed in the articulation, definition, and advancement of national or group interests, to assure its survival in relation to others (Okita 1986).

A good example of the conception and employment of ethnicity as a mobilizing political tool and survival strategy is provided by the proclamation of the Biafran Republic for the largely Igbo-speaking people during the Nigerian Civil War of 1967–70. Commenting on the Biafran struggle, Ojukwu, leader of the attempted secession, states that:

> The proclamation of the Biafran Republic was at best, the delimitation of the people's last defensive position (our last ditch). The territorial delimitation of Biafra was like a series of beacons, search lights, if you will, to help a brutalized and persecuted people identify a safe haven and to inspire them in making the final dash to safety.
> (Odumegwu-Ojukwu 1989: 167)

The issue of the genesis and persistence of ethnic or national identity is an important and basic one that is significant in the lives of individuals, the existence of ethnic groups, and the survival of nation states. It may be noted that just as identity can be defined from a psychological, cultural, or political perspective, its significance for the individual, ethnic group, or nation state also corresponds to these three levels. Psychologically, because identity involves self-perception and projection, it provides self-esteem and empowerment for an individual. Culturally, for an ethnic group, it provides a sense of distinctiveness, and sometimes a tendency toward a feeling of superiority. Politically it creates a sense of patriotism and national pride that makes certain nation states seek power, prestige, and glory, and express them in a manner that undermines those of others. When this happens, it can lead to strained relations among nation states. This situation has more appeal to our sense of nationalism than to our spirit of national unity and integration, when these are under internal threats from ethnicity. This is because the psychological and cultural attachment to our ethnic group is stronger than our political attachment to the nation state.

The reason for having a stronger psychological and cultural attachment to the ethnic group rather than the nation state comes from the character of the state. This is in spite of the fact that characteristics such as common descent, territory, history, language, religion, and way of life are generally associated with the nation state rather than the nation to which they belong (Petersen 1975: 81). The nation state is essentially an artificial creation, a historical product whose boundary can change. This is because the nation state is concerned with the building up, deployment, and management of force, the reconciliation of interests, and the promotion of material and social well-being. However, it lacks "spirit" (Afigbo and Okita 1985: 52). As a result, it has to appeal to those common characteristics normally associated with a nation as the shared experience of its citizenry, in its relationship with other nation states. Therefore, the nation state appropriates from the nation what it lacks, to create the spirit and life that it needs to survive. It is in this context that the significance of the establishment of national museums to create and nourish a spirit of nationalism and a sense of national identity can be appreciated.

Because of the artificial nature of the nation state, it is often seen more in terms of its ability or failure to provide and advance certain common goals. These goals, as noted already, include: the building up, deployment, and management of force to contain internal insurrection and ward off external aggression; the reconciliation of interests; and the promotion of material and social well-being.

Where the state meets these common goals, to secure life and property in ways considered equitable, it can create a sense of identity and a spirit of belonging among the citizenry. However, the deeper sense of psychological attachment is a basic human endowment that appears to be located outside the nation state and usually resides in one's own community. For, after all, while empires rise and fall, and state boundaries change, or people change their citizenship through naturalization, a person's sense of community is a basic and persistent phenomenon. Born of a particular ethnic origin, that deeper sense of psychological attachment tends to remain with its source of origin, irrespective of one's nationality or citizenship. Thus, while every American or Nigerian may be proud of his or her nationality and citizenship, that sense of national pride may not remove the deeper psychological attachment to one's ethnic origin. This has important political and cultural implications.

MULTICULTURALISM: UNITY IN DIVERSITY

The genesis and persistence of ethnic identity continue despite the desire for national unity and integration in multi-ethnic states. According to Boylan:

Few if any states in modern history have been more ferocious in developing and imposing closely defined and all-pervasive official state cultures than the totalitarian regimes of the 1920s to 1950s, whether Mussolini's Italy, Stalin's Soviet Union, Hitler's Germany, Peron's Argentina, or Mao Zedong's China, the latter both before and during what was, of course, officially called the Cultural Revolution. Such official state cultures pervaded all aspects of society and human existence from before conception to beyond the grave, affecting not just museums but architecture, design, literature, music and perhaps above all education and the media.

(Boylan 1990: 244)

Despite the above observation, Boylan also explains that:

In the late 1970s, at the height of the Brezhnev era, the USSR authorities were proudly boasting of the fact that the USSR which had just seven museums at the time of the 1917 Revolution (plus a few more in the Baltic states subsequently annexed) now had over 1,500 museums. However, at about the same time ICOM USSR did a survey that revealed that even in that tightly controlled and regulated system, local groups and individuals had – with no authorization, let alone encouragement, or financial or other support from the state – created no less than 14,000 unofficial museums, reflecting the needs, the history and the cultural identity of their own locality or special interest.

(Boylan 1990: 247)

In the United States of America the earlier expectations of the emergence of one homogeneous culture, epitomized in the idea of the "melting pot," has given way to a new realism of accepting multiculturalism. In different ways federal, state, and local entities make it possible for museums that focus on minority cultures to be established. The support and encouragement from mainstream institutions and relevant professional bodies for this growing multiculturalism in museums are noteworthy.

This trend toward multiculturalism is a global one with only a differing scenario from one place or time to another. In terms of museums' response to multiculturalism, there have been two basic approaches. One of these is a movement toward establishing "exclusive" or separate museums that focus on minority cultures, as is exemplified in the United States. The other trend, symbolized by the situation in Nigeria, is toward establishing national museums that are expected to be "inclusive" and representative of the country's cultural diversity, with emphasis on national unity and integration. It may be noted that the different scenarios often raise different ethical problems, or present themselves in different forms, even where they are similar.

In the case of the area that came to be known as Nigeria, pre-colonial collections related to the culture and history of the different communities and families that existed in various forms. They were secured in the shrines, palaces, and individual homes of family heads and elders of the ethnic groups and nationalities that emerged as Nigerians in 1914. Not unexpectedly, access to, and the roles of, these collections were limited to the communities that owned them, as they represented the culture, history, religious beliefs, and the general ethos of such communities.

However, when public or national museums were established in the second half of the twentieth century, the collections in museums were expected to assume a "Nigerian" or national outlook, irrespective of ethnic origin or role of the collections. Thus, the famous terracottas of the Nok culture and Ife, the Bini bronze and ivory works, and Igbo-Ukwu leaded bronze pieces were claimed as "Treasures of Ancient Nigeria." They were displayed in national museums within the country and shown in museums around the world to enhance national image and prestige, both at home and abroad.

Clearly, there is something contradictory in the roles expected of museums in nation building in a culturally pluralistic society like Nigeria, a country that had to adopt federalism to contain and make provisions for cultural and historical differences among the constituent parts. The issue is one of national unity and integration versus cultural pluralism and ethnic identity on the one hand, and national interest and regional or state loyalty on the other.

Following the Nigerian Civil War of 1967–70, the National Antiquities Commission (now National Commission for Museums and Monuments) made a political decision to establish a national "unity" museum in each state capital of the federation. At the time of that decision there were twelve states in Nigeria. Today there are thirty states. This means there will eventually be thirty national museums located in capital cities alongside the states' own museums. This continuous strong regional attachment raises serious and fundamental political and professional problems which Nigerian museum professionals and their colleagues abroad must address.

The basic question to be examined is: Is it possible to promote the idea of national unity and integration, necessary for nation building, without destroying ethnic identity? Related to this issue is the question of whether it is possible or desirable to transform ethnic collections into a "melting pot" of national unity. If desirable, can that objective be achieved by simply placing objects side by side? Is the seemingly contradictory role of museums in nation building not concili-atory through a collecting policy that represents the culturally pluralistic society and, therefore, capable of promoting unity in diversity? It may be suggested that despite the complex and seemingly contradictory role of museums in nation building, it can still be conciliatory, even in a culturally pluralistic society like Nigeria, if handled with care and imagination. In this way, national unity and integration can be achieved without destroying ethnic identity.

To achieve unity in diversity it is necessary to address the issue of which heritage and whose identity museums should represent, preserve, project, and promote. As noted, while the issue of identity is significant for the individual, ethnic group, and nation state, the need it fulfills is different for each. In a multi-ethnic country like Nigeria, where the national museums are expected to be represen-tative in terms of both the range of collections and the mode of display, the importance of a thematic approach cannot be overestimated. This is because

137

it is the most effective way in which museums can address the ethical problem of which heritage and whose identity museums should collect, conserve, and communicate. With a creative approach, a national museum can address the psychological, cultural, and political needs of an individual, ethnic group, and the nation state. In this way, it can promote unity in diversity, across both vertical and horizontal lines. Where museums are established at the state or local level, rather than national one, creative and imaginative themes can link what may appear to be of only local interest; they can thereby appeal to the rest of humanity at national and international levels.

As an example, an exhibition on "shelter" can center on basic human need through different house types at different historical periods among different peoples of the world. The exhibition also can stress the relationship between humanity and the environment, or culture and environment, showing how dependent humankind is on nature, and, hence, the ethical imperative of protecting the environment. Such an exhibition may be of interest to all sectors of the economy. Participation by communities in formulation of housing policies also can be highlighted. People of various academic and professional backgrounds may find shelter, as a theme, very attractive, as it offers a great deal of scope. Such a theme can address human needs in a manner that reflects a common heritage, while giving recognition to diversity, across vertical and horizontal boundaries, at local, national, and international levels.

GLOBALIZATION: FROM CONQUEST TO COLLABORATION

Imperialism has been described as the highest stage of capitalism. This explains the European search for colonies and the subsequent expansionism in an era that witnessed excessive competition and rivalry among European powers in a manner that led to "unbridled imperialism" or the "scramble for Africa." Today, despite the political independence won by former colonies, Western capitalism still dominates the world – although with a change in tactics. During European expansionism, nation states were concerned with promotion of the material well-being of their citizenry, with the projection of national pride and prestige, as well as imperial power and glory.

However, the emerging nationalism that led to the political independence of former colonies and subsequent political, economic, social, and environmental problems has forced a collective and global approach to the solution of problems. Faced with these new realities, nation states appear prepared to re-examine and redefine the former conventional notion of national sovereignty. They are also prepared to move away from imperial posturing to an attitude of regionalization, globalization, and partnership in order to address certain common political, economic, social, and environmental problems. The previous ultra-nationalistic and competitive spirit, reminiscent of imperialistic nineteenth-century Europe, is being replaced by political and economic cooperation among former rivals and traditional adversaries. The formation of international trading partnerships is an attempt at regionalization and globalization to address common human problems across national boundaries. The general trend emerging from these groupings appears to be a move away from individualism and nationalism to a collective human approach for the advancement and promotion of international interests.

Although the basic national goal is still economic, it is recognized that cultural exchange can promote human understanding and create a better climate for economic and political cooperation. Consequently, the capitalism that led to European expansionism is a major factor in the current move toward regionalization and globalization. The former spirit of competition, driven by the desire for power, prestige, and glory, that looked for lands to conquer, is giving way to mutual benefits. Nation states are searching for new definitions of power, prestige, and glory, and adopting more subtle ways to define and project themselves at home and abroad.

Economic growth to secure for the nation state and its citizenry the material well-being needed to survive is an aim of expansionism. It is equally recognized that increased power and glory can enhance a sense of self-esteem in individuals and the promotion of a strong sense of identity and national pride among groups and national states.

The current movement toward globalization presents a challenge, as well as an ethical responsibility, for museums and nation states alike. As museums are the most appropriate institutions to represent, preserve, present, and promote identity, the nation state also represents the most convenient and viable political unit for the reconciliation of the rather complex and seemingly contradictory role of museums at community, national, and international levels.

Given the basic responsibility of museums to collect, conserve, and communicate, they can help humanity to define and project itself in order to promote harmony with nature and understanding among its peoples. To discharge this ethical responsibility, museums may well benefit from the challenge posed by Ripley, the chief executive officer of the Smithsonian Institute. He wrote:

> Could we not complete the chain of museums on the mall in
> Washington with a final museum, a museum of the Family of Man?
> In such a museum we could perhaps transmit something that has
> eluded museums as collections of objects. We could show the concept
> of the creation of the spirit of man, the development of ideas which
> arise in the human species wherever it happens to exist. Could we show
> the unity of man as an explorer of ideas – in art, science, invention – all
> the stuff of culture, moved by spirit, which occurs in species no matter
> how diverse our environments?
>
> (Alexander 1983: 304)

In the final analysis, it is only when museums can succeed in helping to perceive and project us beyond our communities and countries, by nourishing the common humanity in each of us, and equipping us to meet the challenges of our existence, that a claim to unique ethical responsibility can be justified.

9

Ethics and indigenous peoples

There are certain ideas that are basic to a humanistic view of the world, and the altering of that view transforms all associated activities and perceptions. The actualities of today may have little to do with the realities of tomorrow. Beliefs about many things must change as a result of a revision of the accepted concept of the universe and its relationship to humankind.

Museums are moving away from the individual's personal gratification to a community-wide consciousness and a concern for worldwide issues. No issue is of greater importance or calls for more attention than the one relating to identity. As the world is being compressed by technological means, in many areas the human population is struggling for survival and identity. With the bringing together of all people via the miracle of scientific apparatus, there is a synthesis of expectation without the means of fulfillment for a large segment of humanity. Some people are willing to forfeit their identity in the process of resolving the discrepancy of resources; others seek to retain and enhance their cultural heritage as a means of identity, self-respect, and group empowerment.

Many of the issues relating to the world's indigenous peoples are not situations that can be resolved solely on the economic or political level. They must be enjoined at the people's level. How can museums better serve society and be a positive influence in recognizing the values and merits of all people?

QUESTIONS ABOUT ETHICS AND INDIGENOUS PEOPLES FOR FURTHER CONSIDERATION

1 Socially accepted practices are often used to validate proposed ethical differences among groups of people. However, some researchers argue that differences in social practice are not really based on a difference in basic ethical principles. They contend that the intended outcome is the same regardless of the method of achieving that end. Does this idea argue for or against a transcultural ethical code for museums?

2 Viewed from the perspective of human dignity and the right of a people to preserve their cultural heritage, most people support the idea of repatriation.

140

Emotion aside, are there conflicting ethical issues when cultural materials from museum collections are returned to requesting groups while the original donor is denied the expected continual care and maintenance of his or her collection?

3 Should it be acceptable to act in an unethical manner to promote the good or well-being of an underrepresented segment of society?

4 Some people may believe that if the self-serving actions of a large and wealthy museum should cause harm to smaller and poorer museums, then the larger museum has an ethical duty to compensate those who have been harmed. However, suppose a large museum is requested to give a collection of important objects to several small museums, and they become financially impoverished by providing care for that collection. Does that situation also impose an ethical obligation for compensation from the large museum?

5 If a museum is to be of service to its constituency, should not that audience include all facets of the visiting public, and should not the staff and board of the museum also be representative of that diversity? The question of integration of the museum board has a number of ramifications. Is the board to represent the constituency or aid in the activities of museum governance and fund raising? Is there an ethical conflict between caring for the collections and representing the cultural diversity of the museum's constituency?

Indigenous peoples, museums, and ethics

Amareswar Galla

> We believe in the wisdom of our ancestors and wise people who passed
> on to us their strength and taught us the art of language – enabling us
> to reaffirm the validity of our thousand year old history and the justice
> of our struggle. . . . The International Decade for Indigenous People is
> one more step toward building new relationships between states and
> indigenous peoples on the basis of mutual respect.
>
> (Menchú 1994: 33)

INTRODUCTION

The end of the Cold War and the dismantling of apartheid structures in South
Africa will lead to an increasing focus on the situation of indigenous peoples in
the world. The inauguration of the International Decade of the World's
Indigenous People in December 1994 brings indigenous peoples and their rights
on to the center stage of the global cultural agenda. In 1993, the Year of
Indigenous People provided an international focus on the continuing vulner-
ability of the 300 million aboriginal people in 70 countries. In several parts of
the world, the survival of indigenous people is in danger. For instance, in 1986
there were 10,000 Yanomami in Venezuela: a people whose survival has been
under dire threat. During the droughts of the 1970s nearly 125,000 Tuareg
nomads in the Sahara starved to death as they found it hard to move their herds
to faraway water holes (Menchú 1994). The health conditions of indigenous
peoples are some of the most appalling in the world.

Indigenous peoples have survived despite centuries, and in some instances
millennia, of colonialism, imperialism, and cultural genocide. The resilience
of indigenous peoples is a significant part of the heritage of humanity as it is
symbolic of their capacity for the caring of mother earth in the face of greed
and exploitation. As we move closer toward the turn of the century, the right
to self-determination will be the central principle driving change in all spheres
of life relating to indigenous peoples. The focus of museums, which has been
largely collection-centered, will come under greater scrutiny from indigenous
peoples who have been striving for wider objectives of community-based

cultural conservation and self-determination within the context of social justice strategies. The argument is that there is a direct and primary link between cultural control, heritage, health, and social well-being (Aboriginal Interests Working Group 1991).

The evolution of museums in the past two centuries has inevitably been intertwined with the colonial factors, often disenfranchising and reducing indigenous people as prisoners of collections and archives (Galla 1993a). In several parts of the world, museums and indigenous peoples are beginning to negotiate constructive partnerships and work toward redressing the imbalances in the current practices of cultural heritage management. While the leadership of indigenous people is crucial for future policy approaches, community cultural development ideology will pose a new challenge to museologists. It is in this context that museums have a fundamental role in addressing questions of the erosion of cultural self-esteem and modeling community relations strategies to enhance cross-cultural awareness about indigenous cultures.

In 1972, participants at the meeting of the International Council of Museums (ICOM) in Santiago, Chile, argued that museums should become an integral part of societies around them. This is reflected in the 1974 revision of the ICOM definition with a clear statement that the museum should be an institution in the service of society and its development (ICOM 1989). These changes inform the *Code of Professional Ethics* of ICOM that was ratified in Buenos Aires at its 15th General Assembly on 4 November 1986. This code sets down guidelines that are intended to guarantee "ethical" behavior in all areas of museum activity. It has often been stated that "codes were established because it was felt that there was an urgent need to codify ethical principles in museum affairs. ... [M]useums today need ethical principles in order to meet the challenge of tomorrow" (Schmidt 1992: 257–68). The challenges of cultural justice strategies and the commitment to cultural diversity continue to pose new questions to all public sector institutions. As and when museums endeavor to implement the basic principles of access and equity, museological practice will become increasingly mature and require further refinement of codes of practice.

UN DRAFT DECLARATION ON THE RIGHTS OF INDIGENOUS PEOPLES

This Draft Declaration has important implications for museological practice and the associated codes of conduct. The Working Group on Indigenous Populations (WGIP) held its first session in 1982 in Geneva. The Economic and Social Council of UN, responsible for the creation of the Group, mandated two tasks for WGIP. The first was to review developments pertaining to the promotion and protection of the human rights and fundamental freedoms of indigenous populations. The second task was to give special attention to the evolution of standards concerning the rights of such populations.

The Draft Declaration prepared by the WGIP in 1994 contains nine parts. Part III relates to the cultural, religious, spiritual, and linguistic identity of indigenous

143

peoples. This section that has direct significance to museums and other agencies managing cultural heritage is quoted below. The main purpose of providing the following extract is to challenge museologists to reflect on ways in which their practice could be modified within the framework of international protocol and obligations and their own ethical and professional conduct. Articles are provided from the Draft Declaration. Associated notes are extracted from the respective sections of the Technical Review of the United Nations Draft Declaration on the Rights of Indigenous Peoples (E/CN. 4/Sub. 2/1994/2).

PART III (CULTURE, RELIGIOUS AND LINGUISTIC IDENTITY)

Notes

48 The right of persons belonging to ethnic, religious, or linguistic minorities "in community with the other members of their group, to enjoy their own culture, to profess and practice their own religion, or to use their own language" is protected in Article 27 of the International Covenant on Civil and Political Rights. Part III of the Draft Declaration extends these rights to indigenous peoples. It may be noted that Article 30 of the Convention on the Rights of the Child gives the same rights to children belonging to such minorities but also refers explicitly to children who are "indigenous." It may also be noted that the individual's scientific, literary, or artistic production is protected in Article 15, Paragraph 1 of the International Covenant on Economic, Social, and Cultural Rights.

Article 12

Indigenous peoples have the right to practice and revitalize their cultural traditions and customs. This includes the right to maintain, protect, and develop the past, present, and future manifestations of their cultures, such as archaeological and historical sites, artifacts, designs, ceremonies, technologies, and visual and performing arts and literature, as well as the right to the restitution of cultural, intellectual, religious, and spiritual property taken without their free and informed consent or in violation of their laws, traditions, and customs.

Notes

49 In this Article the right of indigenous peoples to practice and revitalize their cultural traditions and customs includes "the right to the restitution of cultural, intellectual, religious and spiritual property taken without their free and informed consent or in violation of their laws, traditions and customs."

50 It may be noted that Article 24 of the Draft Declaration, which is placed in Part V covering social and economic rights, deals with intellectual property in the specific context of traditional medical knowledge and gives indigenous peoples the "right to the protection of vital medicinal plants, animals, and minerals." Article 29, which is placed in Part VI dealing with land and resources, also protects the cultural and intellectual property of indigenous peoples, but has a broader scope as it refers to "sciences, technologies, and cultural manifestations, including human and genetic resources, seeds, medicines, knowledge of the properties of fauna and flora, oral traditions, literature, designs, and visual and performing arts."

Article 13

Indigenous peoples have the right to manifest, practice, develop, and teach their spiritual and religious traditions, customs, and ceremonies; the right to maintain, protect, and have access in privacy to their religious and cultural sites; the right to the use and control of ceremonial objects; and the right to the repatriation of human remains.

States shall take effective measures, in conjunction with the indigenous peoples concerned, to ensure that indigenous sacred places, including burial sites, be preserved, respected, and protected.

Notes

52 Article 18 of the Universal Declaration of Human Rights contains the right of everyone to freedom of thought, conscience, and religion, which includes freedom "either alone or in community with others and in public or private, to manifest his religion or belief in teaching, practice, worship, and observance."

53 Article 18, paragraph 1 of the International Covenant on Civil and Political Rights uses almost the same wording. The Declaration on the Elimination of All Forms of Intolerance and of Discrimination Based on Religion or Belief in Article 1 also protects this right. However, it should be noted that both instruments allow certain limitations on the right to manifest one's religion or belief if these limitations "are prescribed by law and are necessary to protect public safety, order, health, or morals or the fundamental rights and freedoms of others."

Article 14

Indigenous peoples have the right to revitalize, use, develop, and transmit to future generations their histories, languages, oral traditions, philosophies, writing systems, and literature, and to designate and retain their own names for communities, places, and persons.

States shall take effective measures, whenever any right of indigenous peoples may be threatened, to ensure this right is protected and also to ensure that they can understand and be understood in political, legal, and administrative proceedings, where necessary through the provision of interpretation or by other appropriate means.

Notes

54 The second part of this Article calls on States to ensure that indigenous peoples can understand and be understood in political, legal, and administrative proceedings. A similar provision – although only applying to criminal proceedings – is already contained in Article 14, paragraph 3 (f) of the International Covenant on Civil and Political Rights, which gives a person charged with a criminal offense the right to have the free assistance of an interpreter if he cannot understand or speak the language used in court.

55 Article 12 of ILO Convention No. 169 also obliges States "to ensure that members of these peoples can understand and be understood in legal proceedings, where necessary through the provision of interpretation or by other effective means."

SOME CHALLENGES FOR MUSEUMS

The immediate challenge for museums is to explore the historical background to the relationship between museums and indigenous peoples. This requires museums to address the colonial constructions of what constitutes "indigenous" along with the associated discourse of control and dispossession. Such an introspective approach will enable the development of frameworks for a reassessment of current professional practice. It is important to recognize and focus discussion within the context of the social history of indigenous peoples. The constitutional recognition of disadvantages faced by tribal peoples in India and the bicultural foundation of the rights of the Maori in New Zealand centering around the Treaty of Waitangi, provide critical frameworks for indigenous people in those countries to negotiate. Other forms of public acknowledgment, such as the statement by the prime minister of Australia at the Sydney launch of the IYWIP, are also important first steps for commitment to change. He said:

The starting point might be to recognize that the problem starts with us non-Aboriginal Australians. It begins, I think, with the act of

recognition. Recognition that it was we who did the dispossessing.
We took traditional lands and smashed the traditional way of life. We
brought the diseases. The alcohol. We committed the murders.
We took the children from their mothers. We practiced discrimination
and exclusion. It was our ignorance and our prejudice. And our failure
to imagine these things being done to us.

(Keating 1992)

Museums should also submit to such introspection. It will be crucial for paving
the way toward reconciling the past with the future (Ames 1992).

It is also important to recognize the global distribution of indigenous peoples
and its significance to museums (Burger 1990). There are over 300m (million)
indigenous peoples, about 5 per cent of the world's population. They constitute
over 5,000 distinct peoples living in 70 countries. The largest concentrations are
in China and India, making up roughly 7 per cent or 80m and 65m of their
respective populations. In Central and South Americas there are 13m and 15m
peoples ranging from over 15,000 in Belize and 4,000 in Guyana to 8m in
Mexico to 8.6m in Peru. There are over 25m in Africa. In countries such as
Australia, Aotearoa (New Zealand), USA, and Canada there are 0.25, 0.3, 1.5,
and 1m indigenous peoples respectively. In the Arctic and European region,
there are over 160,000 Inuit and Saami peoples. There are museums all over the
world that represent cultures of these peoples. These museums should recognize
the significance of their collections to the indigenous peoples. They should
negotiate appropriate means of access and also contextualize their collections
with reference to the surviving intangible heritage resources in the respective
communities. However, the community needs to go beyond the development of rescue packages and explorations of the range of access to the existing
collections.

INDIGENOUS PEOPLES
(E/CN. 4 Sub. 2/1993/26/Add.1)

The understanding of the concept of indigenous varies from one country to
another. The United Nations has so far adopted no official definition of indigenous peoples. It has been raised as an issue in several fora, including the first
session of the Working Group in Indigenous Populations in 1982. In May 1994,
at the Symposium entitled Curatorship and Indigenous Peoples held at the
University of Victoria, British Columbia, the definition of indigenous became
a contentious issue. The Commonwealth Association of Museums has undertaken the responsibility to develop a discussion paper on the general usage of
the term "indigenous" by museums in the different Commonwealth countries.
In his report addressing the definition of "indigenous," the Special Rapporteur
of the Sub-Commission of Economic and Social Council (UN) on Prevention of
Discrimination and Protection of Minorities, Josh Martinez Cobo, writes as
follows:

379. Indigenous communities, peoples and nations are those which, having a historical continuity with pre-invasion and pre-colonial societies that developed on their territories, consider themselves distinct from other sectors of the societies now prevailing in those territories, or parts of them. They form at present non-dominant sectors of society and are determined to preserve, develop and transmit to future generations their ancestral territories, and their ethnic identity, as the basis of their continued existence as peoples, in accordance with their own cultural patterns, social institutions and legal systems.

380. This historical continuity may consist of the continuation, for an extended period reaching into the present, of one or more of the following factors:
(a) Occupation of ancestral lands, or at least of part of them;
(b) Common ancestry with the original occupants of these lands;
(c) Culture in general, or in specific manifestations (such as religion, living under a tribal system, membership of an indigenous community, dress, means of livelihood, lifestyle, etc.);
(d) Language (whether used as the only language, as mother tongue, as the habitual means of communication at home or in the family, or as the main, preferred or habitual, general or normal language);
(e) Residence in certain parts of the country, or in certain regions of the world;
(f) Other relevant factors.
(UN Doc E/CN 4/Sub. 2/1986–7 Add. 4, paras 379 and 381)

There has been much resistance among indigenous people to define themselves. At present, the general approach is to allow international practice to determine what constitutes indigenous people.

PRINCIPLES CHALLENGING CODES OF CONDUCT

In rethinking the museum, indigenous peoples should have space, time, and distance to consider very carefully what they want to do with their own communities and lives (Dodson 1991). The following guidelines or principles are essentially an exercise in sharing the emerging global agenda for museums. They could provide the basis for promoting the mutual interests of museums and indigenous communities (Edwards and Stewart 1978). There are some countries that may have addressed some of the following principles and others that are yet to address any of them. These are also relevant to the former Metropolitan centers of imperialist authority in Europe, even if some of them do not have indigenous peoples, as their history is inextricably interwoven with indigenous populations all over the world.

1   The recognition of the cultural rights of indigenous peoples, as expressed in different countries, and the realization of the significance of collections to

community life and development require museums and indigenous peoples to work together to redress the imbalances of cultural representation.

2   The facilitation of the primary role of indigenous peoples and their representative organizations to coordinate the preservation, presentation, continuation, and management of their arts, culture, and heritage. Indigenous terms of reference for control, or negotiated shared control, of policy and administration should be promoted.

3   The promotion of respect and understanding for the cultural diversity of the indigenous peoples with reference to gender, age, economic status, and linguistic, regional, or religious backgrounds.

4   The recognition of indigenous peoples' world view that natural and cultural heritage are integrated as one, and that their perception of, and relationships to, their natural environment are part of their cultural and heritage perceptions.

5   The understanding of museum concepts such as excellence, standards, quality, significance, collections, sites, preservation, interpretation, and living heritage according to community-centered principles.

6   The application of integrated and holistic approaches to the management of all aspects of indigenous arts, culture, and heritage as represented in archaeological, historical, contemporary, and environmental resources. These include movable and immovable, tangible and intangible resources including arts, language, and living heritage. The mutual interests of museum work and indigenous peoples in all the discipline areas, including research, should be explored.

7   The promotion of coordinated and consistent indigenous arts, culture, and heritage policies with terms of reference for all government and other agencies at local, regional, and national levels. This may involve the enactment of laws and ordinances or the development of policy frameworks, with official sanction addressing various essential cultural services such as the establishment of community museums and cultural centers; protection of cultural resources; establishing trust accounts and tax incentives for cultural purposes; reciprocal arrangements between countries regarding illicit export of cultural materials; repatriation of cultural property especially human remains and sacred objects; and the protection of copyright and intellectual property.

8   The development of guidelines for the processes of consultation and negotiation, facilitating meaningful and equitable participation by indigenous peoples in cultural planning and heritage research. These guidelines should consider the mutual appreciation of the cultural and conceptual knowledge of indigenous people and the specialist skills and competencies of academically trained heritage workers.

9   The participation and negotiation by indigenous people in the development of policies regarding funding and other resources. It is important that

149

adequate funding and resources are provided to facilitate community cultural development. Funding agencies should give priority to projects relating to indigenous people that are carried out by or in partnership with indigenous people. Corporate sponsorship in whatever form, activities of cultural tourism, and cooperative marketing by museums and associated heritage agencies must embrace and be consistent with the above-mentioned principles.

10 The promotion of training as access and a means to self-empowerment for indigenous people. Diversity of museum-, academic- and community-based approaches should be recognized with emphasis on cultural context and place, social history, community cultural development, and planning. Diversity of training opportunities should be promoted.

The statement of principles as mentioned above could easily become rhetorical, unless these principles are axiomatic concerns of national cultural policy frameworks. Deborah Doxtator has posed a challenge, to address issues beyond the rhetorical statements that add to the comfort levels of museum professionals and resourcing agencies (Doxtator 1994). My argument is that the outcome of any negotiated policy frameworks between museums and indigenous peoples have to be centered in the national cultural agendas and resourced with priority implementation plans. Otherwise, the outcome of negotiations will only widen the gulf between rhetoric and reality or theory and practice, and perpetuate the cultural hegemony of dominant elites. Moreover, indigenous communities that are already coping with consultation fatigue from the various service providers will lose what little trust they have in negotiating with museums and the respective government agencies.

SOME AREAS OF DISCUSSION FOR PROFESSIONAL CODES OF ETHICS

Recognition of integrated community cultural heritage values

To most indigenous peoples, culture is a map and it is written in the land (Yu 1991). It is a common world view of indigenous peoples that they "belong to the land" as distinct from the general notion that land "belongs to the people." Emerging post-colonial societies must recognize the centrality of land and community cultural reclamation to the individual and community sense of self-esteem and identity. A wide range of activities is encompassed by such an approach: ceremonies, festivals, events of open and restricted local and supralocal significance; preservation, continuation, and management of cultural heritage in the community; the voices, values, and traditions of communities; and the (intangible) contemporary arts movement, including the arts and crafts in all their forms. All these are integral parts of living, dynamic, and adaptive heritage, and of the wider environment, within which communities develop sustainable cultural systems. In short, the perspective is one of holistic preservation and continuation of all aspects of cultural life (Parker 1990). Museums should ensure that their practices are grounded in holistic heritage frameworks.

Cultural centers as foci of cultural conservation

This indigenous heritage movement is often manifested in the forms of keeping places, meeting houses, ceremonial houses, cultural farms, community museums, and cultural and interpretation centers. They are not alternatives to existing museums. They are responses to immediate community needs and in several ways complement the role of existing museums. While keeping places are repositories of items for restricted access, community museums and cultural centers have functions beyond the call of conventional object-centered museums. These community focal points of cultural activity are emerging mechanisms for cultural adaptation, self-empowerment, and the recognition of community leadership, enabling the community's pursuit of a sense of place. Thus they pose a renewed challenge to the museums' world to address post-colonial formations and to become more inclusive, incorporating community cultural development. Museology should include theories of cultural planning that systematically bring in all elements of social and economic impact into an integrated planning process with community terms of reference. What is more important, we must rethink the museum definition in a post-colonial context and include community centers of cultural conservation (Cameron 1992; Eoe and Swadling 1991; Hill and Nicks 1992).

Consultation to cultural action

There are three models of interaction in project development between museums and indigenous peoples. In several ways the same could be said of museum practice in general, with reference to multicultural contexts. The first model is defined by consultation as participation. The project is initiated by the researcher or specialist, usually a museum anthropologist, and the role of the community in participation is limited to that of an informant. Community involvement usually concludes after the anthropologist has received a requisite amount of information. Heritage communication is a one-way process, where the external agency is empowered with the expertise and, with time, the indigenous community is disempowered of its authority on the relevant knowledge. This is a commonly practiced model that is familiar to most museums. It needs to be modified to be more participatory and less exploitative.

The second model articulates participation as a strategic partnership. The project is initiated either by the indigenous community specialist or the external anthropologist. Indigenous people are co-workers in project development and outcomes. Community involvement is ongoing from the initial planning to project development, implementation, and evaluation. Shared decision making underpins the partnership. The specialist knowledge resides with the community and the anthropologist. This approach is mutually empowering, with heritage communication between and among all participants. The project creates a framework for the empowerment of the community to participate in the mainstream. There is an increasing number of such partnerships in several countries largely guided by either family history projects, repatriation arrangements, contractual cultural collections, or the exhibition process. The Museum of Contemporary Art in Sydney recently entered into a cultural agreement involving recognition of proprietary rights of the Aboriginal community. It shares with the Maningrida people of Northern Arnhem Land an ongoing trusteeship. Bernice Murphy, the chief curator at the museum, says that:

> proprietary possession of objects must be understood as a shared and contractual obligation between producers (indigenous societies and custodians) and museums or similar institutions. It must be understood as seeking a reunification (in whatever new and imaginative ways may be facilitated by the cultural institutions acting in good faith) between the producers of the meaning (cultural leaders) and things that have been collected and divorced from their originating contexts.
>
> (Murphy 1994: 22–4)

The third model is characterized by indigenous community cultural action. The project is initiated by community cultural specialists such as elders and other keepers of culture and activists working for community cultural development. Indigenous people control the cultural project and its development. It provides a voice for indigenous community cultural leadership and cultural reclamation. Expertise is a corporate community heritage system. This enables the continuity and adaptation of cultures from generation to generation with the strengthening of community cultural self-esteem. Through such community cultural action and self-empowerment, indigenous people are able to continue in the mainstream of emerging post-colonial societies. Good examples of such practice can be seen in the spirit of the Woodland Cultural Center, Brantford, Ontario and several other community cultural centers and museums around the world. These are often inadequately resourced as they decanter the mainstream control of indigenous peoples' heritage.

An important mechanism for the shift from consultation to community cultural action and from access to engagement is an appropriate museum education and training agenda. The relevance of museum training should be examined with the principles not only of access but also of empowerment to the fore. The nature and development of post-colonial discourse will depend on responsive training strategies catering to the needs of both the industry and the communities. The former requires a revamped approach to cultural education that is not assimilationist. The latter demands a non-intrusive and cultural action methodology. In the face of the realities of visitor statistics and "bed-night dollars" for our local economies, all training should address the significance of cultural and heritage tourism and ensure that there is a consciousness of the need for protection of non-renewable cultural resources. Aggressive and expanding tourism is rapidly becoming the new wave of exploitation of indigenous societies.

International agreements

Several international agreements already govern museum practice across the world. Principles of return and restitution of cultural property recommend adherence to or responsibility for the principles in the UNESCO *Convention on the Means of Prohibiting and Preventing the Illicit Import, Export, and Transfer of Ownership of Cultural Property* (1970) and the terms of the *Convention for the Protection of Cultural Property in the Event of Armed Conflict* (The Hague Convention, 1954). The former recommends return of cultural property on the basis of scientific and professional principles (in preference to action at a governmental or political level). In view of the increasing realization of the rhetoric of community centeredness in museological discourse, it is important that community terms of reference are developed by museums. Given the centrality of the right to self-determination in the Draft Declaration of the Rights of Indigenous Peoples, the enunciation of community terms of reference will become critical for museological practice.

Collections policies

The ethical obligations of the members of the museum profession involving indigenous peoples collections should be further discussed and negotiated with the communities from where the collections have been acquired. The standards of high ethical conduct should be negotiated standards rather than sanitized self-proclamations of moral philosophy. Members of the profession should be prepared to communicate with the respective communities and develop strategies for the creation of a social contract so that the respective museums can become objects of public trust. The quality of service should be not only to the general public but also to the particular communities whose collections are represented in the respective institutions.

The review and revision of collection policies should be undertaken in a meaningful partnership with the respective indigenous communities. The management and care of collections should be negotiated with the respective community agencies or representatives. Museums should endeavor to balance conceptual and physical integrity in conservation (Clavir 1993). It is important that the symbolic significance of collections is not necessarily restricted to sacred and religious objects. Other material culture items could be important focal points for the reclamation of cultural values and the self-esteem of indigenous communities.

Copyright

Copyright regulations should also be applied to intangible cultural values. In general, the particular concerns of indigenous people in relation to copyright should be discussed and negotiated. The following extract from The Mataatua

153

Declaration on Cultural and Intellectual Property Rights of Indigenous Peoples, June 1993, provides direction in terms of the centrality of the concerns of self-determination in relation to copyright.

The Nine Tribes of Mataatua in the Bay of Plenty Region of Aotearoa, New Zealand convened the First International Conference on the Cultural and Intellectual Property Rights of Indigenous Peoples (12–18 June 1993, Whakatane).

We

DECLARE that Indigenous Peoples of the world have the right to self-determination: and in exercising that right must be recognized as the exclusive owners of their cultural and intellectual property;

ACKNOWLEDGE that Indigenous Peoples have a commonality of experiences relating to the exploitation of their cultural and intellectual property;

AFFIRM that the knowledge of the Indigenous Peoples of the world is of benefit to all humanity;

RECOGNIZE that Indigenous Peoples are capable of managing their traditional knowledge themselves, but are willing to offer it to all humanity provided their fundamental rights to define and control this knowledge are protected by the international community;

INSIST that the first beneficiaries of indigenous knowledge (cultural and intellectual property rights) must be the direct indigenous descendants of such knowledge;

DECLARE that all forms of discrimination and exploitation of indigenous peoples, indigenous knowledge and indigenous cultural and intellectual property rights must cease.

CONCLUSION

In several ways, cultural heritage institutions have been at the tail end of a process of social justice agenda of many governments. The challenge has come from the cultural action of both marginalized indigenous peoples and introspective professionals, who are continually endeavoring to rethink the cultural heritage agenda. Institutions managing cultural heritage have to become important focal points for the critical discourse of the borders and subaltern histories in emerging post-colonial societies. They should put into practice the rhetoric of community centeredness and liberate themselves from the colonial bondage to the romanticism of decontextualized objects. The focus should be on cross-cultural heritage consciousness and the crossing of cultural borderlands in the centers of power and authority in the cultural industry. Project-driven approaches on the cultural encounters, integration, dissent, and resistance characterizing border life are challenging, enriching, and rewarding. The above discussion centers around several desultory remarks. Meaningful debates and open discussions with a range of stakeholders are essential for the refinement and modification of existing professional codes of ethics in different museological disciplines and countries (Galla 1993b).

10

Ethics and training

One of the challenges facing the museum community is the training of personnel. In most areas of the world needs assessments call attention to the lack of qualified, professionally oriented museum workers. At the same time, the traditional role of museums in "preserving the material evidence of people" (ICOM 1989) has been expanded. In addressing these issues, museum training must consider the changing nature of both the social and professional roles of museums while stimulating critical thinking and imaginative approaches to the practices of museums.

The loss of important historical and archaeological sites, cultural traditions, and ways of life, compounded by the degradation of the environment, has caused the museum community to reconsider its role and responsibility. Training, retraining, self-determination, funding, marketing, public service, and environmental consciousness are issues included in the professional concerns of the international museum community. To meet these needs, museum training programs have a duty to recognize and respond to the complexities of a rapidly changing social, cultural, and technological world.

Considering the changing nature of the museum community and the variability of world conditions, do traditional values and ethics have a continuing role in the training of museum personnel?

QUESTIONS ABOUT ETHICS AND MUSEUM TRAINING FOR FURTHER CONSIDERATION

1 Contemporary museum training programs should include theoretical as well as practical training. At the same time, technology is rapidly altering traditional concepts about collection care, exhibition techniques, and conservation, causing some students to be uncertain of their role and responsibilities. They may consider ethics as a set of inalterable rules, or as generic standards that may or may not apply. Should ethical practice be a question of opinion?

2 Is it unethical for a museum employee to observe a dereliction of duty that could result in damage to museum collections and do nothing? Is there an

ethical distinction between allowing something inappropriate (wrong) to happen and doing it?

3 How is ethics more specifically defined by and applied to particular professional activities within the museum community? Does this circumstance suggest a form of ethical relativism? Or, is the intended outcome the same with the method (practice) different?

4 Consider the possibility that a museum worker (student) understands that reporting a costly mistake in collection care is his or her ethical duty yet is not motivated to do so. Should museum training address the connection between having a duty and being motivated to perform it? How is it possible to instill a sense of ethical responsibility?

5 It can be argued that a museum training program should provide the most current theories and skills relevant to museum practices. However, is it ethically wrong to prepare students to enter a profession that may be over-populated in the immediate future? Is museum training like most other professions where the well-qualified practitioner always finds employment and job-search responsibility rests with the student?

Ethics and international training of museum personnel

Piet J. M. Pouw
(English translation: Lysbeth Croiset van Uchelen-Brouwer)

Concurrent with the emancipation of the museum to an "institution in the service of society and of its development"(ICOM 1989: 3) is the professionalization of the museum staff. In line with the changing and changed status of museums – that have become public attractions and as such are a factor of significant economic importance – a certain image of the museum profession and museum professionals has been established. That image has been accepted within as well as outside the museum field. The provocative doubts that were cast by Kenneth Hudson (1989) on the concepts of "museum professionals" and "professional standards" have long since been removed by publications (Kavanagh 1991; van Mensch 1989; Weil 1988) delineating the contours of a "museum profession" as well as by the self-image established within the museum field.

As a new academic discipline, museology has been a major factor in establishing the professional image. On an international level this has been boosted by the activities of ICOM through its international committees, both the interdisciplinary committees (International Committee on Museology [ICOFOM] and International Committee for Training of Personnel [ICTOP]) and its disciplinary committees (Committee on Conservation [ICOM CC], Committee on Education and Cultural Action [CECA], Committee on Documentation [CIDOC], Public Relations [MPR], and the International Committee on Museum Security [ICMS]). On the national level, developments have often been initiated by the national museums associations and/or the ICOM national committees.

Professionalization is closely connected with the training of museum personnel. Over the last twenty years the number of institutes and universities offering training and special courses for prospective and incumbent museum personnel has greatly increased, even though this was restricted to Europe, America, and Australia. Minimal museological training is found in Africa, Latin America, the Caribbean, Asia, and the Arab-speaking countries. Thus, from an international point of view, there is a distinct discrepancy, perhaps even a dichotomy, in this regard. The former areas have well-trained, qualified personnel with a professional attitude, whereas in the latter usually only the director and senior staff are trained, often abroad, while the other staff are without qualifications and

158

maintain a low professional status. By entertaining international contacts, participating in congresses and seminars, as well as by attending courses given by foreign experts, professionalization of museum personnel in these countries is being promoted.

ICOM, ICTOP, and some specialized institutes in museology are implementing an active policy in this field of international promotion of expertise. ICOM Latin America and the Caribbean Regional Organization organized a management course in Costa Rica and a museum education course in Ecuador. ICOM and ICTOP have conducted a training program for the senior staff of the new Nubia Museum in Aswan, Egypt. The International Center for the Study of the Preservation and the Restoration of Cultural Property (ICCROM) in Rome has offered PREMA courses in preventive conservation for the museum personnel in sub-Saharan Africa. Texas Tech University in Lubbock, USA, has given a basic training workshop in Barbados for museum employees from ten English-speaking Caribbean countries, and offered courses in Ecuador and Paraguay. The Reinwardt Academie in Amsterdam, the Netherlands, has organized four basic training workshops in Indonesia, a summer course in Vietnam, a museum management course in the People's Republic of China, and a basic course in Cairo, Egypt; the academy is involved in the curriculum development of museology at universities in Mozambique and Costa Rica.

ETHICS AND PROFESSIONALISM

Most professional organizations have codes of ethics, or at least a number of ethical guidelines. These have been formulated by the relevant professional associations and accepted/endorsed by their members. Well-known examples are the codes of doctors, journalists, civil law notaries, and lawyers. Correct conduct requirements are administered by their professional associations and if the ethical rules are violated, sanctions can be imposed that may, in extreme cases, lead to suspension or disqualification from further professional practice. Similarly, several academic disciplines have developed their own ethical sub-disciplines, such as medical ethics, legal ethics, the ethics of science, etc. In social discussions, ethical questions are of increasing importance as ethical positions are defined.

Ethics as the critical theory of moral action focuses more particularly on the standards and values in human behavior. Ethics is concerned with whether or not something is permissible, and with the principles underlying the concept of good and evil. Philosophically speaking, ethics is the science of morals, the art of managing human conduct (Nega 1994).

Professional ethics – including museum ethics – applies general moral standards to a certain professional body. It presupposes constant reflection on professional ethics, with the individual members of the profession trying to answer the questions they encounter during their work. This may lead to a conflict of feelings and interests if the ethics of the individual clash with the general professional ethics.

In the cultural field, codes of ethics were first developed in the museum sector. The first code of ethics was published in 1925 by the American Association of Museums. Internationally, it was widely known within museum circles, updated in 1978, and revised into a new version in 1994. National codes were developed in New Zealand and the United Kingdom in 1977, Canada and Israel in 1979, and Australia in 1982 (van Mensch 1994).

The unanimous acceptance of the *Code of Professional Ethics* during the 15th General Conference of ICOM was an extremely important development for the international museum world. The code was drafted by a committee chaired by Patrick Boylan, director of the Leicestershire Museums and chairman of ICTOP at the time. This *Code* (ICOM 1990) clearly distinguishes between "Institutional Ethics" (chapters 2–4) and "Professional Conduct" (chapters 5–8). The ICOM *Code of Professional Ethics* has been translated into sixteen languages and accepted by scores of countries.

The Dutch translation of the *Code* was introduced to the Dutch museum community by a working party of the Netherlands Museums Association in six meetings in different parts of the country. At each venue lively and sometimes heated discussions took place. Ultimately the definitive version *Gedragslijn voor Museale Beroepsethiek* was published in 1991, with two amendments. One amendment elaborated on the issue of deaccessioning, and the other considered the importance and role of friends of museums organizations.

Research into the actual performance of the code in the Netherlands three years later has shown, however, that implementation is a slow process. Hardly anything has been published about the code, and discussion is at a very low ebb; in fact, communication on the subject seems to have come to a standstill (Weij 1994). The course of implementation by other national museums associations or ICOM national committees has also been difficult at times.

It should be remembered that museum training institutes have an important task in this respect. Lecturers, from their theoretical-philosophical premises, have often been involved one way or another in developing the code and are therefore very interested in the practical possibilities. Teaching and presenting ethical questions and basic principles will assist in the professional training of young museologists, who are to be the new generation of museum professionals. It is therefore a logical conclusion that the subject of ethics and training in museology has been claimed by the ICOM International Committee for Training of Personnel to be one of the cornerstones of professionalism (van Mensch 1989). Several members of this committee are also members of the ICOM Ethics Committee and ICTOP drafted *Standards and Ethics for Museum Training Programs* in 1992.

TRAINING IN ETHICS

The first question that should be answered by museum training programs is why museum ethics should be taught. What is their aim and purpose? Museum ethics and the relevant codes should not be considered bibles proclaiming dogmatic ethical truths. Unfortunately, this tendency can be observed within the conservation community (Talley 1993). Museum ethics should focus on principles, guidelines, standards of conduct, on the presentation of ethical questions, and on methodical research to determine the best outcome for both the museum and the individual in a specific situation.

Museum ethics represents a critical reflection on specific issues by means of existing codes of ethics. These codes should never be conceived as straitjackets, but rather as guidelines indicating how to formulate plans and how to act. Committees or groups appointed to assess a certain course of action in museums should test it against the existing code(s) of ethics and/or the relevant guidelines, but they are not qualified to impose sanctions on a museum or a museum officer. The only sanction "imposed" so far was the one pronounced by the British Museums Association in 1991, when the Derbyshire County Council was expelled because of its "flagrant contravention of the code of practice for museum authorities" (Murdin 1991: 8).

Moreover, in the United Kingdom, the Museums and Galleries Commission can deregister museums from the Registration Scheme, which would result in the museum failing its eligibility for various grants. Each non-profit museum member of AAM in the USA must subscribe to the *Code of Ethics for Museums* as a condition of membership, and must also affirm that it has adopted and promulgated its own separate code of ethics. In the Netherlands each individual, as well as each institutional member of the Netherlands Museums Association, has been asked to endorse the *Gedragslijn voor Museale Beroepsethiek*.

The ICOM Ethics Committee cannot pronounce sentence, as it cannot impose sanctions, but it does express its opinions on specific cases. A case in point is its advice given to the Executive Council on ICOM membership of consultants (Boylan 1994).

Whenever museum training institutes teach museum ethics, the code of ethics will always have to be tested against the national statutory laws; legal obligations always take precedence over ethical obligations. A certain act may be completely within the letter of the law, and at the same time, contrary to all accepted museum ethics. Whenever this is the case, the law must be obeyed, but ethical practice must guide and direct where legal boundaries are limited or ambiguous (Edson 1990; Malaro 1990). This implies that museum studies programs must incorporate courses giving an overview of worldwide museum legislation, international law, and relevant national and local law.

ETHICS IN MUSEUM STUDIES PROGRAMS AND INSTITUTES OF MUSEOLOGY

In museum studies programs and institutes of museology, ethics should be offered at a general introductory level as well as at the level of the different museum disciplines (conservation, registration, education, management, etc.), and subject matters (archaeology, anthropology, art history, history, etc.). All students of museology should attend a course in professional ethics and the general principles of ethics (ICOM 1979). The ICOM *Code of Professional Ethics* – in English or in translation – and the national code, if any, should be compulsory literature. During lectures or study groups these two codes can be analyzed and elaborated upon by means of case studies. In addition, a general survey of the historical development of museum ethics in connection with the professionalization of the museum profession must be offered, including the most important codes. Supplementary literature on the practical ramifications of implementing the codes within the museum field can be offered in a reader or a list of recommended/required reading.

At this stage of their training, students have to develop a capacity for posing ethical questions: to themselves, to the museum, to museum staff, and to the society in which the museum operates. They also have to learn to provide answers to these questions, without aspiring to an ultimate and absolute truth. Questions on the accessioning and deaccessioning policy of the museum, the private collections of museum staff, and the role and responsibility of the museum's governing body may be material for discussion. Notably the issue of collecting policies has given rise to abundant publications, books as well as articles.

After the general course in museum ethics, attention should be given to ethical questions relating to specific museum disciplines. This includes reading, analyzing, and discussing relevant professional literature and practice-based case studies. Reviewing specific codes is often more interesting for students, as they usually contain the profile of a single profession, such as that of the registrar or the conservator-restorer.

From the very beginning, ethical questions have played a major role in the professions of conservators and restorers. In 1963 the *Standards of Practice and Professional Relationships for Conservators* was published in the USA. It was accepted in 1967 by the American Institute for Conservation as the "Code of Ethics for Art Conservators," and in 1980 an updated version entitled the *AIC Code of Ethics and Standards of Practice* was published. *The Conservator-Restorer: A Definition of the Profession*, written by the ICOM Committee for Conservation in 1984 and including a number of recommendations on the training and education of the conservator-restorer, should be compulsory reading. In the Netherlands a code of ethics was published in 1992 by VeRes (an association of restorers). In 1993, Beck and Daley included in their book a "Bill of Rights for a Work of Art" (pages 176–81). This publication is recommended reading for students of art history and art historians.

In *A Code of Ethics for Registrars*, published in 1985 by the Registrar's Committee of AAM (Rose 1985: 42–6), the ethical principles applicable to the specific activities and accountabilities of registrars are defined. Moreover, the role and the professional image of the museum registrar are described. This has given a strong impetus to the emancipation of the profession of registrar within the many new departments of collections management. A few years later, a *Code of Practice for Couriering Museum Objects* (Case 1988) was published, and in 1993 the Museums and Galleries Commission in the United Kingdom promulgated the *Standards for Collection Care*, containing *inter alia* guidelines for security and traveling exhibitions.

Ethics and professionalism are held in high esteem in the USA, as is apparent from the codes published by different AAM committees during the last decade. They are excellent reading material for courses dealing with specific disciplines: museum stores (1981), public relations (1984), museum education (1989), and visitor research and evaluation (1991). Noticeably absent so far in the US are professional standards for museum management and for exhibition design and organization: fields abounding in ethical questions. How does the museum handle cut-backs? How does it handle financial pressure (Schmidt 1992)? What options are chosen in times of financial exigency? What is the influence of sponsors on the museum's policy? To what extent is the content of an exhibition manipulating the visitors, and to what extent is the information given truly informative? Should the use of replicas be allowed in exhibitions? Should exhibitions show, promote and/or initiate social developments? What are the conservation requirements for objects in an exhibition?

A code of ethics for the curator was adopted by the AAM in 1983, comparable with the British Museums Association's *Code of Conduct for Museum Professionals* (Thompson 1992: 716–23). This code was preceded in the 1970s by a *Code of Conduct for Curators*.

Besides the above-mentioned multi- and interdisciplinary codes, there are also codes for the different types of museums and their personnel. Art museums were the first to start formulating a special code of ethics, and not surprisingly the USA again took the lead, with a special *Code of Behavior for Art Museums* in 1966. The code was adjusted and updated in 1972 and 1981. In 1976, a *Draft Set of Principles and Code of Curatorial Conduct* (Merryman and Elsen 1987, vol. II: 707–23) was written especially for art museums.

The ICOM International Committee of Natural History Museums published a draft proposal for a code in 1980 and in that year the ICOM Committee of Ethnography Museums organized a congress on ethics. In its newsletter of August 1994, the ICOM Committee for Museums and Collections of Archaeology and History (ICMAH) published a *Preliminary Report for the Development of a Code of Ethics for Archaeological Research*. Museums of technology, science centers, botanical and zoological gardens, nature reserves, etc., are lamentably missed from this list, since they are major factors in promoting environmental awareness.

During the 1993 ICTOP Congress in Rio de Janeiro, several important contributions on ethics were made. One of the resolutions adopted at that meeting was: "that ICTOP establish a network of museum training programs to develop new training initiatives on environmental research, conservation, and education founded on the principles of established ethical standards" (Edson 1994: 2–4).

The body of these codes, documents, publications, and resolutions concerned with professional and ethical behavior in museums, provides essential teaching material for universities and training institutes offering the academic discipline of museology to students. The same material is also very appropriate for mid-career training programs, continuous training programs, and specialized courses. In general, these training opportunities are aimed at persons already working in museums or specialists working for a limited time in museums on special assignments or projects. An introductory course on general ethical principles (yet unknown as far as could be ascertained), would be extremely useful for museum professionals in many countries.

Courses for museum personnel on one of the specific disciplines or one of the different types of museums should always contain an ethical component and make the incumbent staff aware of the ethical aspects of their jobs. These courses would be the ideal opportunity for participants to consider predicaments from their day-to-day working situations and to discuss them with their lecturers and fellow professionals within the framework of existing literature. Their practical experiences are an excellent starting-point for posing ethical questions and trying to answer them.

TEACHING ETHICS

Education and training in ethics should not be limited to theoretical monologues by the lecturer, but should take place in a workshop where diverse opinions are confronted in discussions. The development of the students' critical sense, their ability to formulate and answer ethical questions and to listen to arguments are important elements in the process of advancing ethical consciousness. At the end of the course students will have to prove – in an oral or written examination based on a special assignment, a case study, and/or the literature studied – that they have acquired sufficient ethical comprehension to become true professionals, or if already working in museums, that they are truly museum professionals.

To the lecturer, who should preferably be trained in philosophy and have sufficient practical experience in the field of cultural and natural heritage, different didactic methods and teaching materials are available. While not suggesting that the following is the ideal program for international training in museum ethics, the elements listed below are considered to be indispensable:

1 a general introduction to ethics as an academic subject, its history, and its methodology (lectures and literature),
2 an introduction to fundamental literature on the subject, such as the ICOM *Code of Professional Ethics*, AIC *Code*, and national codes (lectures and literature),
3 the study of the more specific, discipline-oriented literature (conservation, etc.) and subject-oriented literature (archaeology, etc.) on ethics (lectures and literature),
4 the treatment of some case studies, either oral (discussions with role play) or written (a paper). The case studies can be based on practical museum situations, or, if necessary, be constructed by the lecturer (Glenn and Weil 1990),

5 museum experts can be invited to give a lecture based on their actual experiences, followed by a discussion of relevant ethical questions with the students, and

6 study visits to museum departments (restoration, registration, education, management, etc.) and discussions on specific ethical issues with the museum professionals involved.

There is no such thing as a standard program for teaching museum ethics, nor would it be desirable. The differences in ethical points of view that often harbor subjective opinions on good and bad within one professional category keep this discipline from being one of uniformity or unanimity. Its subjective interpretation by lecturers and students is determined by their personal background, by the cultural background of their country of origin, and their perception of museums as institutes for society and of social development. For the training of museum ethics at a more international level, the exchange of lecturers as well as students between the different countries can be an enormous stimulus. At a national level, a more internationally oriented professional awareness will boost the existing tendency for people working in museums to consider themselves as belonging to a profession. In this light, ethics should be an essential part of every museum training program.

11

Ethics and museology

There are a number of issues related to the museum profession and the concept of common standards that are confusing. It is easy to believe that "the mission of museums as institutions grows out of tradition and is shaped by public need" (Bloom and Powell 1984: 73). With this thought in mind, it is not difficult to understand that contemporary museology gives greater attention to human development as a primary force in society (Weil 1990: 31). However, considering these two assumptions, it is unclear how ethical standards can have universal continuity. To have an impact on the greater museum community, ethics must be an inclusive process that is endorsed by museum workers in all parts of the globe. It would seem that the museological tradition must differ from nation to nation and that the needs and expectations of the public must be equally varied.

Assuming equal application of ethical standards is expected of all museum professionals, then allowing social or cultural circumstances to alter judgment discredits the ethical process and establishes a precedence for disregarding professionally recognized standards of museum practice. The two ideals create a complicated, seemingly conflicting situation. Is endorsement of ethical behavior a common factor for people working in museums in different parts of the world? What are the museological implications of ethical or unethical practices?

QUESTIONS ABOUT ETHICS AND MUSEOLOGY FOR FURTHER CONSIDERATION

1   Contemporary museums are expected to contribute to the collective human experience and to use their collections to enrich the lives of their visitors. In view of the responsibility of museums to enrich public learning opportunities, should they (museums) expect to effect positive ethical changes beyond their walls?

2   Is it ethical to give special considerations, that is, any service or privilege not offered to the public, to major donors, dignitaries, or luminaries? Is ethics a social issue?

3   Is it reasonable to assume that the museum community must have a code of

ethics to maintain a certain acceptable standard, that is, guidelines that are mutually agreed upon and considered appropriate to perpetuate common interests and to reach other community-wide objectives?

4 The challenges facing museums today require significant resources, time, and commitment. Many will change the way they conduct their business and the way they care for collections. In some cases, there may be conflicts between public service and collections care. Will this situation require a redefining of museum ethics or are the current standards as defined by documents such as the ICOM *Code of Professional Ethics* adequately inclusive to allow for changes in museological objectives?

5 With diminishing resources and expanding opportunities, museological expectations are being reformed to meet current trends to what some may consider the detriment of traditional values. Does the museum community have an ethical responsibility (right or wrong) to accommodate new norms, or are they obliged to maintain traditional standards? Where does the duty lie?

Museums, museology, and ethics
A changing paradigm
Tomislav Sola

Many people enter the museum profession almost by chance but stay out of conviction. For some, the reasons for staying are idealistic as other opinions seem circumstatial, that is, without acceptable purpose. However, problems may arise when the profession is composed primarily of persons with such loosely defined reasons for continued involvement. The dedicated may discount the fact that a number of their colleagues remain by chance rather than design, never having had the opportunity for other employment.

The first dilemma of the question about museum ethics and museology is that of the concept of "profession." Few are willing to ask the question: Does a museum profession really exist? There are two possible responses to this question. Recent research in the United Kingdom (Lord *et al.* 1989), indicates that up to 80 per cent of the new employees in museums enter the profession without professional training. By extension, there is probably an even greater percentage of untrained staff already working in museums. This may mean either that the profession can function and exist without training (as may seem apparent from the practices and achievements of the last two centuries), or that it will start to exist in its fullest form only when the percentage of trained personnel reaches a positive proportion. Obviously the museum profession would not define itself in overly simplistic extremes, however, this provocative thesis can serve as a reminder of existing processes.

Much can be said about the museum profession as a process. The idea suggests openness to constant change and implies that no position of its development can be regarded as the final one.

By recounting the basic elements of a profession, it is possible to get a quick summary of the position of the museum profession based on a defined structure. The structural elements are as follows:

1 knowledge and skills (long-term training/education, usually university level),
2 legal regulations,
3 licensing system,
4 codes of ethics,
5 specific professional culture,
6 autonomy,

7 defined performances,
8 mission.

Using these points and considering only the Western world, it is difficult to apply five of the eight structural elements to the museum profession. Although regulatory laws, a licensing system, autonomy, or specific performance measures may be missing in many instances, some museum organizations have failed to endorse any of these elements. That suggests the possible conclusion that the museum profession is in the process of being created, and as such it is still open to definition. Otherwise, it would be difficult to explain why it has only recently established a *Code of Professional Ethics* (ICOM 1990) on the international level. There are a number of countries belonging to the Western cultural attitude, that is having the same concept of museums, where no national code of ethics exists and none is applied apart from diverse rules and regulations that include some ethical elements.

The ICOM *Code of Professional Ethics* (1990) is one of the clear signs of the maturation of the profession. General as it is, it gives direction for further elaboration. It is more a reminder of practices to be followed, and a systematized collection of points of importance with recommendations about how issues should be approached rather than a final professional rule (that is neither expected nor possible on an international level).

Why did it take so long for the museum profession to reach the point of clarifying its ethical duties and attitudes both to itself and to society? The reasons for the delay appear obvious to those willing to analyze the profession. An engineer working in a museum is not a curator but an engineer with curatorial duties. By establishing a goal of making that person a curator, it is necessary to instill the crux of museology – the transfer of the professional experience. It is of no functional importance whether museology is a science or a theory because the goal is the transfer of the expertise and vocational qualities of the profession. As an example, it takes a few months in a military camp to train a recruit in the techniques of combat but a great deal more effort is required to create an urge or instinct for combat. The transfer is disdain for human existence.

At the other end of the spectrum, particularly as it applies to human nature, are museums with their special task of addressing human concerns. Those entering the museum profession with minimal prior knowledge realize that the technical and methodological part of the job can be learned quickly, provided there is qualified instruction. However, to become a true "carer" (a person dedicated to the ideals of the museum profession), requires a commitment beyond the basics of museum practice. Only through long hours of practice and a commitment to the curatorial purpose can a newcomer to the profession have a chance to build an ethical attitude.

The lack of written expectations blurs the ideal ethical profile of a museum curator. However, "caring" means fulfillment of the first two or three duties of the curator: those of collecting, researching, and conserving. Implicit in this fulfillment is the presentation of museum work to the public. These achievements acknowledge the responsibility expected of a public servant and they require little more than technique. To infuse in a "carer" an ethical obligation of commitment requires more than skill and naive ambition – it requires dedication and ardor for museum work.

Therefore, whatever there is in the *Code of Professional Ethics* (1990) applies mainly to attitudes important to the functioning of the profession from the aspect of the "carer," such as a responsible curator, but it goes no further. It could provide more direction by making suggestions such as stating that truth should be the basis of any message or image used in public relations, or that museums exist to serve not only the public but also the relevant community. This implies a moral or ethical obligation to offer services to the non-public, the holistic sense of the constituent community.

That attitude cannot be achieved by a strict professional approach in the traditional sense because it requires creativity, a proactive attitude, and devotion – to things that cannot be learned but depend on the vocational passion. Even if this attitude could be included in a code of ethics, it would sound preposterous to require love, idealism, self-sacrifice, and the spirit of charitable work for contributing to the common welfare. These are moral options that a person either possesses or not. They are qualities that are augmented and contextualized during the process of professional education and fully developed in the circumstances of practice.

A code of ethics adds discussion to the regulated existence of the profession. It helps to discourage wrong-doing and misuse of the profession's special character. However, a code of ethics cannot reach the ethical core of the profession. The ethics that makes the basis for any usable museological theory is more than a conventional or agreeable attitude, it is a way of thinking – a state of mind. A code becomes, in major part, just a set of rules for professional behavior that any person can sign when entering a museum job while remaining unaware of the true nature of the profession. Therefore, the lament of how unknowing (of the profession) most museum workers are, is not quasi-philosophical prepossession of museological theory, but an attempt to explain that the entire profession should be envisaged as an ethical commitment.

Paradoxically, writings on ethics are rare in museological literature. However, there is no harm in this provided everything said or done comes from an ethical background. The entire museological concept begins with two questions: "What?" and "For whom?" All the rest is either elaboration or a question of methods and techniques. Both questions are ethical issues. All the many responsibilities of the museum profession are accepted moral (ethical) obligations or they are not. As in other professions, these issues include the question of freedom of choice, personal attitude, the policies of the particular organization, or the changing nature of profit.

Museology has been a growing annoyance to the effective practitioners of the museum world and they immediately dismiss the case it proposes. With the recent crisis leading to further managerialism in museums and with the authorities forcing museums toward self-reliance, museology has a chance to consolidate the profession from within, enabling it to face severe challenges. It can offer the necessary self-reliance, self-confidence, and a sense of professional strength through a well-defined mission.

The dependence of museum governance on national and international laws – for example, regarding illicit trafficking in museum objects – makes it difficult to insist on high ethical standards when it comes to practice. Consequently, when extremely relevant questions are posed about museum objects and the "responsibility of the museum professional toward the makers and first users," curators offer limited input. It appears that the inherent possessiveness of the institutions does not allow another master to determine what "they" meant and thought while creating or using the object. The fact that the information may be interesting does not oblige anybody to investigate. Yet, is it not the only aim of science to analyze this information and propose how we should use the acquired knowledge for the benefit of our constituents?

This example may remind us of the crucial, basic question of the museum profession: What are we here for? If answered, this question may lead us toward the redefinition of the means used to accomplish our task – namely the museum institution. This is obviously a museological and ethical issue.

It happened logically that the United States has become the leading country when it comes to some idealist projections concerning societal standards, be it the Constitution or museum definitions. The first code of ethics appeared there and, apparently, also the first modern definition of the museum as an institution (that of George Brown Goode – the Smithsonian Museums), at the end of the last century.

Since that time, if traced by sources and by dates of their appearance, the initiatives are less potent and lack the enthusiasm for making the world a better place for living. However, progress has been made and it is considerable. The first ICOM definition of museological terminology to include the idea of visitor 'enjoyment' came in 1956. Next came the Roundtable in Santiago, Chile, where for the first time the idea of museums taking part in development was stated, and from that meeting came the still valid ICOM definition made in 1974.

This is not the time to evaluate different definitions of various professional associations, but one aspect that becomes obvious when measuring their line of progress is that of the growing ethical concern expressed as augmenting the social responsibility of the profession. There could be an easy claim that the changes in theory and definition follow, with little exception, the practice of institutions. If true, this would only testify that our profession is still not concept driven, which is, when it comes to ethics, worse than just a defect.

Any definition should be regarded as a necessary part of governance but otherwise nothing more than the briefest reminder of the state of the profession. I believe the museum community is ready for a conceptual leap that will encompass the entire scope of institutions as they are listed in Article 2 (b) of the ICOM *Statutes* (1989): from natural monuments to the institutions that

171

have some characteristics of a museum. Everything done in museums and related institutions brings ethical consequences and everything said about museums or put into written form is an ethical statement, sometimes embued with the power of law.

Suppose there is a new definition of a "museum." It may be another term that means many things to avoid additions to the definition. It might be called a heritage action unit. It could be defined as: any organized, regular action exercised upon the field of heritage, consisting of collecting, research and preservation of three-dimensional and other information, meant for the communication of the complex human experience. It may be diachronous or synchronous, covering the span of past, present, and future, according to the specific needs and circumstances of its users; contemplative or cybernetic in its effect. It serves to fulfill the constant human need for the pleasure of understanding and widening of experiences, as a virtual set of extensions to human senses, as an amplifier to human abilities of comprehension, sensibility, and will to act toward the wise, harmonious development in the given environment.

With this definition in mind, consider there is still a need for a common basis on which to formulate the theory and practice of the profession. There is a need for forward momentum that will make, even by definition, a clear statement of the ethical basis of the museum profession. Ideally, this will change the entire professional practice. Imagine the past presented in a way that stimulates understanding, tolerance, compassion, co-existence of differences: the past that praises positive action and disdains intolerance, ignorance, and malice. The museums of revolution, scattered across Eastern Europe and the USSR, were early signs of the certain demise of an oppressive system. The amount of misinformation, prejudice, and bias they contained was so resented that they proved to be counter-productive.

Can it be expected that changing ethics and a maturing profession will make a better world? The problem with some museum workers could simply be that they do not see the need for improvement. Unfortunately, they are probably right when viewing their jobs from the formal, contractual perspective. They do not choose to react to the challenges around them – the electronic media, the heritage industry, separate presentational forms, or information networks. The dynamic profession that has clear vision and definition that shows its ethical motivation will be able to compete with greater challenges and require the status with the more convincing authority of the moral obligation it has to fulfill. The difficulties will increase in number and frequency; at the same time, the available space for reaction will decrease.

The theme of museums in crisis can be illustrated by giving an account of the present statistics of the museum world. Growing numbers and increasing outside influence can hardly serve as an argument for crisis. These factors serve to demonstrate the amount of confidence currently assigned to museums, the expectations they should fulfill, and subsequently, the lack of direction caused by this identity crisis. Solutions are being sought for the museum dilemma, because they are still important.

Other initiatives may offer more in more attractive ways; however, a firm ethical perception of the museum's role in contemporary society will keep the profession from staying inefficient (even if technologically disguised) and from imitating harmful examples. Never has it been so necessary for museums as institutions and their perceived missions to undergo an ethical renewal that will distinguish them from the negative aspects of contemporary society and those industries that use the museum disguise to gain relevance.

The profession needs the capacity for rapid adaptation to changing circumstances (strong survival code) and renewed credibility for defending a common cause.

It could be argued that the museum profession is like any other, a profession depending on the subtle laws of demand. This could be partly true but only on the level of the language and syntax of the message. The message itself depends on the user's need, and this element is the responsibility of the institution. That museums belong to the third sector (the public) and are their firmest outer ethical declaration is a given. What remains to be defined, within the theory of their mission (the only science there could be), are the specific ethical responsibilities and aims to be formulated and embellished to meet their ideal contribution to society.

Unlike libraries and archives, museums make a stronger statement. They present a set of selected messages drawn from the enormous pool of possibilities normally located beyond the visitor's reach in some unintelligible interpretation or in the inarticulated information residing in the stored collections. Museums cannot offer themselves to their users the way the other institutions do, where the retrieval is a matter of free will and individual interest. (On the other hand, when a museum tries to be exhaustive like some encyclopedic museums, the user encounters the unique problem of museum fatigue, the condition from which no other institution suffers.)

Deciding which message to provide is one of the major ethical choices to be made in a museum. Of course, it is of the same ultimate importance (although partly implied in deciding which message to offer) to know the user of the message, and the intended impact. Even the least experienced professional knows that making this decision will ultimately formulate the collection policy on one side and the relations with the users on the other. As already mentioned, that action is what museology is essentially about.

The reunification of the world that is happening due to and because of "informatics" – bringing together the museum, archives, and library practices – does the same for their respective theories (thus making museology one of the information sciences and drawing the final and decisive demarcation line toward museography). It has happened and will happen more often, that all three types of repositories together with data banks and telecommunication systems are forming a common network – a data base for commercialization.

The entire scheme can be viewed from the ethical standpoint and there are many questions of importance that can be raised. For instance, the new practice of museums places their interest and information collecting concurrent with living protagonists. Considering the contemporary nature of the material, how should they regulate the dispersal of information? A more important issue is the right of determining the contents of the information being dispersed. In this activity, museums, or the three kindred institutions (museums, libraries, and archives) should have a minimal 51 per cent of the conceptual shares to stay in control.

It is therefore not a code of ethics that will assure accomplishment of the professional mission (or, indeed, formulate that mission) but it will assure the clear moral of the profession, that vocational zest, stemming from the full understanding of the unique invention of human culture, that of heritage preservation.

If told that the final aim of our effort is keeping the evidence of the victorious campaign of our civilization and culture through the accumulation and transfer of knowledge, then the code of ethics will be the set of rules designed to control the greedy and corrupt. If employed to keep certain material evidences alive in spite of the laws of physics and chemistry, then it is not the humanist credo but the task imposed by our directors that make us do our job. Again, the code of ethics is only a part of the contract: something given or induced, and not the visible, formal part of the moral philosophy of the profession.

If, on the other hand, we are here to match the forces of change with the mechanism of regulation and correction, in the true cybernetic sense, in order to give the proper guidance of our planet Earth, then there must be an ethical code that will serve as a clear statement of our role in the society. Museum workers not only follow it like a scribe of its preponderant forces, or trace it like a chronicler, but take an active part in its change. Museums have occupied themselves with analyzing the world while the whole point is to be a part of its transformation, helping the creative forces to function, thus making the change logical and acceptable. Occupying the role of catalyst and amplifier, museums are operating in real time and with real people, as a mechanism through which people correspond with their past, their collective memory, their collective ego, their coded identity, with their fears and hopes. It is an enormous responsibility. To fulfill this obligation, museums have a certain moral right – the right to act protectively and boldly when correct but not understood.

Museums disperse selected, scientifically approved information which is a considerable part of the collective memory. Does this activity bring an immediate obligation to use this resource for the benefit of the society, community, or a group? Who decides when and how it is used? Is the museum a democratic institution by the fact of the free choice offered or by the ambition to play an active part in democratic processes?

Creating knowledge has an implicit element of moral responsibility, but using that knowledge burdens this responsibility with an immense weight. It is therefore far from scientific formalism to ask whether museums are here to act as (one of) the mechanism(s) of approbation of the socio-economic-cultural system or one of the mechanisms of criticism of that same system. This shift creates the ethical potential of heritage-based institutions and museums in all their variety.

If development consists of the parallel forces of change and adaptation, then the disproportion within that duality is the probable essence of any social (maybe even existential) crisis. The profession that is fully aware that it plays an important part in this constant humanization of the society will consciously accomplish its difficult role as a cultural institution: "[C]ulture is somewhat like the moral of science" (Barthes 1980) and science is the basis of the economic and political system (or at least being used by them to generate static patterns of authority, power, and order).

If museums gather such an enormous quantity of historic evidence, they may serve as a mechanism for the productive analysis of the past so the conclusions can be used for living in the present more effectively and for developing a usable future instead of the constant succession of fatal mistakes. The fact is, however, that museums (except the family of ecomuseums) seldom take part in real-life activities, nor do they try to influence the life or destiny of their respective community. The reason is hidden in the deficiencies of their own institutional heritage and expressed in the lack of moral drive.

The prevailing model of museums as an institution is the result of the amalgamated possessiveness and individualism of great collectors, scientific enthusiasm of rationalist scientists, and the frustrations of the world in a dramatic identity crisis. Any outcome of this condition is too far from any idealistic ambition of restoring integrity and moral order of the world – knowledge is quantity, wisdom is quality; one is a contractual responsibility while the other is an ethical obligation.

12

Ethics and the environment

> *The environment does not exist as a sphere separate from human actions, ambitions, and needs, and attempts to defend it in isolation from human concerns have given the very word "environmental" a connotation of naivety in some political circles.*
> (World Commission on Environment and Development 1987: xi)

The inclusion of the word "environment" in the ICOM definition of museums (ICOM 1989: 3), supports the idea that museums, their collections, and the public cannot be isolated from their human or natural surroundings. The role of museums in preservation of the material evidence of people also must give attention to the environment with which humanity is associated. The future existence of the human race may be determined by the manner in which it occupies and uses the environment.

Most people agree there is a need for greater attention to the conservation of the "material evidence of people and their environment" (ICOM 1989: 3); however, the impact of human activities on the ecosystem is often neglected or ignored. Who is responsible for this situation? Do museums have a role in helping to define long-term environmental issues and assessing ways by which the international community can deal more effectively with these concerns?

QUESTIONS ABOUT ETHICS AND THE ENVIRONMENT FOR FURTHER CONSIDERATION

1 Should established ethical practices be pursued even when environmental interest (in the social sense rather than individual) may have to be sacrificed in that pursuit?

2 There are thousands of natural science specimens in museums all over the world. However, biologists continue to collect animals, birds, and reptiles by the hundreds to add to collections. There are valid reasons for biological collections, but is it ethical to continue to destroy living creatures for museums when there is a seeming over-abundance of specimens for study? Does not the ICOM concern for the environment extend to the fauna?

How many specimens are needed and for what purpose? Is it not possible to collect the data without destroying the animal, bird, or reptile?

3 Are social and environmental inequities (in all forms) ethical issues for museums to address? Are cultural relativism and ethical relativism interchangeable concepts?

4 The status of the world environment has been ascribed as suffering from a pervasive "anthropocentric mentality." This attitude has negatively compromised the biosphere, causing potentially catastrophic conditions that will undoubtedly have an impact upon future generations. One method of combating these conditions is by educating the public on the dangers and methods of altering deleterious practices. On the other hand, the principles of act utilitarianism contend that it is correct to act in the way that brings the most good to the most people. Many of the activities that are having a negative impact upon the environment bring many benefits to a great number of people. On the basis of this thinking, should it not be correct, ethically and otherwise, for museums to produce exhibits that support those activities that bring the most good, regardless of the eventual detriment to the environment?

5 With concerns about the biosphere, there are issues about the "human environment." Destruction that results in the loss of "homeland" can have a tragic impact upon the mind, body, and spirit of a people. Displacement, relocation, or other forms of environmental disenfranchisement can deprive a people of their cultural identity. This kind of situation is most obvious in times of armed conflict and natural or human-caused disaster (deforestation, water control, urban renewal, and resettlement for ethnic or cultural segregation). Realizing these activities are a part of many societies, do museums have an ethical responsibility to expose these situations and to include them as part of the social mission of the institution?

Museum ethics and the environment

In search of a common virtue

Tereza Cristina Scheiner

Behave in such a way that you use humanity, in yourself as well as in any other, always and simultaneously as an end and never as a means.

(I. Kant)

Ethics, as a branch of philosophy, encompasses the study of human morals and duties. By definition, ethical questions relate to the morality and behavior of individuals, groups, and societies. They are based on measures of value at the personal and professional levels.

On a personal basis, ethical behavior is influenced by the values formed by the individual and by his or her perception of the adequate conduct required within the group. This perception evolves progressively throughout the process of individual development. It is influenced by social position, societal values, cultural and economical background, family values, education, life experiences, and many other variables. Religion also plays a considerable part in the process, as does the law, a defined code of behavior regulation that must be respected and recognized by all those who are subject to them.

A normal and socially adjusted adult lives and performs under a given set of behavioral conditions, considered as "acceptable" in his or her social and cultural environment. There are no rules of conduct or set of beliefs that can develop into a unique ethical system, relevant to all societies. Across time, philosophers have referred to the many significances of "good" and "bad;" of "vice" and "virtue." To apply these attributes, specific human groups must define which traits will be valued within each group as a basis for cohesion and survival – something like a "common virtue."

Social and professional practices imply that a set of behavioral attitudes, considered as "adequate," relate to the ethical commitment each individual makes at personal, social, and professional levels. A professional who acts ethically is viewed as having personal and professional credibility. This recognition is usually derived from the seriousness of his or her performance, which includes an honest desire to serve.

However, defining adequate behavior on a professional scale is a complex and delicate matter, as many socially accepted behaviors are considered unethical from a professional point of view. This is one of the reasons why professional codes of ethics are developed – as an intent to define which conditions are acceptable, under the realities of each profession. A code of ethics defines general rules of conduct to establish guidelines for professional action, indicating the rights, duties, and limitations for individuals, groups, and professional categories with reference to professional performance. The aim is to confirm the integrity of each profession, guarantee public credibility, and recognize the work being done.

IS THERE A MUSEUM ETHICS RECOGNIZABLE EVERYWHERE?

In the museum field, there is an implicit set of fundamental values recognized and accepted almost everywhere. These values have been serving as a basis for the development of what might be called a "general museum ethics." They include the following:

- search for democracy,
- honesty,
- concern about management and preservation of cultural property, as testimony of human action,
- commitment to world heritage and to group patrimony,
- respect for group identity,
- recognition of cultural plurality,
- emphasis on preservation of patrimony,
- referral to the past as a tool to understand the present and the future, and
- promotion of human well-being, through education and diffusion of knowledge.

Although these values are not exclusive of the museum field, they form the foundation for most museum ethical codes, from the ICOM *Code of Professional Ethics* (1990) to lists of professional standards, and the codes of ethics of specific museums.

Some of these values have been under scrutiny for decades, a few of them for more than a hundred years. Some were recently included and put under consideration – especially after the 1960s, when new paradigms developed and influenced knowledge and behavior throughout the world. The significant changes in museum theory and practice that occurred in Western societies in the last twenty-five years have both exerted influence on and been influenced by such values.

Today a redefinition of the museum universe can be acknowledged, in which new concepts of museum, museology, and of museum practices and responsibilities are under analysis and debate. The working agenda includes a redefinition of museum ethics. In a world where humankind, the environment, and sustainable

179

development are a focal point for international policies, not only in the economic field but also in the field of culture, it is vital to revise the roles and responsibilities of museum professionals and to formulate a new image for the profession.

WHY IS IT SO IMPORTANT THAT MUSEUMS DEAL WITH ENVIRONMENTAL QUESTIONS?

The museum is today, among many other things, a communication agency and a temple for cultural consumption; a political arena for special interest groups and a place for discovery; an intellectual ground for research and for the manifestation of the human genius. It is also a mirror and a synthesis of human society – an instance where reality is decodified into communication signs. It has an extremely important mission: to help societies develop a balanced knowledge about themselves and their significance in the context of planet Earth.

This mission is peculiar, since "museum logic is basically organized around the concept of patrimony" (Davalon *et al.* 1992: 20). Traditionally occupied in identifying the authentic – the tangible as testimony of reality – the museum is now trying to develop a new kind of relationship with the environment. It seeks to establish an agenda where the elements of "nature" are considered patrimony. The recent developments relating to environmental issues have brought

> a double impact on the museum: on one side, the conceptual [r]evolution in the field of Museology; on the other, the new approaches that place the museum facing missions and situations yet unknown.
> To link museum and environment would be, though, more than to work the environment as subject of the museum activity: it would imply the development of an elaborate and careful exam of the social background that influences both the representations of nature established by societies and the evolution of their presentation by the museum.
> (Davalon *et al.* 1992: 21)

Environmental factors that have strongly influenced museum ethics include:

- perception of the total environment as patrimony of humanity,
- respect for communities and societies as responsible for the management and care of such patrimony,
- emphasis in common property, under the responsibility of given communities or social groups,
- respect for communal choice regarding the destiny of patrimony, and
- a renewal of the concept of democracy, where values and beliefs of all social groups are considered equal and important.

In today's ethics agenda, the true patrimony under consideration is life: vegetal and animal life, including human life. Environmental ethics gives priority to quality of life, and often, this means having to cope with values and behaviors that are unusual to the museum field. The policies on sustainable development that now influence museum theory and practice cause a commitment to reduction of economic, educational, and social barriers of all social groups – something not easy to turn into reality, considering that museum professionals still perform under a conceptual model of "museum" derived from the conveniences and prejudices of developed social groups in the Western world.

The reality of this situation presents a serious handicap. In analyzing past and recent experiences, it is seen that museums, as a whole, do not occupy an important place in the center of public interest when considering environmental questions. In truth, "environmental issues have only touched the boundaries of the museum world: museums and museology are hardly referred to in the select club of the agencies that deal with the environmental agenda" (Davalon *et al.* 1992: 14).

During the last twenty years, several museums and museum specialists, mainly in the northern hemisphere, have carried out studies and exchanges about environmental issues. Such experiences reflect a clear rational approach, characterized by extreme care in dealing with the themes being studied. Most of the time such experiences have involved research and exhibition programs about specific communities and/or biomes, undertaken by groups not directly belonging to the realities under study. This happens, in part, because most museum professionals are unfamiliar with the conceptual developments of museology, which represent an important framework for understanding the new roles assigned to the museum.

There is also a certain fear, on the part of the museum community, to approach an issue that generates such a strong political and ideological reference, yet at the same time there is a deep-seated need for a revision of working methods. To work with the environment means to revise the traditional approaches the museum has adopted toward society and to build a new kind of interaction, based on new paradigms (where man integrates with nature as an element, and not as its center) and on new forms of association (where global conception and scales of values for different societies and/or communities have equal importance).

With this approach, it is important to find out how societies develop their representations about the environment. It is also important to define the significance of environmental issues in relation to the social imagery and the symbolic role of each group of "signs," related to the environment in the minds of each group within a particular society. This is the very basis of the relationship between museum ethics and the environment: the immense ethical responsibility, on the part of the museum, to make use of its strength as communication agency and to help societies develop new forms of knowledge and new perceptions about the environment, from inside out.

Such perceptions are linked to the concept of "inner ecology" – the approach of each individual toward his or her own self, based on the balance between the inner energies and the energies of the outside world. It has been acknowledged that societies develop new behaviors because of the pressures of given groups, and that group behavior is strongly influenced by individual change. The development of new forms of self-perception and the understanding of the importance of living in a balanced world is perhaps the strongest catalyst for social, economic, and political change – and this applies also to the museum reality. The museum must use its potential to help generate forms of culture that are genuine and not culturally or politically imposed. This is made possible only when the values of individual change are taken into consideration, and when group and community action aim at promoting a new and more satisfactory relationship with the environment.

In general terms, this was the original purpose of the ecomuseum; most ecomuseums and *musealized* communities still work under those guidelines.

WHAT KIND OF INFLUENCE HAVE ECOMUSEUMS HAD TOWARD MUSEUM ETHICS?

On the basis of the holistic paradigm of science, museology has tried, since the early 1970s, to develop a methodology based on the concept of the "total environment." The United Nations World Conference for Human Environment held in Stockholm in 1972 and the Roundtable in Santiago, Chile, also in 1972, represented a shift in the object of study of museology from the tangible patrimony of humanity to the role of man in the biosphere.

In the field of museology, the ecomuseum has represented a practical experience with the total environment. It has offered a revolutionary option for museum practice. Moreover, it has signified a major change in museum ethics. For the first time, portions of territory were being musealized without much damage to economic activity, and this was happening with the participation of the local communities. The possibility of musealizing human activity *in situ*, and the diffusion of practices that included community choice over museum work, have opened a door to new experiences in the museum field. The experience of the ecomuseum has demonstrated, on a world basis, the possibility of specific human groups creating their own museums. That process has given new meaning to museum ethics, especially to many societies of the southern hemisphere, where the museum has had a traditional role as a vehicle to convey the interests of empowered groups.

With the ecomuseum, an ideology of social museology has evolved that has provoked a random debate about the ethical responsibility of museums toward the total environment. For the first time, museum professionals showed concern in analyzing the ethical importance of alterity, when referring to different social groups and different societal values. The question asked was: "Why not develop museums that emphasize the symbolic importance of cultural practices of different groups, not as scientific subjects, but from the point of view of the groups themselves?" As a result of this appraisal, it was acknowledged that the occidental model of the traditional museum did not apply to many societies, especially those that have endured colonization. From then on, it was necessary to search for a new set of values that could serve as a guideline for museum action.

However, there is a risk in assuming that the ecomuseum (or any other present manifestation of the museum phenomenon) is a response or a solution to the problem of dealing with the environment. No museum can encompass reality as a whole or answer the needs of all societies. To create museums that apply to their needs and expectations, societies (and/or communities) have to organize themselves. They must have an active – not passive – relationship with museums. They must develop museums that are a real synthesis of themselves and in which they can see clearly their many facets.

WHAT WOULD BE AN ADEQUATE APPROACH OF MUSEUMS TOWARD THE ENVIRONMENT?

Since the 1960s, societies have been trying to redefine communal behavior in search of a common ethical perception of the environment. However, environmental issues continue to be appraised either through the study of ecosystems or through the analyses of the relationships between human beings and their natural and social setting. "The fact that nature defines itself through its own laws and dynamics has not been [the] object of much consideration" (Davalon *et al.* 1992: 27).

Another point of consideration is that, according to the region of the world, the environmental agenda presents its own peculiarities. These factors and their influence over general (societal) ethics also have an influence on museum ethics.

Recognizing the many variables, museum specialists have been concerned, in recent years, with programs for environmental education. As a formative process that enables individuals to understand their relationship with nature, it leads to a strong ethical perception of the world. Its basic principles – variety/similarity; patterns; interaction/interdependence; continuity/change; and adaptation/evolution – are in everything related to the principles defined by the holistic paradigm of science:

- **unicity**: the belief that everything is related to everything, a concept that is present in the cultural archetypes of our civilization, from the imagery of primitive societies to Vedic and Taoist texts, in philosophies and religions;
- **mutability**: everything is in a permanent state of change, a transitory state where nothing is definitive and everything is in process; and
- **continuity and adaptation**: forms of interaction of things over time and space.

Environmental education assumes the environment to be a "total system," where dynamic processes are in continuous interaction. It works from the inside out, placing the individual in close contact with himself or herself and with a small parcel of such systems, making use of daily experience and individual perceptions of the universe. Concerned with individual choice of "how to learn and what to learn," it promotes the abandonment of prejudice and of distorted scales of values.

183

Much more than a pedagogy for self-development, environmental education signifies, for museology, one possibility of working with the holistic paradigm. It emphasizes the best characteristics of the museum:

- **liberty**: the capacity of museum action to occur outside areas traditionally considered "museums;"
- **plurality**: recognition that, like society, the museum has many faces and may exist in different forms and spaces simultaneously. Thus there is no "ideal" form of museum; and
- **potential for generating knowledge**: implying two basic assumptions. First, there is not one "knowledge," but several forms of knowledge that vary in time and space, according to societal values; consequently, there is not one moral, one reason, one truth. Second, every museum, no matter how small, how poor, or how deprived of means, has the possibility of producing (not just re-producing) knowledge.

Environmental education, if properly applied to the museum field, is an open invitation to the development of a new concept of museum ethics that considers plurality of values in a context of permanent change. It is an opportunity of promoting individual and social growth, with the museum in the service of building better societies.

This is especially important to societies in less developed regions, where the museum can play a significant role in education for sustainable development. It also may help to develop museums that are locally or regionally appropriate and independent of traditional models. By extension, this approach will help societies understand basic principles of science, which in turn will enable them to make better choices between traditional and new technologies.

WHAT WOULD BE THE ROLE OF MUSEUM CODES OF ETHICS IN SUCH A REALITY?

A code of ethics implies the existence of a fundamental system of behavior "in which the rules of conduct are the same for everyone" (George 1988: 87), delineating the desired commitment to a system of values where virtue resides in "doing the right things" (Able Jr. 1988: 94). Related to the utilitarian principle of building happiness through reason and law created by Bentham (1780), they establish extensive lists of "do's" and "don'ts," and of "rights" and "wrongs," as if it were possible to evaluate the immense complexity of behaviors and situations within such a simplified frame.

Much has already been said about museums having to follow a high standard of ethical conduct in order to deserve public credibility. There is no doubt that museums owe much of their success and audience to public credibility, and that individual and group behavior, on the part of museum professionals, are basic keys to the image of any museum. However, there is a "dark" side to the ethics agenda – represented, in part, by the limits imposed by some codes that use a

184

rigid set of values, leaving few opportunities for development of new practices and methodologies. This situation reflects the lack of knowledge and consideration, on the part of museum professionals, of the immense political importance of museology.

Codes of ethics always refer to the interests of society. However, society is a fictitious entity that includes many groups of individuals, loosely organized into communities. Given this amalgamation, it is often difficult to determine the interest(s) of communities. As Bentham (1780) has stressed: "it is useless to mention the interest of the community if the interest of the individual is not understood."

Museologists, as individuals and citizens of a nation, are subject to personal, social, cultural, and professional rules of conduct that do not always correspond with one another. Many museum codes of ethics have been created and/or renewed in recent years. The positive aspect is the inclusion of a "set of beliefs that places a priority on human dignity and recognizes professional expertise" (George 1988: 87). However, few codes refer to the political, ideological, and practical implications of the relationship between humankind and the total environment, even when acknowledging social, cultural, and political specificities throughout the world.

Even today it is difficult to find, in museum codes of ethics, references to the rights and limits of professional action within the natural environment as well as within specific communities. More than twenty-five years after the birth of "social museology," the search continues for an adequate approach to items such as the relationship between museum specialists and musealized communities.

Most of the codes, from the ICOM *Code of Professional Ethics* (1990) to rules of conduct of specific museums, center their content on behavior about museums and the management and care of cultural property. That is, the *products of culture*, understood as collections belonging to traditional, orthodox museums. The immense ethical responsibility of dealing with the *processes of culture* is hardly considered – although it implies helping to develop new forms of knowledge without interfering with them. No one is exempt from the risks of influencing social groups with values that are not inherited. Another risk is taken by those who deal with *processes of nature* – as they must be permanently aware not to impose anthropocentric paradigms.

In developing countries, professional standards maintain that museum people are supposed to behave ethically toward cultural heritage. However, no mention is made of ethical behavior toward the total environment or specific segments of society, such as native groups, women, and impoverished communities. In any society where the basic needs of the population are not met, it is extraneous to mention the possibility of a common set of values, under the idea of ethics – people are occupied with surviving or lessening social and cultural differences. This model demonstrates the strong political foundation of museum ethics: to deal with the total environment is to discover that "power is necessarily anti-ecological" (Brandão, in *Unger*, 1992: 47). A museum ethics that formalizes environmental affinity implies the recognition of new power relations among societies.

Pierre Weil (in *Unger* 1992: 37–9) points out that it is necessary to establish criteria to define what is ethical and what is not ethical, in reference to the environment. Ethical values would be those that aim to respect and preserve life; unethical values, those that destroy life. Destructive behaviors would imply actions that are harmful to individuals and general health and which menace the mental and emotional balance of populations, social harmony, and understanding among people.

There would be a "superficial ethics," recognizing nature without its own values and as subservient to humankind, and a "profound ethics," recognizing that all things, human and non-human, have a value in themselves. Under which ethics should knowledge and development be produced? Under which ethics should museology exist?

It is true that no code of ethics applies equally everywhere. Moral systems are relative and vary according to societies – no universal morality exists. Behaving ethically toward the environment would signify, for the museum community, a commitment to all things that have a value for humanity. Humanity itself, life on earth, and the health of the planet are this generation's common patrimony and the heritage of future generations.

The aim of museology must be to search for a "common virtue" – a general behavioral code for museum practice toward the total environment: one that defines a commitment to make a better future for humankind and the planet.

13

Ethics and collecting

What, where, and how to collect is an ethical issue that has worldwide implications. No other social institution has the defined responsibility of preserving materials (objects) for future generations. Only museums have this unique assignment. The idea of preserving the "material evidence of people and their environment" (ICOM 1990: 3) should extend beyond the museum to the source of the collections. Museums have an ethical responsibility to preserve the material culture of society as well as the "higher" culture of the humankind. Along with more traditional (movable) museum objects, there is also a need to preserve communities, historic sites, and the ecosystem as generators of culture and daily life.

The acquisition of artifactual material is an ethical issue of immense proportion, and one of the greatest challenges for the museum community. The concepts of stewardship begin with the decision (value judgment) of what is to be selected for inclusion in the museum's collections. From that beginning, decisions made by museum personnel control the destiny of objects and their role as "evidence" of human activity. The ethical ramifications of this element of museum activity are significant and lay the foundation for a major part of all decisions that follow. How are those decisions to be made, who is responsible for their implementation, and why is ethics such an important part of a museum's collection policy?

QUESTIONS ABOUT ETHICS AND COLLECTING FOR FURTHER CONSIDERATION

1   Although ethnocentrism generally is viewed as unacceptable, museums use the premise of ethical relativism to justify retaining collections relevant to other cultures. Can this concept be justified?

2   Illicit trafficking in cultural property is a primary form of income for some people in economically challenged countries. Their motives are survival and a moral responsibility for family. In contrast, the purchasers of the property are often driven by greed. Are the two groups equally responsible from the ethical point of view? Is it possible to empathize with one without condoning the other?

3 A person excavating cultural material from land they own may say it is no one's business what they do with the objects. They may decide to sell the material, give it away, or send it out of the country. For them it is personal property and they contend they are "hurting no one by their actions." Do they have a right to continue this practice or should they be restricted in their activities? Does legal ownership of property supersede the ethical responsibility of cultural preservation?

4 The tourist/traveler is often responsible for illicit trafficking in cultural property. Often, this activity is opportunistic in nature without thought of the long-term implications. An opportunity arises to acquire a "treasure" and it is taken because the person recognizes no duty to do anything other than what is in their own interest. This attitude reflects ethical egoism, and it has both personal and universal implications. What practices (personal and institutional) within the museum community may be driven by this principle?

5 Should the question of monetary value or cultural significance be a factor in determining repatriation of objects such as human remains or spoils of war?

Museum ethics and collecting principles

Paul N. Perrot

The prime and fundamental mission of museums is to collect, preserve, and transmit that part of our tactile heritage, whether manmade or the result of natural phenomena, that can be assembled in an orderly fashion, and which by its study may contribute to a better understanding of our planet's development and the contributions of our ancestors and contemporaries. Museums are storehouses and laboratories. They are also centers where we can contemplate how the inner vision of artists has transmuted the materials at their disposal into objects that rejoice the eye or which provide deeper insights into the human condition, and give tangible reality to past and present fears, hopes, and beliefs.

Museums are centers of lifelong learning – places where assumptions can be measured, talents evaluated, inventions placed in context, and natural phenomena correlated and viewed in perspective. In short they are keepers of the tangible truth that is contained in the existence of holdings against which future generations will gauge their own accomplishments and discoveries. Museums, in a sense, testify to our trust that there will be a future to inherit this legacy. They are also increasingly complex businesses which, in addition to their cultural contributions, have a profound impact on the economies of the communities in which they are located.

If these are the roles that museums play, it follows that in carrying them out, their staff, trustees, and sponsors must be guided in all of their activities by strictly applied ethical principles. For the staff it means avoidance of even the semblance of a conflict of interest; mutual respect among themselves; scrupulous observation of their obligation to be responsive to public expectation; and adherence to the highest standards of accuracy and completeness in fiscal accountability, record keeping, research, presentation, educational programming, and publication. Similar strict requirements extend to the relevance of the museum's shop offerings, the wholesomeness and pricing of the cafeteria or restaurant's menu, as well as the appropriateness of the institution's advertising and public relations, and of its auxiliary activities.

These principles most importantly extend to the relationship of the director to the trustees, their relationship to the staff, and to the manner in which the professionalism of that staff is acknowledged by the trustees, through salaries, benefits, working conditions, or by special recognition.

189

Trustees, as the name implies, are the holders of an institution's assets and the keepers of its reputation. They are the representatives of today's society and tomorrow's public. In all of their activities they must avoid any suggestion of conflict of interest, and be mindful of the differences between setting policy and its implementation. In their hands rests the ultimate responsibility for an institution's image and its financial stability. Unless they recognize their role and adhere to high standards of personal conduct in their relationships with staff and community, they can subtly subvert an institution's reputation and standing.

Unfortunately, the standards of proper stewardship, as suggested above, are sometimes ignored – often with dire consequences. The temptation to submit to pressures, or to what is perceived as an immediate advantage, often takes precedence. This is particularly true with regard to acquisitions and even more so in those that involve the presentation of human remains. In the latter case, something more than preservation or scholarship is involved: it is respect for the departed and for human dignity. These should not be negotiable for they involve fundamental decency.

While all acquisitions should reflect the seriousness of their purpose, as has too frequently been reported in the press, they often reflect greed, manipulation, and sometimes outright falsehood, whether this be in disclosing provenance, exaggerating importance, or winking at inflated valuations. The mistaken belief that the ends justify the means may no doubt prevail in the short range but, equally certain, in the longer perspective something important is lost – a sense of propriety, the lack of which eventually tarnishes an institution's image, reduces the stature and dignity of its staff, and more important, jeopardizes future learning. The result is the betrayal of a trust and frequently also a breach of law, whether national or international.

These considerations apply equally to the products of humankind or to the travail of nature. The acquisition of an illicitly excavated object that has lost its context, and all that could be learned from it, or of an object that has been stolen, is as reprehensible as the raiding of the rare bird's nest that further endangers a species merely to make a collection more complete. In these cases the moral stature of the individuals and the institutions involved is impaired and the confidence that the public should expect in their purpose is weakened.

It is a given understanding that a concern for ethical correctness must extend to every aspect of an institution's activities. Next to collecting, none is more important than preserving. When making an acquisition, whether by purchase, gift, or bequest, a contract is implied. The implication is that the object will be given all the care necessary for its preservation and transmission, and where applicable, that the intentions of the donor will be respected. This respect should go beyond the legally binding and extend, in all but the most extreme cases, to include these intentions. Acceptance on the part of an institution implies the establishment of a trust, whether it be codified in formal documents or merely by precatory suggestions.

190

In the case of those institutions dealing with living things (namely zoos, botanical gardens, and arboreta), there is a further responsibility. They must assure not only that the specimens were obtained legitimately, are well maintained, and that they reproduce but furthermore, in the case of endangered species (where appropriate), they should provide for the reintroduction of the animals into their original habitat or one sufficiently similar in order to assure their survival.

These acquisitions and conservation principles may seem elementary to those who have been sensitized to a higher understanding of what museums should be at the end of the second millennium. Regretfully, there is ample evidence that expediency continues to prevail in far too many cases, casting a cloud on an entire profession and weakening its ability to contribute in a more meaningful way to society's well-being.

WHAT HAVE BEEN THE CONSEQUENCES OF QUESTIONABLE COLLECTION PRACTICES?

Perhaps the most obvious consequences, in the US, have been the growing role of the courts, the increased intrusion of attorney generals into the governance of institutions, more inquisitive internal revenue and customs services, and the ever-present concern of genuine scholars about the destruction of contexts and the attendant loss of evidence. To this must now be added the growing protests of those countries that are rich in cultural or scientific heritage but poor in other resources. These countries now realize that major parts of their national heritage are no longer present within their boundaries to enhance the lives of their peoples.

The realization that the calling of museums is essentially based upon ethical imperatives has been slow to mature. Further, it must be admitted that a code of ethical principles is not immutable. It is intimately related to the growth of knowledge, the emergence of new understandings, the development of new institutional structures, and changing relationships. However, there are principles of behavior that are universal, and notions of decency that remain regardless of time and place. It is these principles that the American Association of Museums attempted to codify when it passed its first *Code of Ethics* in 1925, less than twenty years after the Association's founding.

This document reflected the perceptions of the times. It did not address questions of illicit acquisitions because the notion that such could occur had not yet emerged. The colonies, no matter whose, were there to be exploited – manifest destiny was *de facto* accepted as a mandate. While all men were created equal, some by a strange concept of divine will were granted economic and political dominion over others. With this dominion came ownership, exploitation, and eventual despoliation of heritage.

In the field of the natural sciences the notion that resources could become extinguished had not received general currency. The passing of the passenger

191

pigeon was not interpreted as the harbinger of what today is realized to be an awesome reality – the virtually unchecked diminishing of the biota and an increased specialization that is robbing future generations of a diversity the qualities of which have not yet been identified.

The impact of new discoveries in medicine and agriculture, the flow of new ideas, as well as the fertilizing destructiveness of world wars, and an attendant rise of a sense of nationhood among people who had been previously subjected, have presented new challenges to previously held ideas and assumptions.

Further, the creation of private institutions established for the public good and financed by private benefaction was increasingly encouraged by tax laws that gave special advantages to the donors while strengthening these institutions' ability to serve a larger public. This, in turn, led to a closer examination of how these institutions were using resources that, because a major part came from tax concessions, could be considered public.

These and other factors have led to a growing need to codify behavior and refine principles in every aspect of museum management and especially acquisitions.

It was not until the early 1970s that the American Association of Museums recognized that a code that had remained unaltered for nearly fifty years was no longer responsive to current needs. In Europe, while general principles were discussed by the Museum Division of the League of Nations, nothing substantial emerged before the Second World War.

The creation of the United Nations Educational, Scientific, and Cultural Organization (UNESCO) in 1946 and the subsequent formation of the International Council of Museums (ICOM) as an independent, non-governmental entity charged with fostering the development of museums and of the museum profession was, for the first time, to focus attention on the need to develop basic principles regarding the support, governance, and administration of museums. One of ICOM's first priorities was to deal with the urgent need to protect the patrimony of countries newly freed from colonialism, to establish norms for the protection of archaeological sites, and to prevent a repetition of the wholesale depredation that characterized many prewar excavations whether authorized or not.

Years of study, negotiations, and false starts, led to UNESCO's *Convention on the Means of Prohibiting and Preventing the Illicit Import, Export, and Transfer of Ownership of Cultural Property* adopted in 1970. This recognized that nations have an inalienable right to their patrimony, and for the first time gave a broader juridical framework for the implementation of antiquities and other laws that had been enacted by virtually every culturally rich country and colony but which, for the most part, were either ineffectual or ignored by all parties.

The passage of the Convention, and of a series of recommendations and proposals that preceded and followed it, created a climate favorable for a serious examination of the ethical aspects of museum management. The AAM's rewrite of the 1925 *Code*, after considerable debate, was unanimously passed in 1978. In the interim the major museum-related organizations, the American Association of Museums, the Association of Art Museum Directors, the College Art Association, the Archaeological Institute of America, the American Anthropological Society and others, including individual museums such as the University Museum of the University of Pennsylvania, and Harvard's Department of Anthropology, endorsed the principles of the UNESCO Convention and started to develop new and often stringent acquisition policies.

As these developments were occurring, the international community, led by ICOM with the support of UNESCO, started a comprehensive examination of the possible return or restitution to their country of origin, of those aspects of cultural property that, by general consent and after proper documentation and demonstrated safeguards, were deemed to be important to that country's sense of nationhood.

While many museum professionals strongly voiced their opposition to the Convention and even more questioned return or restitution, none of their dire predictions has proven to be correct. The modalities for the implementation of such instruments are now in the process of being codified by the International Institute for the Unification of Private Law (UNIDROIT), an international organization that specializes in private law unification treaties. This should lead, in time, to a convention that can be fairly applied on the basis of principles that will be in harmony with the national laws of acceding countries.

Thus a gradual evolution of perception has led to a different perspective on the collecting role of museums. They are viewing their activities in a broader international perspective that reflects a heightened concern for ethical propriety. In doing so, it must be realized that history cannot be rewritten and that what are now viewed as errors in long past actions should not be judged by current perceptions. Conversely, as we conduct our current affairs, we need to be mindful that previous actions that we now may regret are not repeated. Thus there is a critical need to review codes and practices and bring them in line with a heightened sense of what is right. This is what the American Association of Museums has attempted to do over the last few years.

Following tormented debates and years of study, a revised code of ethics was enacted in 1994. In several aspects it is less specific than one might like or expect, but in regard to acquisitions it reaffirms the obligation to "comply with applicable local, state, and federal laws and international conventions, as well as with the specific legal standards governing trust responsibilities" (AAM 1994: 4).

The *Code of Professional Ethics* adopted by ICOM in 1986 is more explicit in many ways, yet written in a manner that applies worldwide. It focuses strongly on illicit acquisitions and their destructive impact, and it states:

> A museum should not acquire, whether by purchase, gift, bequest or exchange, any object unless the governing body and responsible officer

are satisfied that the museum can acquire a valid title to the specimen or object . . . and that in particular it has not been acquired in, or exported from, its country of origin and/or any intermediate country in which it may have been legally owned, (including the museum's own country), in violation of that Country's laws.

(ICOM 1990: 27)

The *Code* refers no less strongly to principles relating to field study, human remains, and to the need for museums to have definite acquisition policies, including conflict of interest safeguards.

The Association of Art Museum Directors' *Code of Ethics for Art Museum Directors*, last revised in 1991, is clear on the need to adhere to all pertinent laws in regard to acquisitions. This concern is further emphasized in their *Professional Practices in Art Museums*, last revised in 1992.

These codes and a large number of statements as well as guidelines prepared by different branches of the museum profession and its related fields, all stress the importance of the object, the need for its care, and the social imperative that it be shared as widely as possible.

WHAT DOES THIS MEAN IN PRACTICAL TERMS?

The following are a few guidelines that attempt to summarize some basic requirements.

1 Every museum should have a clearly expressed collection policy. This statement should delineate how the collections reflect the museum's mission and should outline main areas of emphasis, taking into account: the institution's financial ability to assure the proper care of its holdings; the public it is to serve; the extent of comparable resources that may be available in the area; the need (either expressed or perceived) of the region's schools and academic institutions; the availability of spaces that meet environmental and other safety concerns; and the availability of trained staff to oversee and exploit the collections for educational and research purposes. The policy should be broad enough to allow for exceptions where the circumstances warrant, and should be reviewed periodically to ascertain that its provisions are being followed and that they remain responsive to the ideals of the founders and to the evolving requirements of society.

2 All proposed acquisitions should be thoroughly studied to elicit as much information as possible on the nature, history, condition, and requirements of the object, its previous ownership, and past and current legal status. Where any doubt remains concerning the legitimacy of its availability, a thorough search is required. In the case of an archaeological object or specimen on the endangered list, this would entail a formal inquiry by registered letter to the pertinent authorities requesting their comments and/or approbation of the proposed acquisition.

194

3   In considering the deaccessioning of an object acquired by gift or bequest, the first step is an analysis of the documentation recording the original transaction. Any statement implying that the object is to remain permanently in the institution should automatically preclude any further consideration of disposal. If the statement is ambiguous and/or precatory, a careful evaluation should be made of the donor's intention. No disposal should occur unless there are extraordinary mitigating circumstances and only if careful judicial review finds no legal or moral objections. In cases where sale is justified, the proceeds should be used *only* to strengthen the collections and never for operational purposes.

Museum administrators should be mindful that the best deaccession policy is restraint from acquisition. While errors may have been made by our predecessors, it is a hazardous position to use that excuse to speculate on the integrity of past decisions. Tastes change, perspectives alter, and what once may have been on the "most wanted list" may have fallen to the bottom only to re-emerge, sometimes decades later. It is an ethical obligation to consider all possibilities before making any decision.

4   An important aspect of museum responsibility is the manner in which objects are interpreted or even identified. The most scrupulous objectivity should be the goal. Where there is any doubt about an object's authenticity, the information should be carefully recorded on the museum's official record and reflected in the object's labeling. If doubts are credible, the interpretive materials should refer to them. The same should apply to condition. The public should expect to see exactly what the object is alleged to be. It is the moral obligation of staff not to allow donors or viewers to be in doubt about what they have given or what is presented.

These considerations, many of which are discussed in greater detail in the accompanying essays, are part of the ethical correctness that should be expected from institutions of "higher learning." Museums, as the principal keepers of our tactile heritage, have long striven to be recognized as belonging to that august group. The adoption and implementation of strict ethical principles in all their activities are essential components to the continued material and programmatic success of these institutions.

Ethics and preventive conservation

Although the philosophical boundaries of museums change from location to location and will continue to change, one underlying truth should remain constant. That is the notion that all members of the museum staff, paid or non-paid, have a responsibility for the care of collections. Proper concern for artifacts must be a continuing part of every museum worker's personal as well as professional code of ethics.

Most agree that prevention is better, less expensive, less time consuming, and less damaging to the object than conservation or restoration after deterioration or damage has occurred. While the proper care and treatment of objects does not guarantee the prevention of damage, it can greatly reduce the nature and severity of impairment. As all natural and most process-produced materials decay or deteriorate, museums must maintain the best conditions for the maximum "life" of each object. Preventive conservation is a means of retarding the deterioration process by preventing undesirable conditions from occurring.

The future of collections depends on the "prevention of deterioration through control of the environment, in climate, storage, and on exhibition" (Bachmann 1992: 3). Considering the growing body of information available about preventive conservation, what can be done by each member of the museum profession to meet their ethical obligations and ensure the proper care of individual artifacts (ICOM 1990: 32)?

QUESTIONS ABOUT ETHICS AND PREVENTIVE CONSERVATION FOR FURTHER CONSIDERATION

1 Taking steps to prevent damage or reduce the potential for it is preventive conservation. It is a process that pays attention to collection care rather than focusing on the individual object. The idea is that by providing general care for collections, the need for individual treatment can be reduced. However, the effectiveness of properly applied preventive conservation measures is very difficult to validate because as long as they are effective, the object remains unchanged. The absence of effective preventive conservation care is most obvious when the object suffers damage. Do museums have an ethical

responsibility to study the physical nature of objects and to determine ways of protecting them from deterioration? Is there an ethical principle involved in the decision?

2 Once a museum acquires an object, it is assigned a "special" status. If the object is to survive, ways must be found for preventing or slowing its deterioration. An ideal way to protect an object is to keep it in a controlled environment away from the potentially harmful conditions of being on exhibition. However, a museum has an obligation to exhibit the objects it possesses for the benefit of the public. Does the ethical responsibility for preservation outweigh the obligation to exhibit sensitive objects? Should all artifacts housed in the museum be placed on exhibition regardless of the potential damage from light, vibration, handling, and long-term exposure to atmospheric conditions that are not controlled? Is there a conflict between "duty" and "responsibility?"

3 Preventive conservation is not an end unto itself, but a means of assuring the safe keeping and usability of objects left in the care of museums. Sanitizing an object is one way to provide protection. By removing all stains, residues, and "dirt" from an object, there is less potential of damage from material stress or biological agents such as insects or micro-organisms. However, the cleaning process may destroy potentially significant information about the use and users of the object. Is the museum ethically correct to preserve the object at the expense of information lost in the process, or should the information be preserved to the possible detriment of the object? Which is ethically correct?

4 To be effective, preventive conservation must be the responsibility of each member of the museum staff whether custodian, curator, or director. As preservation of the collections is a part of the mission of most museums, staff members not endorsing the basics of preventive conservation may be viewed as unethical. This assumption is based to a degree on the duty incurred through an action (employment in the museum) and the implicit promise to care for collections. If this is true, should not the same ethical requirement apply to all people employed by all museums? Does this support the notion of universally applicable ethics?

5 From the moment objects are created, they begin to deteriorate, and the most common source of deterioration is adverse environmental conditions. Many objects are in a state of continual interaction with their environment. In addition, there are inherent characteristics that cause object degradation. While some materials found in nature have qualities that protect them, manufactured and combined materials may be inherently unstable. Does the museum have an ethical obligation to correct the problems caused by improper or inappropriate creative processes, or should the objects be left to self-destruction – possibly as their originators intended?

Preventive conservation
The evolution of a museum ethic
Stephen L. Williams

The basic functions of a museum include acquisition, preservation, research, interpretation, and exhibition (ICOM 1990). The recognition of the logical sequence of these activities stresses the importance of how the quality of one impacts on subsequent functions. For instance, material must be acquired before it can be preserved, preserved before it can be fully utilized, and researched before information can be communicated. From this perspective it is easy to understand why acquisition serves as the foundation of museum activities, and why this activity is a major issue involving governmental regulation (Malaro 1985; Phelan 1982), endorsement by the museum community (Anonymous 1989), and inclusion in professional ethics (AAM 1994; ICOM 1990). The acquisition function has gained purpose, direction, and credibility from these influences.

Although preservation is the second logical function of museums, it has not received the same attention as acquisition. There are no laws specifying preservation methods. Various disciplinary approaches are not the same nor equally effective (Rose 1977; Williams and Hawks 1992). A preservation ethic is not recognized, and areas of the museum community that have established high standards of practice (for example, the conservation community) tend to be restrictive regarding activities and disciplines. As a result of this disparity and lack of direction, there is a need to give more credibility to the preservation function by identifying common goals and directions, fulfilling the function in a more unified and holistic manner, and developing a preservation ethic for museum professionals. History has shown that the philosophies and practices of preventive conservation can responsibly address this need.

The word "preventive" has been associated with other words, such as medicine and maintenance. Usually, such word combinations refer to activities that avoid predictable, unfavorable effects of a normal course of action. For example, preventive medicine in the form of proper diet and exercise can be important in avoiding expensive and perhaps serious health problems. Also, it is recognized that preventive maintenance for equipment, such as cleaning and lubrication, can prolong utility and avoid costly repairs. Similarly, in the museum setting, preventive conservation is an alternative to costly interventive treatments and loss of collection objects.

Traditionally, preventive conservation has focused on the provision of proper environment, quality storage, and safe handling to lessen the predictable, unfavorable effects of a normal course of action. However, recent interpretations have been broadened to include new strategies, such as assessment, management, and continued education. After an evolution of conceptualization, recognition, acceptance, and implementation of philosophies and practices of preventive conservation by the museum community, the one factor lacking is recognizing the correlation it has with professional ethics.

Preventive conservation is more than a physical activity. It is consistent with philosophies and practices that are basic to ethical standards endorsed by the museum community. Preventive conservation appropriately addresses preservation as a museum function, and clearly demonstrates proper professional conduct that is essential if the museum community is to uphold the integrity of its profession (Malaro 1993). Therefore, it is logical that the philosophies and practices of preventive conservation be incorporated as an important ethic for the museum community.

DEVELOPMENT OF PREVENTIVE CONSERVATION

Preventive conservation has been defined as "the methodology by which the rate of deterioration of collections is reduced by controlling the causes of deterioration" (Duckworth *et al.* 1993). Although the term "preventive conservation" has not been used until recently, methods of mitigating deterioration in research collections have been employed since the early part of the century. For instance, one early application states,

> Specimens . . . should be kept inside cases; specimens left on the tops of cases . . . are subject to injury from dust, insects, and other agents. . . . Extreme care should be exercised in handling specimens. . . . Every effort should be made to keep pests out of the museum offices and laboratories. . . . However, the use of poisons, whether solid, liquid, or gaseous, is never satisfactory, and if museums were properly constructed . . . insecticides could almost be eliminated. By the same process that we could eliminate these obnoxious chemicals, we could increase the life of our specimens. . . . As the remedy I suggest the use of constant temperature rooms.
>
> (Jackson 1926: 113)

Much later, the classical literature of museum conservation (Greathouse and Wessel 1954; Plenderleith 1956; Plenderleith and Werner 1962) promoted similar ideas and incorporated aspects of preventive conservation, such as environment, storage, and handling.

It was not until the mid-1970s that preventive conservation, as a working concept, began building momentum in the museum community. It was becoming increasingly clear that the traditional conservation practices that focused on

199

restoration of objects were not addressing the more pressing problem of deterioration occurring throughout entire collections (Schur 1981). Furthermore, museum professionals questioned the rationale of providing resources for improving the condition of objects when the objects were being returned to the same situations that initially caused problems. More recently, it was recognized that some early conservation practices may have compromised the stability and utility of museum objects (Rose 1988; Schur 1981). These issues led to the development of non-interventive methodologies, which in turn promoted the philosophies and practices of preventive conservation.

In 1976, the concept of preventive conservation for anthropological collections was formally presented at the annual meeting of the American Institute for Conservation in Boston (Carolyn Rose, pers. comm.). This new approach for dealing with museum objects and collections was scrutinized for some time, and several years passed before it was widely accepted by the museum community. This point is illustrated by the general absence of articles and subject listings, specifically for preventive conservation, in the Art and Archaeology Technical Abstracts (AATA) before 1986.

Courses and programs offered through the George Washington University have been influential in shifting methods of collection care toward the philosophies and practices of preventive conservation. Since the late 1970s, this graduate museum studies program has been training and graduating museum professionals that are knowledgeable about this approach to caring for collections (Schur 1981). Other academic training programs (for example, Museum of Texas Tech University and University of Nebraska State Museum) also have incorporated preventive conservation training as part of their graduate degree requirements. Similar training is periodically provided for museum professionals by various conservation laboratories, such as the Getty Conservation Institute and the Canadian Conservation Institute.

During the past decade, the museum community has been developing the working parameters of preventive conservation. A 1986 manual on the subject focused on environmental issues and the needs of various types of objects (Graham-Bell 1986). However, recent interpretations have been more comprehensive in concept. For instance, the National Park Service stated that preventive conservation is:

> an approach to museum collections management that emphasizes a long-term, ongoing program for the preservation of objects and includes the following elements: knowing the causes and recognizing the symptoms of object deterioration; inspecting objects on a regular schedule; monitoring and controlling museum environment (e.g., relative humidity, temperature, light, pests, dust and other pollutants); practicing proper techniques for the handling, storage, exhibit, packing and shipping of objects; providing appropriate security and fire protection for objects; preparing and implementing, when necessary, emergency management plans for objects.
>
> (National Park Service 1990: (3) 2)

This perspective of preventive conservation has far-reaching implications that involve every aspect of the museum, including the management and allocation of resources, personnel roles and responsibilities, and basic operations.

As the working parameters of preventive conservation become better defined and the philosophies and practices become more established in the museum community, it is clear that it has broad application among museum professions and disciplines. This realization has led to the suggestion that preventive conservation should be incorporated in the policies and procedures of museums (Cato and Williams 1993). Special components of preventive conservation, such as collection management, integrated pest management, and emergency preparedness, already have been proposed for museum policies (Jones 1986; Malaro 1985; Zycherman and Schrock 1988). However, a policy specifically for preventive conservation also addresses issues such as turning off unused lights, cleaning up work areas after use, keeping collection objects in designated storage units, and similar responsibilities that normally are expected of individuals (Cato and Williams 1993).

Rose (1988) was the first to associate professional ethics with preventive conservation. This revelation was based on the need to re-focus museum practices from simple "museum object" orientations to those that acknowledge the research potential of museum objects. Rose questioned the professional ethics of treatments that altered or removed "food deposits, wear patterns, charred portions, and native repairs" from artifacts, thus significantly limiting the ability of anthropologists to understand early cultures. It was concluded that the preservation of material stability and research integrity are matters of professional ethics, and that responsible practices include preventive care as well as choosing stabilization over restoration, when appropriate (Rose 1988).

CURRENT STATUS OF PREVENTIVE CONSERVATION

After decades of development, it is surprising that preventive conservation practices are not better established in the museum community. This situation is rapidly changing because of continued collection growth and the need to accommodate advancing technology, which requires new approaches for the management and care of collections.

During the mid-1980s, museum collections were reported to be growing steadily, and two-thirds of the museums surveyed had not assessed the condition of half of their holdings. Available information indicates only 22 per cent of the objects did not require special attention for their continued care; about half of the remainder were in need of special attention, and the needs of the other half were unknown (Slate 1985).

As the size and significance of collections increased, attitudes in the museum community were changing. Some of these changes resulted from the initiatives of professional organizations, such as the National Institute for Conservation. Others were related to major contributions to the museum literature (Applebaum

1991; Malaro 1985; Michalski 1992; National Park Service 1990; Phelan 1982; Thomson 1986; Zycherman and Schrock 1988). As the availability of new and specific information about collection issues increased (McGinley 1993; Rose 1988; Rose and Torres 1993; Schur 1981; Tennent and Baird 1985; Williams 1991; Williams and Hawks 1992; Williams *et al.* 1989), the museum community was more prepared than at any time in the past to make significant modifications in collection care. It became apparent that preventive conservation was the rational method of providing care for collections that were growing faster than available resources (Rose 1988). However, the implementation of preventive conservation practices and programming remained a problem. As a result, the museum community reported that care of collections and training of personnel were among their highest priorities (Slate 1985; Duckworth *et al.* 1993).

Advancing technology is rapidly altering philosophies and practices for caring for collections. Sophisticated research techniques require materials that will provide reliable and complete information. Therefore, objects in research collections that have an unknown history of treatments may have limited value. For example, there is a growing interest in natural science collections because of recent technological advances in biochemistry, genetics, and environmental monitoring of toxic chemicals (George 1987; Herrman and Hummel 1994; Miller 1985). Because organic materials can be altered structurally and chemically by natural causes (such as light, moisture, temperature, and atmospheric materials) and by unnatural causes (for example, application of fumigants and adhesives), there is a need to preserve research integrity by avoiding compromising situations (Webster 1989; Williams and Cato 1995). The need for non-intrusive methods makes preventive conservation practices a logical and appropriate approach for providing the care required for these collections.

The situations described for anthropology and natural science collections are equally applicable for most other museum collections (Hansen and Reedy 1994). For example, new technology has facilitated in-depth analyses of soil, body fluids, and the origin of materials (Cherfas 1989; Johnson 1980; McKusick 1991), thus giving special significance to collections of clothing, textiles, and historical objects. Because there was a time when these applications were not anticipated, it is reasonable to assume that other innovative uses of collections will be developed by future technology. This possibility obligates museum professionals to re-evaluate philosophies and practices that may have negative effects on the future use of collections. This fact should compel the museum community as a whole to make preventive conservation a goal for the profession.

Considering the conceptual evolution of preventive conservation and current definitions (National Park Service 1990), this method of caring for collections is holistic in principle. It involves the intricacies of environment, storage, handling, and other situations that potentially affect collection integrity, such as risk management and responsible use of collection resources. It also includes documented examination, evaluation, problem recognition, solution development, and solution implementation (Rose 1991). This approach requires a knowledge and understanding of the properties of various materials in collections, including how these materials may have been altered and how they may interact with the environment and other materials. Where basic knowledge and understanding are deficient, a non-interventive approach is required (Rose 1988).

As the preventive conservation approach to collection care requires responsible behavior by all museum professionals, it is important for individuals to understand their own limitations as well as those of others (Agrawal 1982). Preventive conservation activities for individuals without proper training must be restricted to providing physical protection for museum objects from agents of deterioration (for example, turning off lights, avoiding the crowding of specimens, putting objects in closed storage units when not in use, and practicing integrated pest management), and properly handling objects as needed. Situations involving interventive practices should be avoided and referred to persons qualified to evaluate the situation and provide the appropriate advice. Unavoidable intervention (such as accidental damage) must be fully documented regarding the situation, basis for action taken, precise materials used (including concentration, dilutants, brand, and supplier), and step-by-step methods applied; reports should include photographic documentation (Rose 1977).

PREVENTIVE CONSERVATION PROGRAMMING AND PRACTICE

Preventive conservation is not a spontaneous attitude or activity. As an ethic for museum professionals, it requires the ongoing application of preventive conservation philosophies and practices as well as continued education. Malaro (1993) states that it requires, "self-education, self-motivation, and peer pressure for the promulgation." As a holistic activity for museums, it requires the continued education of personnel, the assessment of fully documented conditions, and proper management.

Education

Education and training of museum professionals are fundamental requirements of preventive conservation for both the individual and the museum. Museum professionals responsible for collections need to be able to "recognize existing and potential preservation problems" (Rose 1988). This ability requires a basic familiarity with the collections and associated materials. This, in turn, may require material testing to insure suitable products are used in collections. A knowledge of museum environmental conditions, as well as a knowledge of material responses to these conditions, are equally important. This may require systematic monitoring and documentation of environmental conditions, including light, temperature, relative humidity, and pests. The availability of this information provides the basis for responsible decision-making and action in the museum setting.

Because preventive conservation promotes the responsible use of collection resources (that is, personnel, time, space, supplies, and money), museum professionals responsible for collections must understand risk management and be able to manage resources properly for the benefit of collections. These areas of expertise often require appropriate collections care training for individuals having management responsibilities (Cato 1991; Dixon 1987; Williams and Cato 1995).

Assessment

Another basic component of preventive conservation is objectively and critically evaluating the preservation requirements of the collections, as well as the museum's ability to fulfill these needs. The evaluation must include policies and procedures, building structures, collections, exhibits, resources, practices, and other collection-related resources, such as libraries and archives.

For most museums, a conservation assessment is the beginning of a preventive conservation program (Wolf 1990). This usually involves contracting one or more outside conservation professionals to conduct an on-site evaluation and to write a report. Carefully selected outside reviewers insure objectivity and provide the expertise needed for such assessments. The assessment documents existing conditions, including issues that require various levels of action for the benefit of the collections. Once these issues have been identified, it is the responsibility of the museum staff to determine how each will be resolved.

Management

A third basic component of preventive conservation is management, particularly with respect to setting goals, identifying priorities, formulating strategic plans, and effectively using resources to accomplish museum goals. Responsible management is not possible without "clearly and precisely established goals" (Dixon 1987).

The objective of management is the "resolution of conflict between the use of resources, people, goals, different parts of the organization, or competing groups" (Dixon 1987). Fulfilling this objective requires a commitment to purpose and a willingness to "talk frankly with colleagues" (Malaro 1993). Issues of politics, personalities, and conflicting or weakly defined statements of purpose must be put in proper perspective if management is to be effective (Dixon 1987).

Preventive conservation programming depends on effective management if it is to be holistic in its approach. Proper management is important for policy and procedure development, coordination of activities, effective use of resources, and establishing the direction of collection activities. The importance of management in programming has been appropriately summarized:

Lack of management, rather than managing, is truly unethical behavior, the real "immorality." . . . To ignore management of conservation, or to manage it badly . . . is to fail to meet a clear public responsibility, and constitutes unethical and unprofessional behavior.

(Dixon 1987: 2)

CONCLUSION

This chapter shows how preventive conservation has evolved in the museum community to a status that is regarded as a professional ethic. The concept has withstood the "test of time," starting with a history of sporadic applications and reaching levels of broad recognition, acceptance, and application in museum programming and professional training.

Preventive conservation is regarded as a logical and responsible approach for dealing with large, growing collections and making them available for research that is increasingly based on new technologies. Philosophies and practices of preventive conservation rely on documented examination, evaluation, problem recognition, solution development, and solution implementation. For the museum professional, this is achieved with continued education and the application of preventive conservation philosophies and practices. For museums, a holistic approach involves programming based on educated evaluation of fully documented conditions, followed by proper management to achieve established goals.

A museum ethic defines responsible and acceptable conduct among museum professions for the well-being and integrity of the profession (Malaro 1993). Because an important goal of the museum profession is the preservation of collections, it is reasonable to assume that preventive conservation will provide the direction and mechanism for achieving that goal. It preserves the integrity of collections and addresses the preservation function of museums in a rational, responsible, and effective manner.

Preventive conservation is not restricted to specific museum professionals or disciplines. It is a responsibility of all museum professionals associated with collections, whether they be responsible for decision-making, resource allocation, security, house-keeping, structural maintenance, object preservation, or object use.

Considering that ethics is "a sense of professional conduct . . . learned, accepted, and recognized by all" (Vaughn 1977), preventive conservation is in many respects already established within the museum community. Most museum professionals would have serious reservations about knowingly compromising the value or use of a collection, or about using museum resources directly or indirectly in an irresponsible manner, or about applying toxic chemicals in a manner that pollutes the environment and jeopardizes the health and safety of others. The philosophy and practices of preventive conservation responsibly deal with these issues and others.

Because preventive conservation clearly promotes responsible behavior regarding collections and their care, and because it involves the museum community as a whole, serves professional interests and goals, and has reached high levels of recognition and acceptance, there is overwhelming justification for regarding it as an ethic of the museum profession. Therefore, it should be incorporated in the codes of ethics adopted by the museum profession, museum organizations, and museums. Ultimately, it should be part of the ethics practiced by every museum professional.

ACKNOWLEDGMENTS

Sincere appreciation is extended to Carolyn Rose, David Salay, and Robert Waller for useful discussions and for reviewing drafts of this manuscript. Appreciation is also extended to Gary Edson for the invitation, encouragement, and opportunity to present this information.

15

Ethics and conservation

The ethical and philosophical issues associated with conservation are numerous and may vary depending on the beliefs and cultural values of a particular country. However, there are many common factors that form a basis for shared "truths" associated with the preservation of cultural material. It is true that the conservation techniques used to treat certain kinds of artifacts do not vary according to the origin of the object. It is also true that certain forms of deterioration may be treated in basically the same manner regardless of the cultural use or social context of the damaged object.

It is the invasive nature of some forms of conservation that challenges ethical sensibilities. The current approach to conservation is that no harm should be done to the object, and that all treatment must be reversible. However, some conservation techniques alter the aesthetic quality of an object by modifying traditionally held impressions or beliefs. This can occur when an object is cleaned. A painting may present a totally different "feeling" or impression when darkened varnish is removed. A textile may be a different color, and a paper object may have a different appearance when cleaned of spots, stains, or discoloration. Also, cleaning is not reversible.

If present thinking endorses minimal treatment and maintaining objects in a condition as close as possible to original, how are limits determined and are ethical concerns a part of the process?

QUESTIONS ABOUT ETHICS AND CONSERVATION FOR FURTHER CONSIDERATION

1 What are the ethical ramifications of replacing the primary support elements to stabilize a deteriorating historic structure?

2 Some objects of art undergo massive conservation treatment based on technology and materials that may prove to be counterproductive in the future. The museum community currently is dealing with problems that are the result of the well-intended conservation and restoration practices of only a few years ago. In accordance with their ethical responsibility as institutions

of public trust, should museums preserve objects for research and exhibition (regardless of how long they may last) without jeopardizing their eventual safekeeping by subjecting them to potentially unsafe materials or techniques? Ethically, where will the greater good be served?

3   There are many ethical issues to be considered in the conservation process: inoperative machines are made to operate; broken and dilapidated objects are made new; and partly destroyed pieces are made whole. Is it ethically wrong for museums to display objects that are only partly original with the remainder reconstructed by conservation/restoration techniques, or would it be more correct to show a reproduction? Should a building or object be conserved as found or restored to original condition? At what point should conservation stop?

4   Appearance may be a major factor in deciding the level and kind of conservation treatment. This is particularly true for objects valued for aesthetic reasons, but it can apply to other materials as well. For exhibition purposes, appearance can be very important. Does the use of objects that have been extensively conserved constitute a fraud? When does this practice become unethical for museums?

5   Without extensive intervention, many buildings and monuments would no longer exist. However, often the conservation processes of past years were marginally effective and some have caused further damage. Few restored the structures to their original strength and appearance. Nevertheless, in some cases, the conservation work may be important in the context of studying the history of such techniques. In current practice, conservators may remove materials used during former conservation treatments. Has that material become a part of the "fabric" of the building, and should it be retained? Is there an ethical responsibility for the conservator to preserve the past conservation as part of the provenance of the structure?

Ethics and museum conservation

Robert E. Child

ABSTRACT

Ethical museum conservation is not immutable. It changes with the changing needs, fashions, and priorities of museums. However, the fundamental principles of examination (to determine the true nature of an object), conservation (to prevent or retard its deterioration), and restoration (to ameliorate certain aspects of the object), are the basic tenets that define museum conservation. It is in the interpretation and balance of the three principles that controversy is and always will be generated.

INTRODUCTION

> Morality is the custom of one's country and the current feeling of one's peers
> (Butler 1912)

The science of morality is the distinction between right and wrong and gives the ethical perspective to the decisions in life. As with human morality, the ethical point of view can vary with changing fashions, politics, attitudes, and developing circumstances. Samuel Butler continued by saying, "Cannibalism is moral in a cannibal country."

Conservation and restoration ethics developed in museums, galleries, and wealthy households, as a consensus view of those who had an interest in art and antiquities. Therefore, it would be an absurdity to expect that consensus to be unchanging. Similarly, it would be frivolous to expect the same ethical values to be applied to all classes of objects, however even-handed people try to apply them. Depending on fashions and personal preferences, different objects will always evince a different reaction and so their conservation will be, to a degree, subjective. For example, at present, there is a preference for silver and other lustrous metals to be highly polished. However, many institutions are allowing their brass furniture fittings to mellow and patinate with the wood. This attitude follows the present trend in conservation ethics, which is more toward preservation of the inherent nature of an object, rather than its restoration to a subjective former state.

209

There are several published statements on conservation ethics both from institutional bodies such as the International Committee of Museums (ICOM) (AIC 1979; Allen 1984; IIC-CG and CAPC 1986; UKIC 1983) and from concerned specialist conservators and companies (Frost 1980; Harding 1976; Wallis 1988). They show an unremarkable agreement on what is important and as such can be considered the consensus viewpoint of the conservation community.

In order to discuss the current concepts of museum conservation, it is necessary to define and explain the following terms as they are commonly understood by museum conservators:

- **Conservation**: the preservation of an object by retarding or halting the processes of deterioration, without unduly altering the object.
- **Restoration**: the alteration of an object beyond that necessary for its preservation, in order to improve some factor of the object. It is in addition to preservation and should only be undertaken for compelling reasons.

A broken pottery vase needs only correct storage of the fragments for the preservation of the material. Restoration through adhering the pieces back into a unified whole, and applying correct storage/display conditions, will obviously increase the vase's value for research, interpretation, and visual impact. However, further restoration to fill in the cracks and paint the joins to make them invisible, can be considered unnecessary deception, as it does not aid the object's interpretation. This final step denies the observer information about the object. The repaired vase is rendered a fake, as its intent is to deceive the viewer as to its true state and condition.

CONSERVATION ETHICS

The ICOM Committee for Conservation describes the activities of conservation as that of:

- examination,
- preservation, and
- restoration.

Examination is defined in the UKIC *Guidance of Conservation Practice* as, "an adequate examination of the object and all available documentation to record its condition and history, and to establish the causes of its deterioration." The examination of documentation and discussions with outside experts to have the fullest understanding of an object is necessary research before deciding the ethical treatment. The examination of the object, however, has some ethical problems. For instance, often the necessary information on the object's condition can only be obtained through intrusive examination, such as chemical tests, or by extensive dismantling that may, by necessity, damage, remove, or destroy original material. Further, there is often a desire for work to begin on the conservation of objects without completing the necessary preliminary examination and associated records. Time, space, resources, and the over-enthusiasm of the staff put pressure on the examination process.

A basic list of the information needed for the conservation record is as follows:

- **background information**: the history of the object to determine its "curriculum vitae" of storage conditions, details of use, maintenance details, etc.,
- **research date**: operating manuals, manufacturers' catalogues, contemporary oral data and information on similar objects from other museums, specialists, societies, etc., and
- **condition record**: details of materials, fabrication methods, manufacturing information (both from the research data and visual examination), and the deterioration of the object both active and historic should all be recorded in detail.

Before continuing, an evaluation should be made based on the following steps:

1 the proposed conservation treatment, and
2 the additional examination needed to aid the conservation treatment.

If considered dispassionately, any further intrusive examination may not be relevant or necessary. If the object is not unique, such information that might be gleaned will perhaps be gained some other time on another identical article. Most often the examination and initial recording process will be left to the conservator and will often be brief. The curator/conservator dialogue is, however, vital at the end of this procedure to decide the conservation treatment and the proposed end-product.

PREVENTIVE CONSERVATION

The conservation treatment is essentially one of preservation, and in all cases involves what is commonly known as "preventive" or "passive" conservation. This is the provision of an environment that is amicable to the object and provides it with the best possible chance of survival. Normally, it will include the following factors:

- **climatic conditions**: the temperature, humidity, light, etc., that best suit the object. For organic objects, that is usually the climate in which they came to an equilibrium before entering the museum. For inorganic objects, it may be relative humidity low enough to prevent further corrosion.
- **a pollution-free environment**: clean of both gaseous and particular pollutants. Many materials from which showcases and storage boxes are made may emit corrosive fumes, while dust can be hygroscopic and chemically

active, which on absorbing moisture can cause corrosion, staining, and other forms of damage.

- **correct sympathetic storage and materials handling facilities**: to avoid accidental damage through poor handling and the like.

The great ethical advantage of preventive conservation is that it is usually an incontrovertible good for the objects. There is no attempt to alter the object itself, only to provide conditions for its optimum survival. The controversy arises when there is a conflict of interest between the needs of the objects and those of the viewer who wishes to see, handle, and use them. A common complaint of the visitor in museums is the low light levels in costume and picture galleries and the intrusion of glass showcases and glazing over pictures. It is often not well explained (or is conveniently forgotten) that the low light levels and the glass are a compromise between the object and its future, on the one hand, and the requirements of the viewer on the other. Often, the objections arise due to poor design and display techniques which make these compromise safety measures obvious and intrusive. With the options available to conservators, curators, and designers (to use, for instance, high light levels for shorter periods, more frequent rotation of exhibits, filtered air-conditioning, etc.), most ethical conservation restrictions should be surmountable.

INTRUSIVE CONSERVATION

In principle, intrusive or "active" conservation is a treatment that affects the object. It can be as simple as dusting or as complex as the removal of fresco wall paintings in a church. In all cases, the treatment poses a potential risk to the object and this has to be outweighed by the benefit to the object and to the viewer. Often, this includes the application of a protective covering. However, the application of a coating such as varnish, consolidant, paint, etc., is but an inexpensive and expedient alternative to providing the correct environmental and security conditions. When used as such, it is a process to be avoided as it is a short-cut to determining and providing the correct conditions for the object. Also, it is often a non-reversible treatment that may permanently damage or alter the object.

Both Pye and Cronyn (1987) and Horie (1987) note that a basic concept of ethical conservation is the use of reversible treatments – everything that is done should be able to be undone. They go on to demonstrate that although this is a desirable and laudable aim in theory, in practice it is not wholly possible. The treatment of corrosion removal, such as de-rusting, is one obviously irreversible process. However, less obvious is the irreversibility of consolidation, a process where a material is strengthened by impregnation with a hardening agent. In theory the consolidant can be dissolved with the same solvent used to thin it for impregnation. In practice this is not possible because a residue always remains. In the removal of yellowed varnish from paintings or the re-gluing of old glued joints, the original varnish and glue are never completely removed.

Even the lacquers applied to seemingly impermeable metals need drastic solvent treatments to remove most of it, but not all. Furthermore, due to the degradation of the glues, consolidants, varnishes, etc., in time they tend to become increasingly insoluble and irreversible.

An even greater problem of ethics arises with the use of so-called permanent solutions to preservation problems. A backlash to the irreversibility of some processes previously considered reversible is the hard-held opinion of some museum professionals that there are processes that will outlive the life of the object and whose use is thus ethical. Unfortunately, for many of the materials and processes, time has proven them to be less permanent than their proposers had hoped. The subsequent removal of the degraded substance has proved difficult and sometimes impossible. This difficulty is exemplified by the conservator faced with the task of removing epoxy resin glues and polyurethane varnishes.

There is a gray area between what can be defined as active conservation and restoration, and this highlights the conflict between preservation and interpretation. Until recently, it was common conservation practice to clean costumes by various methods to remove dirt, sweat, and other soil that may chemically degrade the fabric or prove an attractant to insect pests or fungi. However, Cooke (1988) shows what evidence can be obtained from crease patterns in costumes and how that information may be lost through washing. Similarly, the removal of rusted layers of iron corrosion will permanently destroy the entrapped original surface with its inherent information and make it irretrievable. Due to the increased understanding of the degradative processes and the ways to overcome them, there are fewer purely preservational reasons for such irreversible processes. If they are used, it is for restoration.

RESTORATION

Restoration, by definition, changes an object from the condition in which it was accepted into the museum. Axiomatically, any change whether through deterioration or restoration diminishes the object's individual integrity. It is a matter of singular importance for any object to be restored, and the goal of such restoration needs to be understood clearly by both curator and conservator. The routine refurbishment of artifacts, and the long accepted customs and practices of restoration such as the importance of clocks to work, cars to "go," and corrosion to be removed, need to be constantly evaluated. This is especially true today when original untouched examples of many museum objects are becoming increasing rare.

The reason for restoration is usually aesthetic, regardless of the truisms that "the significance of a broken object . . . may lie in the damage it has suffered" (Organ 1976). And, "for obvious cultural reasons, it is far more desirable to keep genuine old fabric and workmanship than to replace it with even the highest-quality modern reproduction fabric" (Waite 1976). The tradition of the restorer has evolved from the desire of collectors to own works of art in an immaculate state. When the demand exceeded the supply, the restorer refurbished damaged and deteriorated material for presentation as "in perfect condition." The tradition lives on in collectors of all types who turn to museums to evaluate just how genuine their objects are when compared with the museum's authentic material. Sadly, even museums have restored objects for dubious aesthetic reasons or to improve their financial rather than historic or artistic value.

One of the moral dilemmas facing collectors of usable items such as machinery – clocks, scientific instruments, cars, steam engines, etc. – is the "to run or not to run" problem. Too often, the problem is different from that perceived by the restorer in that the use of replicas is not considered. The restorer may reject this alternative and restore the clock, piano, or car to get an authentic appreciation of its working parts. However, the restoration process by its nature will adapt, repair, modify, and change the original mechanism until there is no guarantee of authenticity beyond general appearance. An accurate facsimile affords a greater chance of reproducing the original working processes because new unworn materials can be used. A further benefit of using a facsimile is that the original is available for comparison.

Many institutions are overcoming the restoration problem by making a register of original items in their collections and keeping them sacrosanct from change. They restore, if appropriate, duplicates. Such an arrangement could be made on a national level to reserve a core of type specimens similar to the methods employed by zoologists and geologists.

Where restoration is determined appropriate, a highly detailed documentation program of the work needs to be completed. This is especially important where outside restorers are used. It will prevent misunderstandings in the treatments planned and assure that the degree of restoration desired is fully understood by both parties. Such a document will exist as a permanent justification for the project and a complete description of the examination, preservation, and restoration work.

For machinery restored to working condition, there must be a schedule of operation that least jeopardizes the safety of the object. For example, this may include operating under low loading limits, or reduced weights in gravity-driven clocks, or slow warm-up times. A complete understanding of the machine and its operative capacities is necessary, and a risk assessment of the museum value of the object against its display use is essential.

There are many manuals, guides, and other publications on the canons of restoration ethics, such as the use of compatible materials, finishes superior to the original, and the transition from restoration to reconstruction. It is easy to get immersed in the minutiae of the moral issues about conservation practice. The general tenets of conservation satisfactorily cover all such points by appealing to the common-sense attitudes of conservators and curators alike to abide by the three main ethical considerations:

- preservation should ideally be the limit of conservation,
- conservation processes should cause the minimum of change and where possible be fully reversible, and

- all relevant information should be fully documented.

It is difficult, if not impossible, to give precise dogmatic criteria for deciding ethical conservation treatments.

As William James said in 1896, "There can be no final truth in ethics any more than in physics, until the last man has had his experience and said his say" (James 1896).

Ethics and exhibitions

The presentation of information in museums, whether through exhibitions, lectures, trunk exhibits, etc., has a reputation of being accepted by the public as inherently accurate and true. A concern is that often what is presented is essentially the opinion of an individual or those of a small group acting in concert to make the presentation. Historically, such offerings have been shown to be less than accurate or, at best, represent only the state-of-the-knowledge at any given time. Although it is evident that this is both acceptable and expected, the question arises whether there is a responsibility on the part of museums to indicate to their audiences that opinion, assumption, and conjecture play an important role in interpretation. Is a statement by the exhibit/lecture/program makers to that effect needed, and if so, how should such a "disclaimer" be presented without becoming an equivocation?

QUESTIONS ABOUT ETHICS AND EXHIBITIONS FOR FURTHER CONSIDERATION

1 In much of the world, the concept of ethnocentrism is viewed as inapplicable. The realization that people in different lands have different beliefs commonly is endorsed. However, the issue of personal beliefs and values is often imposed on critical social custom to challenge museum activities. Is it un-ethical for museums to exhibit objects from a country that holds certain people in a state of servitude? Should such issues be ignored because the beauty and uniqueness of a land or people should not be diminished by social practices?

2 For years the museum community concentrated on exhibiting "real" objects, and the critical issue was authenticity. In contemporary society, the information associated with the object is often more critically assessed than the object. Who owns the truth? Is there an ethical difference between interpretation of events (or objects) to give a certain scholarly perspective and propagandizing to perpetuate a national or ethnic agenda? Should museums do either? Is censorship a part of this issue?

3 Regardless of their subject, are exhibits primarily for entertainment or do

they present certain values associated with the patrimony of a people? Do museums have an ethical responsibility to respond to the pressures of special interest groups by removing material that may be viewed as sensitive or provocative?

4   Should the individual rights of the curator responsible for an exhibition be set aside for the greater requirements of the museum? Can there be a conflict between individual beliefs, duty, and the greatest good for the most people?

5   When exhibiting the work of a living artist, there is often a difference of opinion about how the artwork should be organized and what special arrangements must be made to protect the objects. Does the museum have an ethical responsibility to present and protect the artwork in a museo-logically accepted manner though the artist may demand otherwise? Does personal preference supersede the obligations of the museum staff? What might be the message sent to the viewers?

Ethics and museum exhibitions

David K. Dean

A QUESTION OF HONESTY

The answer to the question, "Does a museum have ethical responsibilities to the public regarding exhibitions?" is of course, "Yes!" Having said this, there is a need for explanation as the response is initially intuitive rather than analytical. Somehow, in any human endeavor, it seems appropriate that ethics be considered. However, beyond this "gut reaction" lie additional ideas worthy of exploration.

The question of responsibility and its simple answer raises two more questions: What ethical principles apply, and, in practical terms, how can a set of standards be applied to what is essentially a creative product – each exhibition being a unique entity? As Richard Rabinowitz comments about exhibitions:

> It is an art we are producing. For all the thematic research invested in the creation of an interpretive exhibit, for all the care spent on curatorial documentation and conservation of the artifacts included, the synthesis of the entire exhibit is a single, composite creative act – a work of conceptual art.
>
> (Rabinowitz 1991: 34)

There are at least two clear obligations facing museums regarding exhibitions for public consumption. For that matter, the same obligations apply to any interpretive communication tool used by museums. The first involves insuring the information is accurate and true within the limitations of current human knowledge. The second concerns the manner of presentation – the willingness to acknowledge the inherent fallibility of any ideas expressed due to their source. A principle, then, is honesty in presenting subjects or objects.

Concerning accuracy and truthfulness in exhibitions, the primary obligation lies in the tacit trust that most visitors have in museums and the information they provide. Public audiences often regard the opinions of researchers and scholars as being established fact and "scientifically" verifiable, therefore, inherently true. Most museums are places where exhibited information is derived from scholarly and scientific pursuits, therefore, the public expectation is that the information presented in museum programs and exhibitions is accurate.

218

Because of this trust, it is incumbent upon the professionals who work in museums to place a high value upon what is offered as fact. The efforts expended in researching and confirming exhibited ideas and information ought to have special priority for exhibit makers. To do less than expend every reasonable effort to obtain and present accurate information is to betray the public trust. This applies not only to new or transient exhibitions, but to "permanent" exhibitions as well. There ought to be a continual review of what is on display to ascertain its accuracy and validity in the light of current knowledge.

Along with the principle of accurate information is the companion obligation for honesty in exhibitions and programs. While the two ideas may seem similar, perhaps even synonymous, they are in reality different. Accuracy refers to presenting up-to-date information, whereas honesty deals with the approach to presenting that information.

Among some museum professionals, there has emerged an advocacy for "signing" exhibitions. Literally interpreted, this involves a publicly visible statement by the exhibit builders confirming that the exhibition and its ideas are products of the creators' thoughts and beliefs – their intellectual progeny, so to speak. Such a statement might then be followed by the names of those individuals actually involved in creating the exhibition.

Along a more figurative line, "signing" might involve, in an opening statement near the entrance to an exhibition, the makers' assertion that the exhibition is as accurate and true as the current state-of-the-knowledge allows, or a statement to the effect that speculative materials are included in the presentation. While it may sound as though both types of "signing" are nothing more than disclaimers or equivocations, in reality, they can be forthright efforts to inform the museum's audience, thereby respecting their right to know the truth. Both approaches have validity at times.

Beyond the question of whether or not to sign an exhibition, there exist other advantages for a strategy of honesty. In an exhibition or program depicting the current judgments of scholarly research, a literal signing in the catalog, lecture abstract, or the title panel can serve to credit the originator or originators, just as does the author's name in a book or the artist's signature on a painting. While serving to provide appropriate recognition, it also stresses the basis and possible biases for the presentation's content.

Also, admitting the speculative or theoretical nature of the material presented serves to defuse any resistance on the viewer's part by allowing them to decide upon their own views about the subject. This is less threatening than giving the impression that to disagree with the exhibition or program content is to be intellectually inferior.

Another advantage involves showing respect for the museum visitor as a thinking being, someone worthy of taking the effort to inform fully. No one likes to feel intellectually inadequate to understand what they experience. Such feelings are uncomfortable and unproductive, usually discouraging future visits. Whereas some people might not be affected by intellectual snobbery, in today's consumer-oriented climate, many patrons do appreciate an institution dealing honestly with them, in turn affirming their trust and promoting further participation.

This is especially true for exhibitions that portray ideas derived from the best-informed speculations of researchers. It is probably wise to include a statement alerting the audience that what they are about to experience is, at least in part, enlightened conjecture. The electronic media often provide such "disclaimers" at the beginning of speculative programs, clearly stating the nature of the information offered for consideration. Might it not be true that what is good in one medium is sometimes appropriate for another? There is nothing inherently wrong nor intellectually shameful about informed speculation. It is the basis for human exploration and learning. The important point is that scholarly "guesstimates" need to be presented openly, not allowed through omission to pose as established fact. The responsibility of museums as public educators is to provide audiences with accurate and truthful information, honestly presented, even if that means admitting that best guesses are all we have to offer at present.

All of this is not to say that every exhibition in every circumstance needs to be "signed." Some things are what they are. It is not really necessary for a museum to explain in every instance why a particular painting, garment, or mineral specimen was chosen for display. Most people understand that such choices are the purview of a museum's specialists. However, these professionals must not use that as license for patronizing their audiences. They need to ponder the information exhibited with the ethical sword dangling where it belongs – directly over their intellectual heads – lest complacency set in.

RECONTEXTUALIZING THE WORLD

For the most part, museums rely upon their most unique assets – collections – to tell their story. The choice and presentation of objects presented are fraught with subtle dangers lying at the heart of the decision making process. Namely, any object placed on exhibition is put in a context that is often completely foreign to its origins. It is "recontextualized." As Susan Vogel remarks, "Almost nothing displayed in museums was made to be seen in them. Museums provide an experience of most of the world's art and artifacts that does not bear even the remotest resemblance to what their makers intended" (Vogel 1991: 191).

The ethical concern is that recontextualizing is a subtle and powerful manipulator of public values and opinions. This fact has far-reaching implications for exhibit makers. The placement of objects is capable of communicating an infinite variety of messages. Speaking of the arrangement of objects (in this case Dutch landscape paintings), Svetlana Alpers observes, "Of course we know that any order we place on material is ours [the museum professional's] not necessarily theirs [the object's creator]" (Alpers 1991: 27).

Discussing cultural representation in museums, Alpers points out, "Museums turn cultural materials into art objects. The products of other cultures are made into something that we can look at. It is to ourselves, then, that we are representing things in museums" (Alpers 1991: 27). It might be added that the same is true for items drawn from the dominant culture of the area in which the museum is located. For example, farming implements were not intended to be put on exhibit, but used for the purposes for which they were made. Yet, how many agricultural exhibitions recontextualize such objects?

The power of museums to instruct, color, and rearrange opinions is incalculable. Susan Vogel sums this up nicely in the following paragraph from her article in *Exhibiting Cultures*.

> The museum is teaching – expressly, as part of an education program and an articulated agenda, but also subtly, almost unconsciously – a system of highly political values expressed not only in the style of presentation but in myriad facets of its operation. The banners in front of the building tell the visitor what really matters before he or she has entered the display. The museum communicates values in the types of programs it chooses to present and in the audiences it addresses, in the size of staff departments and the emphasis they are given, in the selection of objects for acquisition, and more concretely in the location of displays in the building and the subtleties of lighting and label copy. None of these things is neutral. None is overt. All tell the audience what to think beyond what the museum ostensibly is teaching.
>
> (Vogel 1991: 200)

The power that museums have to transfer knowledge and shape opinions points out the dangers. Not only do people *trust* the information they receive in museum exhibitions and programs, but they *believe* what they are taught. The responsibility for the exhibitor that such a situation entails is self-evident. Certainly, not all visitors enter museums entirely credulous, but it might be argued that, for most, the presentation of ideas and theories in an exhibition is accepted. So then, if a statement is made about the benefits of certain nutritional regimens, or the planetary threat posed by the destruction of rain forests, or the true nature of the universe and time, or even who shot President Kennedy, then a majority of the public who receive the message are generally accepting of the opinions expressed. Consequently, an unreflective attitude regarding exhibition or program messages is inadmissible.

In developing an interpretive concept, the public trust must be considered of paramount importance. Therefore, knowing the audience is essential. What audience does the museum serve? What levels of information do they bring with them? What prevailing attitudes flavor how they will react to new information? These and many other questions should be answered in the planning of exhibitions or programs. All of which is to say that the originating of exhibition or programming ideas is a central issue in serving the public. There are no substitutes for careful deliberation and planning, and there is no such thing as a simple exhibit.

221

THE POWER OF CONTENT

Once an idea or concept has been settled upon, then a process ensues, sometimes arduous, involving decisions about how best to present ideas and information, and what objects to use. This embraces the actual content of the presentation. Usually, there is far more information available, both factual and conjectural, than is possible or practical to use in an exhibition or program. Determinations must be made about how to prune and shape content to achieve the desired results. Here again, there is an obligation to the audience to weigh carefully such matters and to arrive at a presentation configured to match the visitor's needs and expectations as closely as possible.

After content has been decided, perhaps even while the process is ongoing, appropriate deliberation must be applied to the information delivery methods to be used. It is proper to ask such questions as: Is exhibition really the best means of communicating an idea? Would a workshop or living history re-enactment better serve as a channel for communicating information and shaping opinions? The options open to museum professionals to promulgate ideas are many. The decision to employ one or another channel must be based upon experience, a thorough knowledge of the community, and an appreciation for indigenous values.

Almost any idea is communicable if the audience is willing to receive it. The concept of audience receptivity must rest upon an appreciation of that group's inherent values and belief systems. A theory that challenges popular belief will often be rejected, without due consideration being given to the idea, despite the worthiness of the scholarship and research behind its formulation. Consider the degree of resistance originally faced by the now accepted theory that dinosaurs were extinguished by an asteroid strike 65 million years ago.

An appreciation for prevailing world views is essential in communicating any new or radical ideas. The principle that works well is to start with the familiar and move the audience toward new concepts in easily digestible increments. To assail the constituency's values and beliefs unexpectedly is not responsible, to them or the idea. Museums must be sensitive to their communities and give constituency values and beliefs their proper credit, even if the staff does not share them.

ARRANGING FOR LEARNING

Beyond these considerations lies the matter of how concepts are physically presented – the visual and verbal expression of the ideas in the exhibition or program. The planner can manipulate – subtly or otherwise – an audience's opinions by altering environmental and psychological factors. Shades of color, tone of voice, the gallery's comfort, the ease or difficulty of reading or under-standing text are elements that impact upon visitor attitudes. The docent's verbal delivery, the use of hands-on materials, or the kinds of handouts provided affect the way a participant feels about the subject presented, their willingness to learn, and their satisfaction with the experience.

Knowing the cultural norms is the key to creating presentations that will satisfy public needs and expectations. Design elements such as color, texture, form, line, and the like, carry with them cultural associations as well as aesthetic ones. As an example, color combinations have particular meanings in various cultures. The colors pink and blue are typically associated with gender in the US. Black and white are colors that have different associations depending on the cultural context.

The placement of objects in a gallery can have unexpected results. Consider the difficulties that arose in connection with the US flag being displayed on the floor of a well-known art museum. Although the museum's leadership felt this presentation was appropriate and respected the artist's freedom of expression, nonetheless the community's reaction was strongly felt. If such a controversial presentation is contemplated, the museum's obligation is to weigh carefully perceived community benefits against the possible backlash and detriment to the institution.

There are a myriad of possibilities and pitfalls inherent in the interpretive process. It is not enough to put an object on a pedestal and open the doors. Everything around the object has an impact on how the visitor reacts, interprets, and assimilates the presentation. It is this power to affect the visitor that the planner must take into account. The degree of care, thought, and concern for one's audiences should be a museum professional's first and most lasting concern.

IN CONCLUSION

To summarize, museum exhibition and program planners and workers need to be aware of the impact their efforts have on a largely accepting and expectant public. If what is presented in exhibitions and programs is seen as inherently reliable and accurate, then honesty and openness should be the museum's proactive approach to presentation. If the context carries messages about values and attitudes, then the utmost consideration must be applied to what exhibitions and programs are meant to communicate, and actually do communicate. To create communication media for the public without adequate thought given to the implications is inexcusable and unacceptable for a publicly oriented institution.

Does all of this mean that museum professionals should throw up their hands in despair? Of course not! What it means is that museums must be aware of the attitudinal and informational potential that exists in what they present, and dedicate themselves to making decisions about presenting exhibitions in a manner consistent with such an awareness. If that process includes providing the audience with an overt statement about the how, why, and who of an exhibition's creation, then so be it.

Museums have no need to apologize for what they are and do. Theirs is a long and fruitful history of public service, enlightenment, education, and entertainment to millions of people. However, it behooves museum professionals, both paid and volunteer, to consider the ethical implications of presenting any subject or object in a museum context. Such deliberations should take first priority whenever museum staffs engage in exhibit or program planning and production. In fact, the results from a close scrutiny of the audience's needs and expectations, and a museum staff's own ethical self-examination, will be appreciated by the public, even if unknowingly, by supporting them intellectually and enhancing the museum experience.

Ethics and public programs

"The contemporary museum strives to be a forum where the genius of the times and the spirit of the people find expression" (Solana 1981: 17). Museums fulfill this responsibility through programming that includes an enormous variety of different public-oriented activities. These activities may include formal talks, tours, lectures, informal family walks or excursions, cultural events of all kinds including films, concerts, crafts demonstrations, mobile exhibitions, outreach programs, and research. Each of these programs is a part of fulfilling the ethical responsibility of the museum.

Most visitors consider public programming and exhibits to be the primary mission of museums. These activities normally occupy the public areas of the museum and are often the only activity the public observes. The public is also beginning to view museums as institutions of social responsibility and to acknowledge their role as servants of society. Consequently, museums ought to take every opportunity to develop programmatic resources available to all segments of the constituency they intend to serve.

Considering the changing nature of the museum public and their expectations, is public programming becoming the primary function of museums, causing social service to eclipse all other museological duties?

QUESTIONS ABOUT ETHICS AND EDUCATION FOR FURTHER CONSIDERATION

1 As uniquely qualified institutions of learning, museums can stimulate visitors to initiate their own encounters with objects and ideas. In fulfilling this role, do museums have an ethical responsibility to develop educational opportunities for school-age visitors and adults that reflect associated learning styles? Or, is educational programming a collateral activity that is valuable but not totally necessary to the purpose of the museum? Are museums unethical for not providing education-based learning opportunities?

2 As part of the museum community's commitment to education, rigorous standards of scholarship should be maintained. In this way, the validity and

integrity of the educational programs can be assured. At the same time, most museums recognize that curators, scholars, and researchers bring certain biases to their research. Is it an ethical responsibility of the museum to validate every program or is it appropriate to allow each program to be presented on its own merits allowing the initiator to be held responsible (for right or wrong information)?

3 Young people acquire beliefs about the world, and attitudes toward other people, from their families and the culture in which they live. As socially oriented institutions, museums can play an important role in transmitting cultural issues because a part of preserving the cultural heritage of a people is sharing it through the educational process. If this is true, it may be assumed that education is concerned with a people's attitude, feelings, and character as well as their intellectual growth. Therefore, museums would seem to have a very broad and inclusive social responsibility that should apply equally to all their constituents. With this in mind, is it ethically correct to focus programming content on those parts of society that are traditional supporters of the museum, knowing they will underwrite the activities, or should financial consideration be ignored in favor of social service? Should the issue of museum survival to serve the greater "good" of the community take priority over the needs of an individual constituency group?

4 Museums have a legal as well as ethical duty to their collections as objects held in public trust. However, at the present, most museum advocates place the educational mission of museums as a primary duty. Are people the most important responsibility of museums or does the ethical obligation to the collections take precedence? From the perspective of ethics, where does the true duty of museums reside?

5 The idea of marketing is gaining greater acceptability in the museum community. Institutions are advertising their exhibits, programs, and related activities by proclaiming them to be exciting and culturally enlightening. Normally, the museum does not call attention to the flaws in the programs or the inconsistencies in an exhibition. Does the principle of "consumer (visitor) beware" apply, or should the public expect more ethical practices from museums?

Ethics and public programs
For the visitor's global experience

Johanne Landry
(Written with the collaboration of Annick Poussart;
translation from French by Terry Gillett)

In our daily existence, each of us strives to live in harmony with our values –
our personal code of ethics. It takes time for these values to emerge, and it
would be presumptuous to assert that our convictions will forever remain
unchanged. Life *is* change, and a single striking experience can prompt us to
call those values into question. I had such an experience, years ago, back when
I felt I knew it all.

At the time, I was part of a multimedia team composed of people driven, as I
was, by a consuming environmental faith. Our budget was meager but our
imagination boundless, and we had decided to sensitize the public to the beauty
of nature by staging a show that would have them experience a thunderstorm
in a pine forest.

After weeks of rehearsal, the big night arrived. While projectors and loud-
speakers boomed, thunder and lightning flashed, and the ventilation system
wafted a subtle odor of pine through the room. I, dressed all in black, made
my way up and down the aisles, sprinkling a fine rain on the spectators. The
audience was enchanted. People burst out laughing. After the show it was
our turn to be deluged with compliments. We were awash in our euphoria
when one spectator, recognizing me as the one who had made it rain, laced
into me for getting his shirt wet. At first I thought he was joking, but he was
not. He obviously felt he had been assailed, and spared no words in venting
his displeasure.

I was 20. My first reaction was one of shock and dismay. However, the
experience taught me something. I learned that even with the best of intentions,
our actions can be construed totally differently by others. I became aware that
a product meant for the public cannot ignore the feelings and reactions of the
individuals that make up that public. I did not know then that I would one day
conceptualize exhibitions, or be led to reflect on the ethics of museums, and
more particularly with regard to public programs. My professional experiences
since that "stormy" evening none the less confirm the importance of the issue
to a museum's daily operations. Its significance is such that I would like to

present my thoughts on the subject. As a foreword, though, allow me to define what I mean here by ethics by citing this definition:

> Ethics: Moral position adopted by an individual in his soul and conscience. . . . Because they arise from convictions, these ethics determine the professional behavior of the individual and can bring him into conflict with his profession's code of ethics or with the accepted morality of the society in which he lives.
>
> (Internal government report 1994)

Ethics is thus a matter of conscience and of choice. In the general acceptance of the word, that conscience is individual. Considering this particular context of reflection, however, I will deal here essentially with institutional ethics.

INSTITUTIONAL ETHICS: THE AFFIRMATION OF VALUES

Like an individual, a museum is constantly called upon to make choices, take actions, and, in so doing, measure its values – its ethics – against reality. None of its activities escapes this preoccupation. It applies to financial management, which must meet recognized accounting and administrative procedures. It also applies to the management of human resources; in this sense, we are talking about equity, empowerment of personnel, and individual autonomy. However, for a museum, beyond these areas where the need for rules is manifest, ethics govern the institutional philosophy – both content and message – as well as the means used to impart them to various visitors. This is the primary preoccupation of public programs.

I will use the Biodôme as an example. The argument is all the more pertinent since it is a museum with a "message." To make myself clearly understood, I would like to outline – briefly, since that is not the purpose of this essay – what this message consists of and how it is conveyed.

The Biodôme de Montréal devotes most of its exhibitions to the painstaking representation of four natural settings: the tropical rain forest, the Laurentian forest, the St Lawrence marine ecosystem, and the polar world. Each of these "ecosystems" has been recreated with the most stringent possible respect for the biological and physical features of each environment. As such, every plant and animal in the Biodôme – all alive – belongs to these ecosystems in the wild. Although manmade, the rocks were created with meticulous attention to detail to look like typical rock formations. The lighting, ambient temperature and humidity, among other things, have allowed different climates to be recreated under one roof.

Visitors undergo an intense sensory experience as they walk along the pathways of the "ecosystems" – hearing, smelling, scrutinizing, breathing this nature. Other aspects of the experience are added in layers. The discovery center, Naturalia, gives young and old a hands-on opportunity to examine, play with, and ask questions about specimens to understand better the adaptation of living beings to their environments. Temporary exhibitions on various environmental themes are posted here and there. Environment Place shows short films and stages activities about the challenges our planet faces. Environmental News is the setting for exhibitions that are regularly renewed and emphasize the importance of "thinking globally, acting locally." All of these elements and activities work through the senses, the intellect, and the emotions to impart a real "message" of awareness without appearing to do so. They have proved quite effective, judging by visitors' comments. The Biodôme is thus a museum in which each space is put at the service of a greater message, a message that can be found on the last panel posted at the end of the pathway: "Nature is beautiful, complex, fragile, and vulnerable. We are a part of it, and it is our responsibility, as well as within our power, to look after it."

Each gesture made by the Biodôme is inspired by environmental values. They guide its actions around three complementary fields of endeavor: scientific research, conservation, and education on the environment. Each of these areas, in turn, is based on values that form the "code of ethics" of the Biodôme and guide every person who works there.

This code of ethics is unwritten, yet it exists. In fact, shortly after opening, the Biodôme published a statement of its mission, objectives, and means, thereby giving itself a frame of reference for its actions. For the people who designed the Biodôme and those who supported this bold undertaking, the publication of this framework was a gesture of fundamental importance, because a museum must affirm its values. In an economic context of shrinking resources, it is very tempting to forgo the intentions and desires that gave a museum institution its life-force in exchange for short-term financial profitability. The continuous evolution of the public also demands that museums become ever more conscious of their interventions, more sensitive to the needs and expectations of visitors, and more vigilant with regard to their actions.

Among the changes observed are the rising level of education among the museum-going public, an increase in female visitors, and the appearance of elderly visitors. The latter are generally financially secure, active, curious, have been to other museums, and have traveled. They have deliberately chosen to visit a museum and have precise expectations.

To continue along its path and sustain its progress, therefore, it is as important for a museum as for an individual to identify goals and how they are to be attained. The museum must give itself a framework that guides the choice of themes, the treatment of content, and relations with visitors that fall in large part to its public programming. (The term "public programs" should be understood as being all the actions and means used to convey the institutional message to a diverse visitor base.)

To address the issue of the links between ethics and public programs, I have chosen to structure my thoughts starting, not from principles, but from daily actions. (Anyone who has ever worked to install an exhibition, coordinate an advertising campaign, develop a new by-product, find sponsorships, or decide to grant permission to a film crew to shoot an ad in the midst of a collection will relate to this position.) Let us set out on this eventful journey, and see if, in the end, museum and visitor meet.

VISITOR SERVICES: WELCOME TO THE MUSEUM!

On the one side, the museum. On the other, the potential visitor. The first strives to attract the second.

Initially, this is accomplished through marketing. Once an advertising campaign has convinced them that an event is worth attending, visitors will inquire about the way to the museum and undertake to get there. Upon arrival, they must locate the admission counter, buy a ticket, and, finally, get into the desired exhibition or conference.

During each of these steps, the visitor's experience will either be satisfying or frustrating. If finding parking is too difficult or the main entrance (not to mention the museum itself!) is hard to locate, they will certainly not enter the institution with an open mind. Visitors to a new place appreciate being treated as though their arrival were eagerly awaited, rather than being treated merely as consumers. If the reception staff look surly; if there's an hour-long line-up; if no one seems to notice their presence at all; if they cannot pay with a credit card; if they cannot be served in their own language; if there is no coat check – then everything is in place to dispel the magic the visit might have held, no matter how interesting the activity at hand might be. After dealing with a maze of peripheral constraints, the public cannot be expected to grasp the message the curators have devoted time and effort to convey. They are there physically, but they are not emotionally receptive. They will not enjoy the visit, will not return to the museum, and worse still, will express their frustration to friends and family.

Taken individually, these points may seem trivial. In reality, they bring to light one of the essential rules of museum ethics: each visitor must be treated with warmth and courtesy. Training front-line personnel from the ticket agent to the security guard is therefore of primordial importance.

MEDIUM AND MESSAGE: RESPECTING THE VISITOR

To approach the question of ethics and the message, I shall talk about the medium favored by museums: the exhibition, a place where knowledge, experience, and values are shared.

For whom is an exhibition created? For the public, of course! Or, as is often said, for the average visitor. Defining this "average visitor" is an impossible exercise. In fact, no two visitors are alike, even if, for obvious reasons, we lump them together into relatively homogeneous profiles.

Indeed, there are as many ways to tour an exhibition as there are, for instance, ways to appreciate a dinner. If you invite a group of people to dinner, you can be fairly sure some of them will be allergic to certain foods. Others, for religious or personal health reasons, will not eat certain dishes. Others will eat, concentrating on identifying the ingredients. Still others will rave about a sauce without asking for the recipe, and some, simply pleased to be in good company, will eat whatever you put in front of them.

Analogies of this kind are always somewhat awkward. The fact remains that an exhibition, like a meal, can be savored in many different ways – by lingering over it, sampling every offering, or selectively snacking. In fact, the behaviors and motivations are numerous. As Paulette McManus has said,

> Though visitors still politely respond to our surveys – when asked about the reason of their visit, they answer with the inevitable "educational purpose" – research has shown that visiting a museum is nevertheless largely a social event.
>
> (Schouten 1993: 382)

In the same fashion, an infinite possible number of topics and paths are open to us. Under these conditions, what ethics do we adopt? First and foremost is respect for the visitor.

Respecting visitors means being conscious of the fact that they do not arrive at the museum as blank slates, but rather as scores on which music is already written. The museum generally does the "talking," but this exclusivity of message does not mean truth. It therefore behooves the museum to show sufficient judgment and humility and recognize that the visitor knows, experiences, and feels. Each human being has culture, even if it is not always that conferred by a university diploma. Each human being has a wealth of experience, even if some of it does not mirror the values of society. Each human being has values, despite the fact that they may not always be linked to recognized systems.

Respecting visitors means addressing them as intelligent beings, offering them content based on meticulous research, a clear and logical itinerary, and a balanced message that appeals to the heart as well as the intellect. It means showing a concern for rigor and avoiding excess – both sensationalistic and moralistic – at all costs.

Respect means giving visitors the freedom to discover in their own fashion. It is recognizing that, like French author Daniel Pennac's appeal on behalf of reading, the visitor has the right to tour an exhibition in a half-hour, to see only a part of it, to start at the end, or to simply sit and gaze at a painting or an aquarium for the sheer pleasure of contemplation. It is taking into account the fact that we do not all follow an itinerary the same way, and that if reading a text or trying an interactive display is a chore for some, others take great pleasure in it. It means avoiding over-solicitation, granting solitude to those who desire it, not forcing unwanted activities on them.

In terms of sharing values, it means asking questions without denying the right to different answers. It involves being wary of preconceptions, that are sometimes expressed so subtly that they go unnoticed by most people. It is being conscious that we are not dealing with curators on one side and visitors on the other, but with human beings who share a common desire to communicate, learn, and enjoy.

Exhibitions help people to see things and, better still, to observe them together. Here, ethics takes the form of respect, vigilance, and awareness, down to the respect for the role of each artist and the right to intellectual property. All of this may seem obvious. But do we always keep it in mind?

EDUCATIONAL ACTIVITIES: FOR EVERYONE

The young are often introduced to museums through the scholastic network's educational activities. Here, too, we have many options from which to choose. Should the content of educational activities be developed in line with scholastic programs? Or should they differ as much as possible? I personally believe that the museum is not, and should not be, the school. Of course, both institutions contribute to educate children in the real sense of the word education: "to develop" or guide to a growing awareness, an openness to oneself and the world. As such, I expect a museum's educational activities to allow children to experience something other than they would at school, both in terms of content and approach. The museum has a thousand ways to interest children and help them express their potential. Just as a good teacher can be an extra-ordinary source of motivation for a child, or just as a captivating object or documentary can stimulate curiosity about new subjects, an enjoyable visit to the museum can do wonders! Games, exploration, discovery, role-playing, humor, and laughter can all be turned to good account. Pleasure is the best stimulant!

I also think that, in this process, teachers must be thought of as partners. No one can say teachers do not care, that a day at the museum is a day off for them, that the outing is no more than "a treat for the kids." I believe that a teacher who goes to the trouble of organizing a day at a museum shows more dynamism than laziness!

For that matter, why not organize activities for adults and families? Educational departments often limit themselves to preparing programs for students. However, visitors who decide of their own volition to come to the museum are just as entitled to a setting in which learning and experimentation are emphasized through activities designed specifically for them.

Lastly, it is important to think of those visitors who do not come to the museum – a challenge to meet the social responsibility of our institutions.

A museum belongs to its community. It must take sustenance from the community and nourish it in return by being intellectually, physically, and economically accessible. This preoccupation can be expressed by specific services or spaces designed for different categories of visitors in relation to particular societal challenges. In Paris, for example, the Cité des sciences et de l'industrie de la Villette has established the "Cité des métiers," a resource and reference center on the trades. It is used notably by young dropouts and people looking for jobs: individuals who are not usually museum-goers.

PUBLIC RELATIONS AND PROMOTION: SAYING IT LIKE IT IS

The role of public relations and promotion is to inform and to promote the museum. This dual mandate contains an intrinsic conflict. Information implies transparency and objectivity; yet promotion, almost by necessity, involves stressing the positive. On the very fine line known as the "happy medium," the tone provides the equilibrium. If the tone is credible and if the message, because it is based on the reality of fact, has the ring of truth, chances are that even the most suspicious of recipients will recognize its validity. That includes journalists. They are regularly faced with an invariably positive and optimistic "institutional" version of things. They tend to seek a researcher or someone on the reception staff as a moderator rather than the museum's official spokesperson when trying to take the pulse of an issue.

For the spokesperson, then, ethics entails having a clear awareness of the stakes involved. On the one hand, the public must be accurately informed, especially given that the museum is a public institution. On the other hand, the spokesperson must manifest loyalty to the institution and support its efforts to progress, while being able to explain clearly the positions taken by the institution. The facts must not be embellished, but stated as they are: stressing qualities and successes without glossing over difficulties, constraints, and misjudgments. Finally, in my opinion, there is also the question of personal ethics. I find it hard to imagine how an individual whose values do not agree with those of the museum can accomplish a professional communication job.

The people in charge of promotion face the same challenges when planning an advertising campaign. One cannot sell a museum – that is, a service institution with educational objectives – as one sells breakfast cereal. Yes, we must attract attention, and we must do so by being imaginative enough to make a visit to the museum stand out among a host of increasingly diverse leisure activities. Yet here, too, it is how you do it that matters. You must entice without soliciting, intrigue without mystifying, highlight without exaggerating, and be humorous without being coarse. The campaign must match the museum's personality and values, even if that means sending the creative team back to the drawing board. An accurate vision of things is thus important. Luckily, constraints are also stimuli to the creative process.

MARKETING: IN HARMONY WITH VALUES

As is true of sponsorship, marketing a museum's spaces and services can bring about ethical dilemmas. Here again, I will cite the Biodôme as a case in point.

We are often asked if film crews can shoot footage in the unique setting the "ecosystems" provide.

These requests are extremely diverse. When the project is a nature documentary or children's programs, the educational aim is obvious. When it involves advertising fur coats with cameo appearances by the penguins in the polar world, or promoting a new line of swimwear in the tropical rain forest, however, granting permission is somewhat less clear-cut. On the other hand, productions like these offer tempting financial benefits and public visibility.

Faced with an influx of requests, it soon became apparent that the Biodôme would have to formulate a policy concerning filming on its premises. To arrive at this, the personnel from different departments discussed the advantages and limitations of these activities and the possibilities of integrating them harmoniously into life at the Biodôme – that is, guaranteeing respect for the health of the living collections of plants and animals as well as the comfort and safety of the public. The resulting filming policy – that is sent to the shoot director and spelled out in the contract between both parties – begins by stating certain fundamental principles that are part of the ethics of the Biodôme. The policy notably gives priority to film projects whose content reinforces the attainment of the Biodôme's educational objectives.

SPONSORSHIP: MUSEUM FOR HIRE?

Everyone knows it, and it's true: Money is scarce. Major corporations have become sources of financing and objects of increasing solicitation from all sides, including museums. But does teaming up with a sponsor mean a loss of institutional freedom?

The question of financing through sponsorship, and more broadly of self-financing, is the one in which ethics run the risk of making themselves felt the most. Yet in this area, as elsewhere, moderation is the rule of thumb.

Allow me to mention one happy sponsorship venture, this time involving the Planétarium de Montréal. In the winter of 1993, the institution decided to make the May 1994 solar eclipse a scientific event of broad appeal and insure that it took place under the safest possible conditions. To achieve this, the Planetarium mapped out a specific sponsorship strategy. With the help of a magazine that popularizes scientific topics for young readers, it created a poster and an observation kit and turned out 45,000 copies of each through a network of distributors and retailers. The Planetarium also enlisted the help of provincial ophthalmologists and optometrists, who informed people about the dangers of looking directly at the eclipse and gave advice on safe ways to observe the phenomenon.

This "marriage of sponsors" – public institution, private corporation, professional associations, and the scientific press – was a complex undertaking. However, all were unanimous in declaring it successful. Everyone came out a winner, and the eclipse received widespread media coverage.

The budget for this operation was very small when we consider the importance of the resulting benefits. Behind this success lay a set of clear ethical guidelines that were endorsed by each participant: the desire of each to benefit from the project; the willingness to participate in a beneficial cause for the population as a whole; and the recognition of each other's role.

MUSEUMS: PARTNERS RATHER THAN COMPETITORS

Shrinking budgets have hit large institutions hard. Imagine how they have affected small museums! Museum ethics must consider the disparity of resources and lead museums, both large and small, to express their solidarity and work together, rather than view each other as competitors.

Although I can think of a number of examples that demonstrate the positive progress of thinking in this regard, I will content myself with mentioning two. The first involved a project for an itinerant exhibition for which the Biodôme had received a government subsidy. To mount the exhibit, the institution joined forces with a regional museum specialized in the field, rather than a design firm. The exhibition thus became a co-production that both museums could then display. Another major Québec museum was also appointed to do the formative assessment of the proposed concept. In this way, the expertise of each institution – be it modest or major – was put to best use and the respective strengths of each recognized. The second example I would cite concerns the joint promotion efforts undertaken by museums in Montréal and other cultural areas, the strategy being to encourage the visitors of one to go to the others. These are signs that museums have growing confidence in the quality of their offerings.

TOWARD A NEW CODE OF ETHICS?

Museums are places of coming together and sharing. Will they always be thus? As new technologies emerge, so does the specter of learning in isolation, discovery through the imagination. As information multiplies, technology finds more ways to access it quickly, even simultaneously. Consequently, direct contact between people may seem to be on the wane.

What new ethics will these technological changes call into play? Will the fact of being linked to millions of virtual visitors and visiting the collections at the Louvre through one's personal computer change the way we operate and the way we convey our museological message? To what extent will institutions agree to universal access to their content? Will the profitability of services prevail over universal access to information? Will the museum's accessibility increasingly become the privilege of those with the means and possibility to plug themselves into the global village? Like many people, I ask myself these questions. I am not overly worried, however. The desire to communicate with one's peers, express one's convictions, and compare them with those of others

235

are needs so profound that they transcend even the most revolutionary technologies.

The museum is no longer what it was just twenty years ago. One hopes to be able to say the same twenty years from now. But whatever changes come to pass, I trust that one thing stays intact, the thing that animates and inspires the museum: the hope that each visitor finds within it food for thought, for discovery, for personal growth, and for wonderment.

Appendix: ICOM Code of Professional Ethics

(The ICOM *Code of Professional Ethics* is published with the permission of the International Council of Museums, Elisabeth des Portes, Secretary General.)

I PREAMBLE

The ICOM *Code of Professional Ethics* was adopted unanimously by the 15th General Assembly of ICOM meeting in Buenos Aires, Argentina on 4 November 1986.

It provides a general statement of professional ethics, respect for which is regarded as a minimum requirement to practice as a member of the museum profession. In many cases it will be possible to develop and strengthen the *Code* to meet particular national or specialized requirements and ICOM wishes to encourage this. A copy of such developments of the *Code* should be sent to the Secretary General of ICOM, Maison de l'Unesco, 1 rue Miollis, 75732 Paris Cedex 15, France.

For the purposes of Articles 2 para. 2, 9 para. 1(d), 14 para. 17(b), 15 para. 7(c), 17 para. 12(e) and 18 para. 7(d) of the ICOM *Statutes*, this *Code* is deemed to be the statement of professional ethics referred to therein.

---

1 Definitions

1.1 The International Council of Museums (ICOM)

ICOM is defined in Article 1 para. 1 of its *Statutes* as "the international non-governmental organization of museums and professional museum workers established to advance the interests of museology and other disciplines concerned with museum management and operations."

The objectives of ICOM, as defined in Article 3 para. 1 of its *Statutes*, are:

(a) To encourage and support the establishment, development and professional management of museums of all kinds;
(b) To advance knowledge and understanding of the nature, functions and role of museums in the service of society and of its development;
(c) To organize co-operation and mutual assistance between museums and between professional museum workers in the different countries;

(d) To represent, support and advance the interests of professional museum workers of all kinds;

(e) To advance and disseminate knowledge in museology and other disciplines concerned with museum management and operations.

1.2 Museum

A museum is defined in Article 2 para. 1 of the Statutes of the International Council of Museums as:

> a non-profit making, permanent institution in the service of society and of its development, and open to the public which acquires, conserves, researches, communicates and exhibits, for purposes of study, education and enjoyment, material evidence of people and their environment.
>
> (a) The above definition of a museum shall be applied without limitation arising from the nature of the governing body, the territorial character, the functional structure or the orientation of the collections of the institution concerned.
>
> (b) In addition to institutions designated as "museums" the following qualify as museums for the purposes of this definition:
>
> > (i) natural, archaeological and ethnographic monuments and sites of a museum nature that acquire, conserve and communicate material evidence of people and their environment;
> >
> > (ii) institutions holding collections of and displaying live specimens of plants and animals, such as botanical and zoological gardens, aquaria and vivaria;
> >
> > (iii) science centres and planetaria;
> >
> > (iv) conservation institutes and exhibition galleries permanently maintained by libraries and archive centres;
> >
> > (v) nature reserves;
> >
> > (vi) such other institutions as the Executive Council, after seeking the advice of the Advisory Committee, considers as having some or all of the characteristics of a museum, or as supporting museums and professional museum workers through museological research, education or training.

1.3 The museum profession

ICOM defines the members of the museum profession, under Article 2 para. 2 of its *Statutes*, as follows:

> Professional museum workers include all the personnel of museums or institutions qualifying as museums in accordance with the definition in Article 2 para. 1 (as detailed under para 1.2 above), having received specialized training, or possessing an equivalent practical experience, in any field relevant to the management and operations of a museum, and privately or self-employed persons practising in one of the

museological professions and who respect the ICOM *Code of Professional Ethics.*

1.4 *Governing body*

The government and control of museums in terms of policy, finance and administration, etc., varies greatly from one country to another, and often from one museum to another within a country according to the legal and other national or local provisions of the particular country or institution.

In the case of many national museums the Director, Curator or other professional head of the museum may be appointed by, and directly responsible to, a Minister or a Government Department, whilst most local government museums are similarly governed and controlled by the appropriate local authority. In many other cases the government and control of the museum is vested in some form of independent body, such as a Board of Trustees, a society, a non-profit company, or even an individual.

For the purposes of this *Code* the term "Governing Body" has been used throughout to signify the superior authority concerned with the policy, finance and administration of the museum. This may be an individual Minister or official, a Ministry, a local authority, a Board of Trustees, a Society, the Director of the museum or any other individual or body. Directors, Curators or other professional heads of the museum are responsible for the proper care and management of the museum.

II INSTITUTIONAL ETHICS

2 Basic principles for museum governance

2.1 *Minimum standards for museums*

The governing body or other controlling authority of a museum has an ethical duty to maintain, and if possible enhance, all aspects of the museum, its collections and its services. Above all, it is the responsibility of each governing body to ensure that all of the collections in their care are adequately housed, conserved and documented.

The minimum standards in terms of finance, premises, staffing and services will vary according to the size and responsibilities of each museum. In some countries such minimum standards may be defined by law or other government regulation and in others guidance on and assessment of minimum standards is available in the form of "Museum Accreditation" or similar schemes. Where such guidance is not available locally, it can usually be obtained from appropriate national and international organizations and experts, either directly or through the National Committee or appropriate International Committee of ICOM.

2.2 Constitution

Each museum should have a written constitution or other document setting out clearly its legal status and permanent, non-profit nature, drawn up in accordance with appropriate national laws in relation to museums, the cultural heritage, and non-profit institutions. The governing body or other controlling authority of a museum should prepare and publicize a clear statement of the aims, objectives and policies of the museum, and of the role and composition of the governing body itself.

2.3 Finance

The governing body holds the ultimate financial responsibility for the museum and for the protecting and nurturing of its various assets: the collections and related documentation, the premises, facilities and equipment, the financial assets, and the staff. It is obliged to develop and define the purposes and related policies of the institution, and to ensure that all of the museum's assets are properly and effectively used for museum purposes. Sufficient funds must be available on a regular basis, either from public or private sources, to enable the governing body to carry out and develop the work of the museum. Proper accounting procedures must be adopted and maintained in accordance with the relevant national laws and professional accountancy standards.

2.4 Premises

The board has specially strong obligations to provide accommodation, giving a suitable environment for the physical security and preservation of the collections. Premises must be adequate for the museum to fulfil within its stated policy its basic functions of collection, research, storage, conservation, education and display, including staff accommodation, and should comply with all appropriate national legislation in relation to public and staff safety. Proper standards of protection should be provided against such hazards as theft, fire, flood, vandalism and deterioration, throughout the year, day and night. The special needs of disabled people should be provided for, as far as practicable, in planning and managing both buildings and facilities.

2.5 Personnel

The governing body has a special obligation to ensure that the museum has staff sufficient in both number and kind to ensure that the museum is able to meet its responsibilities. The size of the staff, and its nature (whether paid or unpaid, permanent or temporary), will depend on the size of the museum, its collections and its responsibilities. However, proper arrangements should be made for the museum to meet its obligations in relation to the area of the collections, public access and services, research, and security.

The governing body has particularly important obligations in relation to the appointment of the Director of the museum, and whenever the possibility of terminating the employment of the Director arises, to ensure that any such action is taken only in accordance with appropriate procedures under the legal or other constitutional arrangements and policies of the museum, and that any such staff changes are made in a professional and ethical manner, and in accordance with what is judged to be in the best interests of the museum, rather than any personal or external factor or prejudice. It should also ensure that the same principles are applied in relation to any appointment, promotion, dismissal or demotion of the personnel of the museum by the Director or any other senior member of staff with staffing responsibilities.

The governing body should recognize the diverse nature of the museum profession, and the wide range of specializations that it now encompasses, including conservator/restorers, scientists, museum education service personnel, registrars and computer specialists, security service managers, etc. It should ensure that the museum both makes appropriate use of such specialists where required and that such specialized personnel are properly recognized as full members of the professional staff in all respects.

Members of the museum profession require appropriate academic, technical and professional training in order to fulfil their important role in relation to the operation of the museum and the care for the heritage, and the governing body should recognize the need for, and value of, a properly qualified and trained staff, and offer adequate opportunities for further training and re-training in order to maintain an adequate and effective workforce.

A governing body should never require a member of the museum staff to act in a way that could reasonably be judged to conflict with the provisions of this *Code of Ethics*, or any national law or national code of professional ethics.

The Director or other chief professional officer of a museum should be directly responsible to, and have direct access to, the governing body in which trusteeship of the collections is vested.

2.6 Educational and community role of the museum

By definition a museum is an institution in the service of society and of its development, and is generally open to the public (even though this may be a restricted public in the case of certain very specialized museums, such as certain academic or medical museums, for example).

The museum should take every opportunity to develop its role as an educational resource used by all sections of the population or specialized group that the museum is intended to serve. Where appropriate in relation to the museum's program and responsibilities, specialist staff with training and skills in museum education are likely to be required for this purpose.

The museum has an important duty to attract new and wider audiences within all levels of the community, locality or group that the museum aims to serve, and should offer both the general community and specific individuals and groups within it opportunities to become actively involved in the museum and to support its aims and policies.

2.7 Public access

The general public (or specialized group served, in the case of museums with a limited public role), should have access to the displays during reasonable hours and for regular periods. The museum should also offer the public reasonable access to members of staff by appointment or other arrangement, and full access to information about the collections, subject to any necessary restrictions for reasons of confidentiality or security as discussed in para. 7.3 below.

2.8 Displays, exhibitions and special activities

Subject to the primary duty of the museum to preserve unimpaired for the future the significant material that comprises the museum collections, it is the responsibility of the museum to use the collections for the creation and dissemination of new knowledge, through research, educational work, permanent displays, temporary exhibitions and other special activities. These should be in accordance with the stated policy and educational purpose of the museum, and should not compromise either the quality or the proper care of the collections. The museum should seek to ensure that information in displays and exhibitions is honest and objective and does not perpetuate myths or stereotypes.

2.9 Commercial support and sponsorship

Where it is the policy of the museum to seek and accept financial or other support from commercial or industrial organizations, or from other outside sources, great care is needed to define clearly the agreed relationship between the museum and the sponsor. Commercial support and sponsorship may involve ethical problems and the museum must ensure that the standards and objectives of the museum are not compromised by such a relationship.

2.10 Museum shops and commercial activities

Museum shops and any other commercial activities of the museum, and any publicity relating to these, should be in accordance with a clear policy, should be relevant to the collections and the basic educational purpose of the museum, and must not compromise the quality of those collections. In the case of the manufacture and sale of replicas, reproductions, or other commercial items adapted from an object in a museum's collection, all aspects of the commercial venture must be carried out in a manner that will not discredit either the integrity of the museum or the intrinsic value of the original object. Great care must be taken to identify permanently such objects for what they are, and to ensure accuracy and high quality in their manufacture. All items offered for sale should represent good value for money and should comply with all relevant national legislation.

2.11 Legal obligation

It is an important responsibility of each governing body to ensure that the museum complies fully with all legal obligations, whether in relation to national, regional or local law, international law or treaty obligations, and to any legally binding trusts or conditions relating to any aspect of the museum collections or facilities.

3 Acquisitions to museum collections

3.1 Collecting policies

Each museum authority should adopt and publish a written statement of its collecting policy. This policy should be reviewed from time to time, and at least once every five years. Objects acquired should be relevant to the purpose and activities of the museum, and be accompanied by evidence of a valid legal title. Any conditions or limitations relating to an acquisition should be clearly described in an instrument of conveyance or other written documentation. Museums should not, except in very exceptional circumstances, acquire material that the museum is unlikely to be able to catalogue, conserve, store or exhibit, as appropriate, in a proper manner. Acquisitions outside the current stated policy of the museum should only be made in very exceptional circumstances, and then only after proper consideration by the governing body of the museum itself, having regard to the interests of the objects under consideration, the national or other cultural heritage, and the special interests of other museums.

3.2 Acquisition of illicit material

The illicit trade in objects destined for public and private collections encourages the destruction of historic sites, local ethnic cultures, theft at both national and international levels, places at risk endangered species of flora and fauna, and contravenes the spirit of national and international patrimony. Museums should recognize the relationship between the marketplace and the initial and often destructive taking of an object for the commercial market, and must recognize that it is highly unethical for a museum to support in any way, whether directly or indirectly, that illicit market.

A museum should not acquire, whether by purchase, gift, bequest or exchange, any object unless the governing body and responsible officer are satisfied that the museum can acquire a valid title to the specimen or object in question and that in particular it has not been acquired in, or exported from, its country of origin and/or any intermediate country in which it may have been legally owned (including the museum's own country), in violation of that country's laws.

So far as biological and geological material is concerned, a museum should not acquire by any direct or indirect means any specimen that has been collected, sold or otherwise transferred in contravention of any national or international wildlife protection or natural history conservation law or treaty of the museum's own country or any other country except with the express consent of an appropriate outside legal or governmental authority.

So far as excavated material is concerned, in addition to the safeguards set out above, the museum should not acquire by purchase objects in any case where the governing body or responsible officer has reasonable cause to believe that their recovery involved the recent unscientific or intentional destruction or damage of ancient monuments or archaeological sites, or involved a failure to disclose the finds to the owner or occupier of the land, or to the proper legal or governmental authorities.

If appropriate and feasible, the same tests as are outlined in the above four paragraphs should be applied in determining whether or not to accept loans for exhibition or other purposes.

3.3 Field study and collecting

Museums should assume a position of leadership in the effort to halt the continuing degradation of the world's natural history, archaeological, ethnographic, historic and artistic resources. Each museum should develop policies that allow it to conduct its activities within appropriate national and international laws and treaty obligations, and with a reasonable certainty that its approach is consistent with the spirit and intent of both national and international efforts to protect and enhance the cultural heritage.

Field exploration, collecting and excavation by museum workers present ethical problems that are both complex and critical. All planning for field studies and field collecting must be preceded by investigation, disclosure and consultation with both the proper authorities and any interested museums or academic institutions in the country or area of the proposed study sufficient to ascertain if the proposed activity is both legal and justifiable on academic and scientific grounds. Any field program must be executed in such a way that all participants act legally and responsibly in acquiring specimens and data, and that they discourage by all practical means unethical, illegal and destructive practices.

3.4 Co-operation between museums in collecting policies

Each museum should recognize the need for co-operation and consultation between all museums with similar or overlapping interests and collecting policies, and should seek to consult with such other institutions both on specific acquisitions where a conflict of interest is thought possible and, more generally, on defining areas of specialization. Museums should respect the boundaries of the recognized collecting areas of other museums and should avoid acquiring material with special local connections or of special local interest from the collecting area of another museum without due notification of intent.

3.5 Conditional acquisitions and other special factors

Gifts, bequests and loans should only be accepted if they conform to the stated collecting and exhibition policies of the museum. Offers that are subject to special conditions may have to be rejected if the conditions proposed are judged to be contrary to the long-term interests of the museum and its public.

3.6 Loans to museums

Both individual loans of objects and the mounting or borrowing of loan exhibitions can have an important role in enhancing the interest and quality of a museum and its services. However, the ethical principles outlined in paras 3.1 to 3.5 above must apply to the consideration of proposed loans and loan exhibitions as to the acceptance or rejection of items offered to the permanent collections: loans should not be accepted nor exhibitions mounted if they do not have a valid educational, scientific or academic purpose.

3.7 Conflicts of interest

The collecting policy or regulations of the museum should include provisions to ensure that no person involved in the policy or management of the museum, such as a trustee or other member of a governing body, or a member of the museum staff, may compete with the museum for objects or may take advantage of privileged information received because of his or her position, and that should a conflict of interest develop between the needs of the individual and the museum, those of the museum will prevail. Special care is also required in considering any offer of an item either for sale or as a tax-benefit gift, from members of governing bodies, members of staff, or the families or close associates of these.

4 Disposal of collections

4.1 General presumption of permanence of collections

By definition one of the key functions of almost every kind of museum is to acquire objects and keep them for posterity. Consequently there must always be a strong presumption against the disposal of specimens to which a museum has assumed formal title. Any form of disposal, whether by donation, exchange, sale or destruction, requires the exercise of a high order of curatorial judgment and should be approved by the governing body only after full expert and legal advice has been taken.

Special considerations may apply in the case of certain kinds of specialized institutions such as "living" or "working" museums, and some teaching and other educational museums, together with museums and other institutions displaying living specimens, such as botanical and zoological gardens and aquaria, which may find it necessary to regard at least part of their collections as "fungible" (i.e. replaceable and renewable). However, even here there is a clear ethical obligation to ensure that the activities of the institution are not detrimental to the long-term survival of examples of the material studied, displayed or used.

4.2 Legal or other powers of disposal

The laws relating to the protection and permanence of museum collections, and to the power of museums to dispose of items from their collection, vary greatly from country to country, and often from one museum to another within the same country. In some cases no disposals of any kind are permitted, except in the case of items that have been seriously damaged by natural or accidental deterioration. Elsewhere, there may be no explicit restriction on disposals under general law.

Where the museum has legal powers permitting disposals, or has acquired objects subject to conditions of disposal, the legal or other requirements and procedures must be fully complied with. Even where legal powers of disposal exist, a museum may not be completely free to dispose of items acquired: where financial assistance has been obtained from an outside source (e.g. public or private grants, donations from a Friends of the Museum organization, or private benefactor), disposal would normally require the consent of all parties who had contributed to the original purchase.

Where the original acquisition was subject to mandatory restrictions these must be observed unless it can be clearly shown that adherence to such restrictions is impossible or substantially detrimental to the institution. Even in these circumstances the museum can only be relieved from such restrictions through appropriate legal procedures.

4.3 De-accessioning policies and procedures

Where a museum has the necessary legal powers to dispose of an object, the decision to sell or otherwise dispose of material from the collections should only be taken after due consideration, and such material should be offered first, by exchange, gift or private treaty sale, to other museums before sale by public auction or other means is considered. A decision to dispose of a specimen or work of art, whether by exchange, sale or destruction (in the case of an item too badly damaged or deteriorated to be restorable) should be the responsibility of the governing body of the museum, not of the curator of the collection concerned acting alone. Full records should be kept of all such decisions and the objects involved, and proper arrangements made for the preservation and/or transfer, as appropriate, of the documentation relating to the object concerned, including photographic records where practicable.

Neither members of staff, nor members of the governing bodies, nor members of their families or close associates, should ever be permitted to purchase objects that have been de-accessioned from a collection. Similarly, no such person should be permitted to appropriate in any other way items from the museum collections, even temporarily, to any personal collection or for any kind of personal use.

4.4 Return and restitution of cultural property

If a museum should come into possession of an object that can be demonstrated to have been exported or otherwise transferred in violation of the principles of the UNESCO *Convention on the Means of Prohibiting and Preventing the Illicit Import, Export, and Transfer of Ownership of Cultural Property* (1970) and the country of origin seeks its return and demonstrates that it is part of the country's cultural heritage, the museum should, if legally free to do so, take responsible steps to co-operate in the return of the object to the country of origin.

In the case of requests for the return of cultural property to the country of origin, museums should be prepared to initiate dialogues with an open-minded attitude on the basis of scientific and professional principles (in preference to action at a governmental or political level). The possibility of developing bilateral or multilateral co-operation schemes to assist museums in countries that are considered to have lost a significant part of their cultural heritage in the development of adequate museums and museum resources should be explored.

Museums should also respect fully the terms of the *Convention for the Protection of Cultural Property in the Event of Armed Conflict* (The Hague Convention 1954), and in support of this *Convention*, should in particular abstain from purchasing or otherwise appropriating or acquiring cultural objects from any occupied country, as these will in most cases have been illegally exported or illicitly removed.

4.5 Income from disposal of collections

Any moneys received by a governing body from the disposal of specimens or works of art should be applied solely for the purchase of additions to the museum collections.

III PROFESSIONAL CONDUCT

5 General principles

5.1 Ethical obligations of members of the museum profession

Employment by a museum, whether publicly or privately supported, is a public trust involving great responsibility. In all activities museum employees must act with integrity and in accordance with the most stringent ethical principles as well as the highest standards of objectivity.

An essential element of membership of a profession is the implication of both rights and obligations. Although the conduct of a professional in any area is ordinarily regulated by the basic rules of moral behaviour which govern human relationships, every occupation involves standards, as well as particular duties, responsibilities and opportunities that from time to time create the need for a statement of guiding principles. The museum professional should understand two guiding principles: first, that museums are the object of a public trust whose value to the community is in direct proportion to the quality of service rendered; and, secondly, that intellectual ability and professional knowledge are not, in themselves, sufficient, but must be inspired by a high standard of ethical conduct.

The Director and other professional staff owe their primary professional and academic allegiance to their museum and should at all times act in accordance with the approved policies of the museum. The Director or other principal museum officer should be aware of, and bring to the notice of the governing body of the museum whenever appropriate, the terms of the ICOM *Code of Professional Ethics* and of any relevant national or regional *Codes* or policy statements on Museum Ethics, and should urge the governing body to comply with these. Members of the museum profession should also comply fully with the ICOM *Code* and any other *Codes* or statements on Museum Ethics whenever exercising the functions of the governing body under delegated powers.

5.2 Personal conduct

Loyalty to colleagues and to the employing museum is an important professional responsibility, but the ultimate loyalty must be to fundamental ethical principles and to the profession as a whole.

Applicants for any professional post should divulge frankly and in confidence all information relevant to the consideration of their applications, and if appointed should recognize that museum work is normally regarded as a full-time vocation. Even where the terms of employment do not prohibit outside employment or business interests, the Director and other senior staff should not undertake other paid employment or accept outside commissions without the express consent of the governing body of the museum. In tendering resignations from their posts, members of the professional staff, and above all the Director, should consider carefully the needs of the museum at the time. A professional person, having recently accepted a new appointment, should consider seriously their professional commitment to their present post before applying for a new post elsewhere.

5.3 Private interests

While every member of any profession is entitled to a measure of personal independence, consistent with professional and staff responsibilities, in the eyes of the public no private business or professional interest of a member of the museum profession can be wholly separated from that of the professional's institution or other official affiliation, despite disclaimers that may be offered. Any museum-related activity by the individual may reflect on the institution or be attributed to it. The professional must be concerned not only with the true personal motivations and interests, but also with the way in which such actions might be construed by the outside observer. Museum employees and others in a close relationship with them must not accept gifts, favours, loans or other dispensations or things of value that may be offered to them in connection with their duties for the museum (see also para. 8.4 below).

6 Personal responsibility to the collections

6.1 Acquisitions to museum collections

The Director and professional staff should take all possible steps to ensure that a written collecting policy is adopted by the governing body of the museum, and is thereafter reviewed and revised as appropriate at regular intervals. This policy, as formally adopted and revised by the governing body, should form the basis of all professional decisions and recommendations in relation to acquisitions.

Negotiations concerning the acquisition of museum items from members of the general public must be conducted with scrupulous fairness to the seller or donor. No object should be deliberately or misleadingly identified or valued, to the benefit of the museum and to the detriment of the donor, owner or previous owners, in order to acquire it for the museum collections nor should be taken nor retained on loan with the deliberate intention of improperly procuring it for the collections.

6.2 Care of collections

It is an important professional responsibility to ensure that all items accepted temporarily or permanently by the museum are properly and fully documented to facilitate provenance, identification, condition and treatment. All objects accepted by the museum should be properly conserved, protected and maintained.

Careful attention should be paid to the means of ensuring the best possible security as a protection against theft in display, working or storage areas, against accidental damage when handling objects, and against damage or theft in transit. Where it is the national or local policy to use commercial insurance arrangements, the staff should ensure that the insurance coverage is adequate, especially for objects in transit and loan items, or other objects, which are not owned by the museum but which are its current responsibility.

Members of the museum profession should not delegate important curatorial, conservation, or other professional responsibilities to persons who lack the appropriate knowledge and skill, or who are inadequately supervised, in the case of trainees or approved volunteers, where such persons are allowed to assist in the care of the collections. There is also a clear duty to consult professional colleagues within or outside the museum if at any time the expertise available in a particular museum or department is insufficient to ensure the welfare of items in the collections under its care.

6.3 Conservation and restoration of collections

One of the essential ethical obligations of each member of the museum profession is to ensure the proper care and conservation of both existing and newly acquired collections and individual items for which the member of the profession and the employing institutions are responsible, and to ensure that as far as is reasonable the collections are passed on to future generations in as good and safe a condition as practicable having regard to current knowledge and resources.

In attempting to achieve this high ideal, special attention should be paid to the growing body of knowledge about preventative conservation methods and techniques, including the provision of suitable environmental protection against the known natural or artificial causes of deterioration of museum specimens and works of art.

There are often difficult decisions to be made in relation to the degree of replacement or restoration of lost or damaged parts of a specimen or work of art that may be ethically acceptable in particular circumstances. Such decisions call for proper co-operation between all with a specialized responsibility for the object, including both the Curator and the Conservator or Restorer, and should not be decided unilaterally by one or the other acting alone.

The ethical issues involved in conservation and restoration work of many kinds are a major study in themselves, and those with special responsibilities in this area, whether as Director, Curator, Conservator or Restorer, have an important responsibility to ensure that they are familiar with these ethical issues, and with appropriate professional opinion, as expressed in some detailed ethical statements and codes produced by the Conservator/Restorer professional bodies. ("The Conservator-Restorer: A Definition of the Profession" *ICOM News*, Vol. 39, No. 1, 1986, pp. 5–6.)

6.4 *Documentation of collections*

The proper recording and documentation of both new acquisitions and existing collections in accordance with appropriate standards and the internal rules and conventions of the museum is a most important professional responsibility. It is particularly important that such documentation should include details of the source of each object and the conditions of acceptance of it by the museum. In addition, specimen data should be kept in a secure environment and be supported by adequate systems providing easy retrieval of the data by both the staff and by other *bona fide* users.

6.5 *De-accessioning and disposals from the collections*

No item from the collections of a museum should be disposed of except in accordance with the ethical principles summarized in the Institutional Ethics section of this *Code*, paras 4.1 to 4.4 above, and the detailed rules and procedures applying in the museum in question.

6.6 *Welfare of live animals*

Where museums and related institutions maintain for exhibition or research purposes live populations of animals, the health and well-being of any such creatures must be a foremost ethical consideration. It is essential that a veterinary surgeon be available for advice and for regular inspection of the animals and their living conditions. The museum should prepare a safety code for the protection of staff and visitors which has been approved by an expert in the veterinary field, and all staff must follow it in detail.

6.7 *Human remains and material of ritual significance*

Where a museum maintains and/or is developing collections of human remains and sacred objects these should be securely housed and carefully maintained as archival collections in scholarly institutions, and should always be available to qualified researchers and educators, but not to the morbidly curious. Research on such objects and their housing and care must be accomplished in a manner acceptable not only to fellow professionals but to those of various beliefs, including in particular members of the community, ethnic or religious groups concerned. Although it is occasionally necessary to use human remains and other sensitive material in interpretative exhibits, this must be done with tact and with respect for the feelings for human dignity held by all peoples.

6.8 *Private collections*

The acquiring, collecting and owning of objects of a kind collected by a museum by a member of the museum profession for a personal collection may not in itself be unethical, and may be regarded as a valuable way of enhancing professional knowledge and judgment. However, serious dangers are implicit when members of the profession collect for themselves privately objects similar to those which they and others collect for their museums. In particular, no member of the museum profession should compete with their institution either in the acquisition of objects or in any personal collecting activity. Extreme care must be taken to ensure that no conflict of interest arises.

In some countries and many individual museums, members of the museum profession are not permitted to have private collections of any kind, and such rules must be respected. Even where there are no such restrictions, on appointment, a member of the museum profession with a private collection should provide the governing body with a description of it, and a statement of the collecting policy being pursued, and any consequent agreement between the Curator and the governing body concerning the private collection must be scrupulously kept. (See also para. 8.4 below.)

7 Personal responsibility to the public

7.1 Upholding professional standards

In the interests of the public as well as the profession, members of the museum profession should observe accepted standards and laws, uphold the dignity and honour of their profession and accept its self-imposed disciplines. They should do their part to safeguard the public against illegal or unethical professional conduct, and should use appropriate opportunities to inform and educate the public in the aims, purposes and aspirations of the profession in order to develop a better public understanding of the purposes and responsibilities of museums and of the profession.

7.2 Relations with the general public

Members of the museum profession should deal with the public efficiently and courteously at all times, and should in particular deal promptly with all correspondence and inquiries. Subject to the requirements of confidentiality in a particular case, they should share their expertise in all professional fields in dealing with inquiries, subject to due acknowledgment, from both the general public and specialist inquirers, allowing bona fide researchers properly controlled but, so far as possible, full access to any material or documentation in their care, even when this is the subject of personal research or special field of interest.

7.3 Confidentiality

Members of the museum profession must protect all confidential information relating to the source of material owned by or loaned to the museum, as well as information concerning the security arrangements of the museum, or the security arrangements of private collections or any place visited in the course of official duties. Confidentiality must also be respected in relation to any item brought to the museum for identification and, without specific authority from the owner, information on such an item should not be passed to another museum, to a dealer, or to any other person (subject to any legal obligation to assist the police or other proper authorities in investigating possible stolen or illicitly acquired or transferred property).

There is a special responsibility to respect the personal confidences contained in oral history or other personal material. Investigators using recording devices such as cameras or tape recorders or the technique of oral interviewing should take special care to protect their data, and persons investigated, photographed or interviewed should have the right to remain anonymous if they so choose. This right should be respected where it has been specifically promised. Where there is no clear understanding to the contrary, the primary responsibility of the investigator is to ensure that no information is revealed that might harm the informant or his or her community. Subjects under study should understand the capacities of cameras, tape recorders and other machines used, and should be free to accept or reject their use.

8 Personal responsibility to colleagues and the profession

8.1 Professional relationships

Relationships between members of the museum profession should always be courteous, both in public and in private. Differences of opinion should not be expressed in a personalized fashion. Notwithstanding this general rule, members of the profession may properly object to proposals or practices which may have a damaging effect on a museum or museums, or the profession.

8.2 Professional co-operation

Members of the museum profession have an obligation, subject to due acknowledgment, to share their knowledge and experience with their colleagues and with scholars and students in relevant fields. They should show their appreciation and respect to those from whom they have learned and should present without thought of personal gain such advancements in techniques and experience which may be of benefit to others.

The training of personnel in the specialized activities involved in museum work is of great importance in the development of the profession and all should accept responsibility, where appropriate, in the training of colleagues. Members of the profession who in their official appointment have under their direction junior staff, trainees, students, and assistants undertaking formal or informal professional training, should give these the benefit of their experience and knowledge, and should also treat them with the consideration and respect customary among members of the profession.

Members of the profession form working relationships in the course of their duties with numerous other people, both professional and otherwise, within and outside the museum in which they are employed. They are expected to conduct these relationships with courtesy and fair-mindedness and to render their professional services to others efficiently and at a high standard.

8.3 Dealing

No member of the museum profession should participate in any dealing (buying or selling for profit), in objects similar or related to the objects collected by the employing museum. Dealing by museum employees at any level of responsibility in objects that are collected by any other museum can also present serious problems even if there is no risk of direct conflict with the employing museum, and should be permitted only if, after full disclosure and review by the governing body of the employing museum or designated senior officer, explicit permission is granted, with or without conditions.

Article 7 para. 5 of the ICOM *Statutes* provides that membership of ICOM shall not be available, under any circumstances, to any person or institution that is dealing (buying or selling for profit) in cultural property.

8.4 Other potential conflicts of interest

Generally, members of the museum profession should refrain from all acts or activities which may be construed as a conflict of interest. Museum professionals by virtue of their knowledge, experience, and contacts are frequently offered opportunities, such as advisory and consultancy services, teaching, writing and broadcasting opportunities, or requests for valuations, in a personal capacity. Even where the national law and the individual's conditions of employment permit such activities, these may appear in the eyes of colleagues, the employing authority, or the general public, to create a conflict of interest. In such situations all legal and employment contract conditions must be scrupulously followed, and in the event of any potential conflict arising or being suggested, the matter should be reported immediately to an appropriate superior officer or the museum governing body, and steps must be taken to eliminate the potential conflict of interest.

Even where the conditions of employment permit any kind of outside activity, and there appears to be no risk of any conflict of interest, great care should be taken to ensure that such outside interests do not interfere in any way with the proper discharge of official duties and responsibilities.

8.5 Authentication, valuation and illicit material

Members of the museum profession are encouraged to share their professional knowledge and expertise with both professional colleagues and the general public (see para. 7.2 above).

However, written certificates of authenticity or valuation (appraisals) should not be given, and opinions on the monetary value of objects should only be given on official request from other museums or competent legal, governmental or other responsible public authorities.

Members of the museum profession should not identify or otherwise authenticate objects where they have reason to believe or suspect that these have been illegally or illicitly acquired, transferred, imported or exported.

They should recognize that it is highly unethical for museums or the museum profession to support either directly or indirectly the illicit trade in cultural or natural objects (see para. 3.2 above), and under no circumstances should they act in a way that could be regarded as benefiting such illicit trade in any way, directly or indirectly. Where there is reason to believe or suspect illicit or illegal transfer, import or export, the competent authorities should be notified.

8.6 Unprofessional conduct

Every member of the museum profession should be conversant with both any national or local laws, and any conditions of employment, concerning corrupt practices, and should at all times avoid situations which could rightly or wrongly be construed as corrupt or improper conduct of any kind. In particular no museum official should accept any gift, hospitality, or any form of reward from any dealer, auctioneer or other person as an improper inducement in respect of the purchase or disposal of museum items.

Also, in order to avoid any suspicion of corruption, a museum professional should not recommend any particular dealer, auctioneer or other person to a member of the public, nor should the official accept any "special price" or discount for personal purchases from any dealer with whom either the professional or employing museum has a professional relationship.

References

INTRODUCTION

Bukkyo Dendo Kyokai (1966) *The Teaching of Buddha*, Tokyo: Bukkyo Dendo Kyokai.

Burcaw, G. E. (1983) *Introduction to Museum Work* (2nd edn), Nashville, TN: American Association for State and Local History.

International Council of Museums (1989) *Statutes*, Paris: ICOM.

CHAPTER 1: ETHICS

American Association of Museums (1925) *Code of Ethics for Museum Workers*, Washington, DC: AAM.

Bowne, B. P. (1892) *The Principles of Ethics*, New York, Cincinnati, and Chicago: American Book Company.

Brown, M. T. (1990) *Working Ethics: Strategies for Decision Making and Organizational Responsibility*, San Francisco and Oxford: Jossey-Bass Publishers.

Caplan, A. L. and Callahan, D. (eds) (1981) *Ethics in Hard Times*, New York and London: Plenum Press.

Capra, F. (1991) *The Tao of Physics* (3rd edn), Boston: Shambhala.

Everett. W. G. (1918) *Moral Values: A Study of the Principles of Conduct*, New York: Henry Holt & Company.

Fagothey, A. (1972) *Right and Reason: Ethics in Theory and Practice* (5th edn), St Louis, MO: The C. V. Mosby Company.

Fuller, B. A. G. (1945) *A History of Philosophy* (revised), New York: Henry Holt & Company.

Guy, M. E. (1990) *Ethical Decision Making in Everyday Work Situations*, New York/London: Quorum Books.

Holmes, R. L. (1992) *Basic Moral Philosophy*, Belmont, CA: Wadsworth Publishing Company.

International Council of Museums (1990) *Code of Professional Ethics* (revised), Paris: ICOM.

Jevons, F. B. (1927) *Philosophy: What Is It?* London: Cambridge University Press.

Pepper, S. C. (1960) *Ethics*, New York: Appleton-Century-Crofts, Inc.

Pojman, L. P. (1990) *Ethics: Discovering Right and Wrong*, Belmont, CA: Wadsworth Publishing Company.

Rescher, N. (1987) *Ethical Idealism*, Berkeley: University of California Press.

Tasnoff, R. A. (1955) *Ethics* (revised edn), New York: Harper & Brothers.

van Mensch, P. (ed.) (1989) *Professionalising the Muses*, Amsterdam: AHA Books.

CHAPTER 2: ETHICS AND THE PROFESSION

American Heritage Electronic Dictionary (1991) Houghton Mifflin Company, copyright (1992) Word Star International Inc., US Pat. No. 4,724,523.

Aristotle (1985) *Nicomachean Ethics* (translation and notes by T. Irwin), Indianapolis: Hackett Publishing Company.

Beauchamp, T. L. (1989) *Case Studies in Business, Society, and Ethics* (2nd edn), Englewood Cliffs, NJ: Prentice-Hall.

International Council of Museums (1990) *Code of Professional Ethics* (revised), Paris: ICOM.

Kultgen, J. (1988) *Ethics and Professionalism*, Philadelphia: University of Pennsylvania Press.

Lewis, C. I. (1955) *The Ground and the Nature of Right*, New York: Columbia University Press.

Lovin, R. (1992) "What is Ethics?". Unpublished paper presented at an American Association of Museums Board Meeting, Washington, DC.

McDowell, B. (1991) *Ethical Conduct and the Professional's Dilemma*, New York and London: Quorum Books.

Messenger, P. (ed.) (1989) *The Ethics of Collecting Cultural Property*, Albuquerque: University of New Mexico Press.

Pojman, L. P. (1990) *Ethics: Discovering Right and Wrong*, Belmont, CA: Wadsworth Publishing Company.

Titus, H. H. (1947) *Ethics for Today* (2nd edn), New York: American Book Company.

CHAPTER 3: ETHICS AND MUSEUMS

Banner, W. A. (1968) *Ethics: An Introduction to Moral Philosophy*, New York: Charles Scribner's Sons.

Bowne, B. P. (1892) *The Principles of Ethics*, New York, Cincinnati, and Chicago: American Book Company.

Brown, M. T. (1990) *Working Ethics: Strategies for Decision Making and Organizational Responsibility*, San Francisco and Oxford: Jossey-Bass Publishers.

Caplan, A. and Callahan, D. (eds) (1981) *Ethics in Hard Times*, New York and London: Plenum Press.

Garnett, A. C. (1960) *Ethics: A Critical Introduction*, New York: The Ronald Press Company.

Guy, M. E. (1990) *Ethical Decision Making in Everyday Work Situations*, New York and London: Quorum Books.

Holmes, R. L. (1992) *Basic Moral Philosophy*, Belmont, CA: Wadsworth Publishing Company.

International Council of Museums (1989) *Statutes*, Paris: ICOM.

—— (1990) *Code of Professional Ethics* (revised), Paris: ICOM.

Lewis, C. W. (1991) *The Ethics Challenge in Public Service*, San Francisco and Oxford: Jossey-Bass Publishers.

MacIntyre, A. (1966) *A Short History of Ethics*, New York: The Macmillan Company.

McKechnie, J. L. (general supervisor) (1977) *Webster's New Twentieth Century Dictionary of the English Language* (2nd edn) William Collins/World Publishing Co., Inc.

McInerney, P. K. and Rainbolt, G. W. (1994) *Ethics*, New York: HarperCollins Publishers, Inc.

Moore, G. E. (1902) *Principia Ethica* (republished 1988), Buffalo, NY: Prometheus Books.

Mount, E. (1990) *Professional Ethics in Context*, Louisville, KY: Westminster/John Knox Press.

Patterson, C. (1949) *Moral Standards: An Introduction to Ethics*, New York: The Ronald Press Company.

Pojman, L. P. (1990) *Ethics: Discovering Right and Wrong*, Belmont, CA: Wadsworth Publishing Company.

Sommers, C. H. (1986) *Right and Wrong: Basic Readings in Ethics*, New York: Harcourt Brace Jovanovich, Publishers.

Titus, H. H. (1947) *Ethics for Today* (2nd edn), New York: American Book Company.

CHAPTER 4: ETHICS AND DUTY

Banner, W. (1968) *Ethics: An Introduction to Moral Philosophy*, New York: Charles Scribner's Sons.

Bayles, M. (1981) *Professional Ethics*, Belmont, CA: Wadsworth Publishing Company.

Brandt, R. B. (1979) *A Theory of the Good and The Right*, New York and Oxford: Oxford University Press.

Gowans, C. W. (ed.) (1987) *Moral Dilemmas*, New York and Oxford: Oxford University Press.

Guy, M. E. (1990) *Ethical Decision Making in Everyday Work Situations*, New York and London: Quorum Books.

Hare, R. M. (1952) *The Language of Morals*, Oxford: The Clarendon Press.

Hughes, E. "Professions," in: Callahan, J. (1988) *Ethical Issues in Professional Life*, Oxford: Oxford University Press.

International Council of Museums (1990) *Code of Professional Ethics* (revised), Paris: ICOM.

Kant, I. [1785] (1993) *Grounding for the Metaphysics of Morals* (trans. J. W. Ellington, 3rd edn), Indianapolis: Hackett Publishing Company, Inc.

Lamont, W. (1981) *Law and the Moral Order*, Aberdeen: The University Press.

Lewis, C. W. (1991) *The Ethics Challenge in Public Service*, San Francisco and Oxford: Jossey-Bass Publications.

McDowell, B. (1991) *Ethical Conduct and the Professional's Dilemma*, New York and London: Quorum Books.

McKechnie, J. (general supervisor) (1977) *Webster's New Twentieth Century Dictionary of the English Language* (2nd edn), William Collins/World Publishing Co., Inc.

Pojman, L. P. (1990) *Ethics: Discovering Right and Wrong*, Belmont, CA: Wadsworth Publishing Company.

Sommers, C. H. (1986) *Right and Wrong: Basic Readings in Ethics*, New York: Harcourt Brace Jovanovich, Publishers.

Van Wyk, R. (1989) *Introduction to Ethics*, New York: St Martin's Press, Inc.

Wheelwright, P. (1959) *A Critical Introduction to Ethics* (3rd edn), New York: The Odyssey Press, Inc.

CHAPTER 5: ETHICS AND TRUTH

Allen, B. (1993) *Truth in Philosophy*, Cambridge and London: Harvard University Press.

Bahm, A. J. (1974) *Ethics as a Behavioral Science*, Springfield, IL: Charles C. Thomas Publisher.

Banner, W. (1968) *Ethics: An Introduction to Moral Philosophy*, New York: Charles Scribner's Sons.

Bowne, B. P. (1892) *The Principles of Ethics*, New York, Cincinnati, and Chicago: American Book Company.

Brown, M. T. (1990) *Working Ethics: Strategies for Decision Making and Organizational Responsibility*, San Francisco and Oxford: Jossey-Bass Publishers.

Ellis, B. (1990) *Truth and Objectivity*, Cambridge and Oxford: Basil Blackwell Ltd.

Fagothey, A. (1972) *Right and Reason: Ethics in Theory and Practice* (5th edn), Saint Louis, MO: The C. V. Mosby Company.

Finnis, J. (1983) *Ethics and Society*, New York: New York University Press, 1980.

Fried, C. (1978) *Right and Wrong*, Cambridge, MA and London: Harvard University Press.

Guy, M. E. (1990) *Ethical Decision Making in Everyday Work Situations*, New York and London: Quorum Books.

Holmes, R. L. (1992) *Basic Moral Philosophy*, Belmont, CA: Wadsworth Publishing Company.

International Council of Museums (1989) *Statutes*, Paris: ICOM.

Joachim, H. H. (1906) *The Nature of Truth*, Oxford: The Clarendon Press.

Lamont, W. (1981) *Law and the Moral Order*, Aberdeen: The University Press.

Patterson, C. H. (1949) *Moral Standards: An Introduction to Ethics*, New York: The Ronald Press Company.

Pojman, L. P. (1990) *Ethics: Discovering Right and Wrong*, Belmont, CA: Wadsworth Publishing Company.

Rachels, J. (1993) *The Elements of Moral Philosophy* (2nd edn), New York: McGraw-Hill, Inc.

Titus, H. H. (1947) *Ethics for Today* (2nd edn), New York: American Book Company.

Tsanoff, R. A. (1955) *Ethics* (revised edn), New York: Harper & Brothers.

Westermarck, E. (1971) *The Origin and Development of the Moral Idea*, (vols I and II) (revised), Freeport, NY: Books for Libraries Press.

CHAPTER 6: ETHICS AND THE MUSEUM COMMUNITY

Aristotle (1980) *Nicomachean Ethics* (trans. and introduced by D. Ross) Oxford: Oxford University Press.

Brandt, R. B. (1966) "Two Tests of Ethical Principles: Consistency and Generality," in: Titus, H. H. and Keeton, M. T. (eds), *The Range of Ethics*, New York, American Book Company.

Fuller, B. A. G. (1947) *A History of Philosophy* (revised), New York: Henry Holt & Company.

Garnett, A. C. (1960) *Ethics: A Critical Introduction*, New York: The Ronald Press Company.

Goldman, A. H. (1980) *The Moral Foundations of Professional Ethics*, Totowa, NJ: Rowman & Littlefield.

International Council of Museum (1990) *Code of Professional Ethics*, (revised) Paris: ICOM.

McInerney, P. K. and Rainbolt, G. W. (1994) *Ethics*, New York: HarperCollins Publishers, Inc.

Moore, G. E. (1903) *Principia Ethica* (republished 1988) Buffalo, NY: Prometheus Books.

Pepper, S. C. (1960) *Ethics*, New York: Appleton-Century-Crofts, Inc.

Rand, A. (1964) *The Virtue of Selfishness*, New York: The New American Library.

Rawls, J. (1971) *A Theory of Justice*, Cambridge, MA: The Belknap Press of Harvard University Press.

Rescher, N. (1987) *Ethical Idealism*, Berkeley, Los Angeles, and London: University of California Press.

Russell, B. (1955) *Human Society in Ethics and Politics*, New York: Simon & Schuster.

Sommers, C. H. (1986) *Right and Wrong: Basic Readings in Ethics*, New York: Harcourt Brace Jovanovich, Publishers.

CHAPTER 7: ETHICS AS A CODE

Bloom, J. and Powell, E. (eds) (1984) *Museums for a New Century*, Washington, DC: American Association of Museums.

Everett, W. G. (1918) *Moral Values: A Study of the Principles of Conduct*, New York: Henry Holt & Company.

Garnett, A. C. (1960) *Ethics: A Critical Introduction*, New York: The Ronald Press Company.

Garrett, T. M. (1968) *Problems and Perspectives in Ethics*, New York: Sheed & Ward, Inc.

George, A. "Ethics in Management," *Museum News*, Nov./Dec. 1988, American Association of Museum, Vol. 67, No. 2, p. 87.

Guy, M. E. (1990) *Ethical Decision Making in Everyday Work Situations*, New York and London: Quorum Books.

International Council of Museums (1990) *Code of Professional Ethics* (revised), Paris: ICOM.

Kant, I. [1785] (1983) *Grounding for the Metaphysics of Morals*, (trans. J. W. Ellington, 3rd edn) Indianapolis and Cambridge: Hackett Publishing Company, Inc.

Kultgen, J. (1988) *Ethics and Professionalism*, Philadelphia: University of Pennsylvania Press.

Lewis, C. W. (1991) *The Ethics Challenge in Public Service*, San Francisco and Oxford: Jossey-Bass Publishers.

Malaro, M. (1990) "What Is an Ethical Obligation?," in: *Museum Training as Career-Long Learning in a Changing World*, Proceedings of the ICOM Committee on Training of Museum Personnel, Washington, DC: Smithsonian Institution.

Phelan, M. (1994) "A Synopsis of the Laws Protecting Our Cultural Heritage," *New England Law Review*, New England School of Law, Vol. 28, No. 1.

Sheldahl, T. (1979) "A Logical Structure for Codes of Professional Ethics," *Working Paper Series* WP 79–18, Management Research Center, Syracuse, NY: Syracuse University School of Management.

Westermarck, E. (1971) *The Origin and Development of the Moral Idea*, (vols I and II, revised), Freeport, NY: Books for Libraries Press.

PART II: INTRODUCTION

Bryce, H. J. (1992) *Financial and Strategic Management for Nonprofit Organizations* (2nd edn), Englewood Cliffs, NJ: Prentice-Hall, Inc.

CHAPTER 8: ETHICS AND CULTURAL IDENTITY

Afigbo, A. E. and Okita, S. I. O. (1985) *The Museum and Nation Building*, Owerri: New Africa Publishing Co. Ltd.

Alexander, E. P. (1983) *Museum Masters – Their Museums and Their Influence*, Nashville, TN: American Association for State and Local History.

Boylan, P. J. (1990) "Museums and Cultural Identity," Presidential Address to the Annual Conference of the Museums Association, Glasgow, July 10, 1990 in *The Source Book* 1993 Annual Meeting of the American Association of Museums, Washington, DC: American Association of Museums.

International Council of Museums (1989) *Statutes*, Paris: ICOM.

Odumegwu-Ojukwu, E. (1989) *Because I Am Involved*, Ibadan, Owerri and Kaduna: Spectrum Books Ltd.

Okita, S. I. O. (1986) "Ethnic Identity and the Problem of National Integration in Nigeria," paper presented at the National Seminar on the National Question in Nigeria: Its Historical Origin and Contemporary Dimension, Abuja, August 4–9, 1986 – organized by the Federal Ministry for Special Duties, Lagos and Ahmadu Bello University, Zaria.

Petersen, W. (1975) "On the Subnation of Western Europe," in: Glaser, N. and Moynichen, D. P. (eds), *Ethnicity: Theory and Practice*, Cambridge, MA: Harvard University Press.

CHAPTER 9: ETHICS AND INDIGENOUS PEOPLES

Aboriginal Interests Working Group, Towards a Co-ordinated Aboriginal Heritage Policy for Western Australia (1991) *Into the Twenty-First Century*, The Report of State Task Force on Museum Policy, Western Australia, Perth.

Ames, M. (1992) *Cannibal Tours and Glass Cases: The Anthropology of Museums*, Vancouver: UBC Press.

Assembly of First Nations and Canadian Museums Association (1992) *Turning the Page: Forging New Partnerships between Museums and First Peoples*, Ottawa: Assembly of First Nations and Canadian Museums Association, Ottawa.

Burger, J. (1990) *The Gaia Atlas of First Peoples*, London: Gaia Books Ltd.

Cameron, D. F. (1992) "Getting Out of Our Skin: Museums and a New Identity," *MUSE*, Summer/Fall, pp. 7–10.

Clavir, M. (1993) *An Examination of the Conservation Codes of Ethics in Relation to Collections from First Peoples*, Vancouver: UBC Museum of Anthropology.

Dodson, P. (Commissioner) (1991) *The Royal Commission into Aboriginal Deaths in Custody*, National Report, Overview and Recommendations by Commissioner Elliott Johnson, QC, Australian Government Publishing Service, Canberra.

Doxtator, D. (1994) "The Implications of Canadian Nationalism on Aboriginal Cultural Autonomy," *Curatorship: Indigenous Perspectives in Post-Colonial Societies*, Symposium Papers, April, 1994, pp. 19–25.

E/CN.4 Sub. 2/1993/26/Add.1. For discussion of the use of the phrase "peoples," see the document by Erica-Irene A. Daes, chairperson of the Working Group on Indigenous Populations.

Edwards, R. and Stewart, J. (eds) (1978) *Preserving Indigenous Cultures*, Canberra: Aboriginal Educational Consultative Group.

Eoe, S. M. and Swadling, P. (1991) *Museums and Cultural Centres in the Pacific*, Port Moresby: Papua New Guinea National Museum.

Galla, A. (1993a) "Some Challenges for Reconciling the Past with the Future," in: the

Bulletin of the International Council of Museums, Vol. 46, No. 2, pp. 3–6.

—— (1993b) *Heritage Curricula and Cultural Diversity*, Office of Multicultural Affairs, Prime Minister and Cabinet, Canberra: Australian Government Publishing Service. (For detailed discussion relating to the issues mentioned and the associated professional training and practice.)

Hill, T. and Nicks, T. (1992), "The Task Force on Museums and First Peoples," *MUSE*, Summer/Fall, pp. 81–4.

International Council of Museums (1989) *Statutes*, Paris: ICOM.

Keating P. J. (1992) The Hon. Prime Minister, MP, speech at the launch of the International Year for the World's Indigenous People, Redfern, 10 December 1992.

Menchú, R. (1994) "Special Contribution, The International Decade of Indigenous People," *Human Development Report 1994*, UNDP, New York: Oxford University Press.

Murphy, B. "New Partnerships: Aboriginal Art within and beyond the Museum," *Art Monthly Australia*, April 1994, pp. 22–4.

Museums Australia (1992) *Previous Possessions and Present Obligations*, Melbourne: Museums Australia, Melbourne.

Parker, P. L. (compiler) (1990) *Keepers of the Treasures: Protecting Historic Properties and Cultural Traditions on Indian Lands*, Washington, DC: National Park Service.

Schmidt, F. (1992) "Codes of Museum Ethics and the Financial Pressures on Museums," in: *Journal of Museum Management and Curatorship*, No. 11, pp. 257–68.

UN Doc. E/CN 4/Sub. 2/1986/7 Add. 4, *Study of the Problem Against Indigenous Populations*, Vol. 5, *Conclusions, Proposals and Recommendation*.

Yu, P. (compiler) (1991) *The Crocodile Hole Report*, Derby: Kimberley Land Council and Warringarri Resource Centre.

CHAPTER 10: ETHICS AND TRAINING

Beck, J. and Daley, M. (1993) *Art Restoration. The Culture, the Business and the Scandal*, New York and London: W. W. Norton & Company.

Boylan, P. J. (1994) "The Status and Role of 'Consultants' among ICOM's Membership," unpublished paper presented at the ICOM Advisory Committee, Paris, June.

Case, M. (ed.) (1988) *Registrars on Record*, Washington, DC: Smithsonian Institution.

Edson, G. (1990) "Ethics and Professionalism in Museums," in: *Museum Training as Career-Long Learning in a Changing World* (1990), Proceedings of the ICOM Committee for the Training of Personnel, Washington, DC: Smithsonian Institution.

—— (1994) "Proceedings of ICTOP Conference," unpublished report from ICTOP meeting in Rio de Janeiro, Brazil. For the resolution see: *it*, Newsletter ICTOP 19, June, pp. 2–4.

Glenn, J. and Weil, S. (1990) "Pat Barga's Discovery," An example of a constructed case study in: *Museum Training as Career-Long Learning in a Changing World* (1990), Proceedings of the ICOM Committee for the Training of Personnel, Washington, DC: Smithsonian Institution.

Hudson, K. (1989) "The Flipside of Professionalism," *Museums Journal*, Vol. 88, No. 4, pp. 188–90.

International Council of Museums (1979) *Basic Syllabus for Professional Museum Training*, Paris: ICOM.

—— (1989) *Statutes*, Paris: ICOM.

Kavanagh, G. (ed.) (1991) *The Museums Profession*, Leicester and New York: Leicester University Press.

Malaro, M. (1990) "What Is an Ethical Obligation?," in: *Museum Training as Career-Long Learning in a Changing World*, Proceedings of the ICOM Committee for the Training of Personnel, Washington, DC: Smithsonian Institution.

Merryman, J. H. and Elsen, A. E. (1987) *Law, Ethics and the Visual Arts*, Philadelphia: University of Pennsylvania Press.

Murdin, L. (1991) "Museums Association Expels Derbyshire," *Museums Journal*, Vol. 91, No. 5, p. 8.

Nega, V. (1994) "Preliminary Report for the Development of a Code of Ethics for Archaeological Research," in: *ICMAH Information*, International Committee on Archaeology and History.

Rose, C. (1985) "A Code of Ethics for Registrars," *Museum News*, Vol. 63, No. 3, pp. 42–6.

Schmidt, F. (1992) "Codes of Museum Ethics and the Financial Pressure on Museums," in: *Museum Management and Curatorship*, 2nd edn, London: Butterworth Heinemann pp. 257–68.

Talley, M. K. (1993) "Ethics and the Morality of Conservation/Restoration Practices," in: P. Berghuis and P. A. Terwen (eds) *How Safe is Your Object? A Concise Manual of Preventive Conservation*, Amsterdam: Reinwardt Academie.

Thompson, J. M. A. (ed.) (1992) *Manual of Curatorship* (2nd edn), London: Butterworth Heinemann.

van Mensch, P. (ed.) (1989) *Professionalising the Muses*, Amsterdam: AHA Books.

—— (ed.) (1994) *Ethics in Museology*, Amsterdam: Reinwardt Academie.

Weij, A. (1994) "Functioneren van de Gedragslijn voor Museale Beroepsethiek," (unpublished paper) Amsterdam: Reinwardt Academie.

Weil, S. (1988) "The Ongoing Pursuit of Professional Status. The Progress of Museum Work in America," *Museum News*, Vol. 67, No. 2, pp. 30–4.

CHAPTER 11: ETHICS AND MUSEOLOGY

Barthes, R. (1980) "Editorial," *Culture et Communication*, Paris, March, p. 8.

Bloom, J. and Powell, E. (eds) (1984) *Museums for a New Century*, Washington, DC: American Association of Museums.

International Council of Museums (1990) *Statutes and Code of Professional Ethics* (revised), Paris: ICOM.

Lord, B., Lord, G. D., and Nicks, J. (1989) *The Cost of Collecting*, London: HMSO.

Weil, S. (1990) *Rethinking the Museum and Other Meditations*, Washington, DC, and London: Smithsonian Institution Press.

CHAPTER 12: ETHICS AND THE ENVIRONMENT

Able Jr, E. H. (1988) "Ethical Standards Today," *Museum News*, Nov./Dec., Vol. 62, No. 2, p. 94.

Arruda, A. (1992) "Ecologia e desenvolvimento," in: *O conhecimento no cotidiano* (as representações sociais na perspectiva da psicologia social). Brasiliense.

Bentham, J. (n.d.) "Uma introdução aos principios da Moral e da Legislação," Trans. Luis João Baraúna, *Abril Cultural*, São Paulo, pp. 9–13.

COFEM (Conselho Federal de Museologia – Brasil) (1992) *Código de Ética Profissional do Museólogio*, Rio de Janeiro, October.

Davalon, J., Grandmont, G., and Schielle, B. (1992) "L'environnment entre au musée," *Collection Muséologies*, Lyon: Presses Universitaires de Lyon.

George, A. (1988) "Ethics and Management," in: *Museum News*, Nov./Dec., Vol. 67, No. 2, p. 87.

International Council of Museums (1989) *Statutes*, Paris: ICOM.

—— (1990) *Code of Professional Ethics* (revised), Paris: ICOM.

Kant, I. (n. d.) "Critica da razão pura e outros textos filosóficos," (ed. Marilena Chuaui Berlinck), *Abril Cultural*, São Paulo.

Macdonald, R. (1993) "A Code of Ethics for United States Museums," in: *Museum International*, Paris: UNESCO, Vol. XIV, No. 1, pp. 53–6.

Scheiner, T. (ed.) (1991) "Interação museu-comunidade pela educação ambiental," *Tacnet Cultural*, Rio de Janeiro.

Unger, N. M. (ed.) (1992) "Fundamentos filosóficos do pensamento ecológico," *Ed. Loyola*, São Paulo, 1992.

World Commission on Environment and Development (1987) *Our Common Future*, Oxford and New York: Oxford University Press.

CHAPTER 13: ETHICS AND COLLECTING

American Association of Museums (1994) *Code of Ethics*, Washington, DC: AAM.

International Council of Museums (1990) *Code of Professional Ethics* (revised), Paris: ICOM.

CHAPTER 14: ETHICS AND PREVENTIVE CONSERVATION

Agrawal, O. P. (1982) "Errors in Organization: Laboratory without Trained Staff," *Museum*, Vol. 34, No. 1, p. 44.

American Association of Museums (1994) *Code of Ethics*, Washington, DC: AAM.

Anonymous (1989) "Collecting Thoughts," *Museum News*, Vol. 68, No. 5, pp. 53–7.

Applebaum, B. (1991) *Guide to Environmental Protection of Collections*, Madison, CT: Sound View Press.

Bachmann, K. (ed.) (1992) *Conservation Concerns: A Guide for Collectors and Curators*, Washington, DC: Smithsonian Institution Press.

Cato, P. S. (1991) "Summary of a Study to Evaluate Collection Manager-Type Positions," *Collection Forum*, Vol. 7, No. 2, pp. 72–94.

Cato, P. S. and Williams, S. L. (1993) "Guidelines for Developing Policies for the Management and Care of Natural History Collections," *Collection Forum*, Vol. 9, No. 2, pp. 84–107.

Cherfas, J. (1989) "Science Gives Ivory a Sense of Identity," *Science*, Vol. 246, No. 4934, pp. 1120.

Dixon, B. (1987) "Conservation Management: Possible or Necessary?," in: *Conservation Management*, Kingston, Ontario: Queen's University, pp. 1–8.

Duckworth, W. D., Genoways, H. H., and Rose, C. L. (1993) *Preserving Natural Science Collections: Chronicle of our Environmental Heritage*, Washington, DC: National Institute for the Conservation of Cultural Property.

George, S. B. (1987) "Specimens as Bioindicators of Environmental Disturbance," in: Genoways, H. H., Jones, C., and Rossolimo, O. L. (eds),

Mammal Collection Management Lubbock, TX: Texas Tech University Press, pp. 65–73.

Graham-Bell, M. (1986) *Preventive Conservation: A Manual* (2nd edn), Handbook of British Columbia Museums Association, Vol. 2, pp. 1–87.

Greathouse, G. A. and Wessel, C. J. (eds)(1954) *Deterioration of Materials. Causes and Preventive Techniques*, New York: Reinhold Publishing Corporation.

Hansen, E. F. and Reedy, C. L. (eds) (1994) *Research Priorities in Art and Architectural Conservation*, Washington, DC: American Institute for Conservation of Historic and Artistic Works.

Herrman, B. and Hummel, S. (1994) *Ancient DNA*, New York: Springer-Verlag.

International Council of Museums (1989) *Statutes*, Paris: ICOM.

—— (1990) *Code of Professional Ethics* (revised), Paris: ICOM.

Jackson, H. H. T. (1926) "The Care of Museum Specimens of Recent Mammals," *Journal of Mammalogy*, Vol. 7, No. 2, pp. 113–19.

Johnson, R. I. (1980) "Scientists Examine the Shroud of Turin," *Industrial Research/Development*, Vol. 22, No. 2, pp. 145–50.

Jones, B. G. (1986) *Protecting Historic Architecture and Museum Collections from Natural Disaster*, London: Butterworths.

Malaro, M. C. (1985) *A Legal Primer on Managing Museum Collections*, Washington, DC: Smithsonian Institution Press.

—— (1993) "Laws, Ethics, and Conservation Concerns," in: Rose, C. L., Williams, S. L., and Gisbert, J. (eds), *Current Issues, Initiatives, and Future Directions for the Preservation and Conservation of Natural History Collections*, Madrid: Ministerio de Cultura, pp. 339–43.

McGinley, R. J. (1993) "Where's the Management in Collections Management?," in: Rose, C. L., Williams, S. L., and Gisbert, J. (eds) *Current Issues, Initiatives, and Future Directions for the Preservation and Conservation of Natural History Collections*, Madrid: Ministerio de Cultura, pp. 309–38.

McKusick, V. A. (1991) "Abraham Lincoln and Marfan Syndrome," *Nature*, Vol. 352, No. 6333, p. 280.

Michalski, S. (1992) *A Systematic Approach to the Conservation (Care) of Museum Collections*, Ottawa: Canadian Conservation Institute.

Miller, E. H. (1985) "Museum Collections: Their Roles and Future in Biological Research," British Columbia Provincial Museum, *Occasional Paper Series*, Vol. 25, pp. x, 1–219.

National Park Service (1990) *Museum Handbook, Part 1. Museum Collections*, Washington, DC: National Park Service.

Phelan, M. (1982) *Museums and the Law*, Nashville, TN: American Association for State and Local History.

Plenderleith, H. J. (1956) *The Conservation of Antiquities and Works of Art*, London: Oxford University Press.

Plenderleith, H. J. and Werner, A. E. A. (1962) *The Conservation of Antiquities and Works of Art* (2nd edn), London: Oxford University Press.

Rose, C. L. (1977) "An Introduction to Museum Conservation," *The American Indian Art Magazine*, Vol. 3, No. 1, pp. 30–1, 83, 104, 106.

—— (1988) "Ethical and Practical Considerations in Conserving Ethnographic Museum Objects," in: *The Conservation of Ethnographic Objects In Museums*. Senri Ethnological Studies, Vol. 23, pp. iii, 1–290.

—— (1991) "The Conservation of Natural History Collections: Addressing Preservation Concerns and Maintaining the Integrity of Research Specimens," in: Cato, P. S. and Jones, C. (eds) *Natural History Museums: Directions for Growth*, Lubbock, TX: Texas Tech University Press, pp. 51–9.

Rose, C. L. and Torres, A. R. (eds) (1993) *Storage of Natural History Collections: Ideas and Practical Solutions*, Pittsburgh, PA: Society for the Preservation of Natural History Collections.

Schur, S. E. (1981) "The Anthropology Conservation Laboratory, Smithsonian Institution," *Technology & Conservation*, Vol. 6, No. 4, pp. 26–35.

Slate, J. (1985) "A National Study Assesses Collections Management, Maintenance and Conservation," *Museum News*, Vol. 64, No. 1, pp. 38–45.

Tennent, N. H. and Baird, T. (1985) "The Deterioration of Mollusca Collections: Identification of Shell Efflorescence," *Studies in Conservation*, No. 30, pp. 73–85.

Thomson, G. (1986) *The Museum Environment* (2nd edn), London: Butterworth.

Vaughn, T. (1977) "A Simple Matter of Standards," *Museum News*, Vol. 55, No. 1, pp. 32–4, 45.

Webster, L. (1989) "Altered States: Documenting Changes in Anthropology Research Collections," *Curator*, Vol. 33, No. 2, pp. 130–60.

Williams, S. L. (1991) "Investigations of the Causes of Structural Damage to Teeth in Museum Collections," *Collection Forum*, Vol. 7, No. 1, pp. 13–25.

Williams, S. L. and Cato, P. S. (1995) "Serving the Long-term Interests of Natural History Collections," *Collection Forum*.

Williams, S. L. and Hawks, C. A. (1992) "The Condition of Type Specimens of *Peromyscus*," *Journal of Mammalogy*, Vol. 73, No. 4, pp. 731–43.

Williams, S. L., Walsh, E. A., and Weber, S. G. (1989) "Effects of DDVP on Museum Materials," Vol. 32, No. 1, pp. 34–69.

Wolf, S. J. (ed.) (1990) *The Conservation Assessment: Tool for Planning, Implementing, and Fund Raising*, Los Angeles and Washington, DC: Getty Conservation Institute and the National Institute for the Conservation of Cultural Property.

Zycherman, L. A. and Schrock, J. R. (eds) (1988) *Guide to Museum Pest Control*, Washington, DC: Association of Systematics Collections and the American Institute for Conservation.

CHAPTER 15: ETHICS AND CONSERVATION

AIC Committee on Ethics and Standards (1979) *Code of Ethics and Standards of Practice*, Washington, DC: American Institute for the Conservation of Historic and Artistic Works.

Allen, N. (ed.) (1984) *Scottish Conservation Directory*, Glasgow Conservation Bureau, Scottish Development Agency.

Butler, S. (1912) *Elementary Morality*, London: Notebooks.

Cooke, W. (1988) "Creasing in Ancient Textiles," *Conservation News*, No. 35, pp. 27–30.

Frost, M. (1980) "Care and Conservation of Machinery," *Saskatchewan Museum Quarterly*, Vol. 7, No. 8, pp. 11–18.

Harding, K. (1976) *A Code of Ethics for Restorers in Antiquarian Horology*, London: Keith Harding.

Horie, V. (1987) *Materials for Conservation*, London: Butterworth.

ICOM (1984) *The Conservator-Restorer; A Definition of the Profession*, Paris: ICOM.

IIC-CG and CAPC (1986) *Code of Ethics and Guidance for Practice*, Ottawa: Ottawa International Institute for Conservation/Canadian Group and Canadian Association of Professional Conservators.

James, W. (1896) "The Moral Philosopher and the Moral Life," *The Will to Believe*, London.

Organ, R. M. (1976) *Discussion, Preservation and Conservation: Principles and Practices*, Washington, DC: The Preservation Press.

Pye, E. and Cronyn, J. (1987) *The Archaeological Conservator Re-examined*, London: Institute of Archaeology Jubilee Conference Proceedings.

Standing Commission on Museums and Galleries (1980) *Conservation: Report by a Working Party 1980*, London: HMSO.

UKIC (1983) *Guidance for Conservation Practice*, London: United Kingdom Institute for Conservation.

Waite, J. G. (1976) *Architectural Metals: Their Deterioration and Stabilization, Preservation and Conservation: Principles and Practices*, Washington, DC: The Preservation Press.

Wallis, G. (1988) *Dorothea Restorations Ltd, Conservation Policy Statement*, Bristol: Dorothea Restorations Ltd.

CHAPTER 16: ETHICS AND EXHIBITIONS

Alpers, Svetlana (1991), "The Museum as a Way of Seeing," in: Karp, I. and Lavine, S. (eds) (1991) *Exhibiting Cultures*, Washington, DC, and London: Smithsonian Institution Press.

Rabinowitz, R. (1991) "Exhibit as Canvas," *Museum News*, Vol. 70, No. 2, March/April.

Vogel, Susan (1991), "Always True to the Object, in Our Fashion," in: Karp, I. and Lavine, S. (eds) *Exhibiting Cultures*, Washington, DC, and London: Smithsonian Institution Press.

CHAPTER 17: ETHICS AND PUBLIC PROGRAMS

Schouten, F. (1993) "The Future of Museums," *Museum Management and Curatorship*, London: Butterworth Heinemann, 12, 381–6.

Special report: "L'éthique ou qui ose encore faire du bon journalisme?" *Suites*, magazine for UQAM graduates, May 1994.

Solana, F. (1981) "Inaugural Address by the Minister of Public Education of México," in: Bochi, A. and Valence S. (eds) *Proceedings of the 12th General Conference and 13th General Assembly of the International Council of Museums*, Paris: ICOM.

REFERENCES FOR GLOSSARY

American Heritage Electronic Dictionary © (1991) Houghton Mifflin Company. US Pat. No. 4,724,523. WordStar © International Incorporation.

Aristotle (1941) *Metaphysics*, in *The Basic Works of Aristotle* (R. McKeon ed.), New York: Random House.

Brown, M. (1990) *Working Ethics*, San Francisco and Oxford: Jossey-Bass Publishers.

Guy, M. (1990) *Ethical Decision Making in Everyday Work Situations*, New York and London: Quorum Books.

International Council of Museums (1990) *Statutes and Code of Professional Ethics* (revised), Paris: ICOM.

Martin, H. and Henningan, P. (1982) *Applying Professional Standards and Ethics in the '80s*, Washington, DC: American Society for Public Administration Publishers.

Nietzsche, F. (1924) *The Will to Power*, trans. by

A. M. Ludovici in *The Complete Works of Nietzsche*, New York: The Macmillan Company.

Pojman, L. (1990) *Ethics: Discovering Right and Wrong* (quoting J. Ladd, *Ethical Relativism*, Wadsworth, 1973, p. 1) Belmont, CA: Wadsworth Publishing Company.

Rand, A. (1964) *The Virtue of Selfishness*, New York: The New American Library.

Russell, B. (1955) *Human Society in Ethics and Politics*, New York: Simon & Schuster.

Scheiner, T. (1994) statement prepared for this publication, Rio de Janeiro, Brazil.

Solomon, R. (1992) *Ethics and Excellence*, New York: Oxford University Press.

Taylor, P. (1975) *Principles of Ethics: An Introduction*, Encino, CA: Dickenson Publishing Company, Inc.

Wheelwright, P. (1959) *A Critical Introduction to Ethics* (3rd edn), New York: The Odyssey Press Inc.

United Nations Educational, Scientific, and Cultural Organization (UNESCO) (1970) *Convention on the Means of Prohibiting and Preventing the Illicit Import, Export and Transfer of Ownership of Cultural Property*, Paris: UNESCO.

Glossary

Language is the basis for truth as each word, regardless of the idiom, conveys a pre-established message. Communication is achieved only when that definition is understood by the user and the receiver. Once mutual comprehension has been established, it serves as a foundation for trust based on the knowledge that each time that particular word is used, it will have the same (or similar) meaning.

absolute a concept associated with ethical idealism.

accountability accepting the consequences of personal actions and accepting the responsibility for decisions – being accountable.

act deontology an approach to ethical reasoning that considers each act to be a unique ethical experience. Act deontologists contend each person must decide right and wrong in each situation based on personal values (intuition or conscience) separate from consideration of established rules. Those persons perpetuating the act-deontological theory are divided into two groups. One group is called intuitionists and the other decisionists. Intuitionists maintain that each person must consult their intuition to determine the right thing to do. Decisionists contend there is no right decision until a person decides on what is right or wrong in a particular situation. Decisionists are also called existentialists (Pojman 1990). French writer, philosopher, and political activist Jean-Paul Sartre (1905–80) was an existentialist.

act utilitarianism the theory that an act is right (good) if it maximizes happiness and that otherwise it is wrong, or that it results in as much good as any available alternative. An act that promotes the greatest good of (or for) the greatest number (of people, objects, ideas, things, etc.).

aestheticism the belief that the aesthetic experience is the highest form of human experience and that ethical and moral observances are secondary to art. The theory that the pursuit of beauty is the basic principle from which all other principles are derived and that art and artists are held to have no obligation other than striving for beauty.

altruism the promotion of the good of others by unselfish acts. This attitude is contrasted with egoism.

anticipatory socialization the process of adjusting to the beliefs, dress, and values to accommodate new settings prior to interaction (Guy 1990).

a priori principles and judgments valid without reference to sense impressions; proceeding from cause to effect; deductive reasoning: the opposite to *a posteriori*.

canon a basis for judgment; the standard against which an act or actions can be measured.

caring treating people as ends in themselves, not as means to an end, and having compassion.

category "one of the highest classes to which the objects of knowledge or thought or experience can be reduced" (Wheelwright 1959: 386). Value is a basic category of ethics.

categorical imperative the concept of an absolute ethical (moral) law that German philosopher Immanuel Kant (1724–1804) believed to be the foundation for all ethical (moral) conduct. A theory that recognizes the imperial status of ethical obligation.

CECA International Committee for Education and Cultural Action, a standing committee of ICOM.

CIDOC International Committee for Documentation, a standing committee of ICOM.

conflict of interest those acts or activities that may be construed to be contrary to ethical museum practices based on knowledge, experience, and contracts gained through conditions of employment.

267

cultural absolutism the premise that all people everywhere are accountable to certain universal moral standards, and that if not all societies recognize these standards, it is the result of moral ignorance.

cultural heritage a tradition, habit, skill, art form, or institution that is passed from one generation to the next.

cultural property the material manifestation of the concepts, habits, skills, art, or institutions of a specific people in a defined period of time.

> cultural property means property which, on religious or secular grounds, is specifically designated by each State as being of importance for archaeology, prehistory, history, literature, art or science and which belongs to the following categories:
>
> (a) rare collections and specimens of fauna, flora, minerals and anatomy, and objects of paleontological interest;
> (b) property related to history, including the history of science and technology and military and social history, to the life of national leaders, thinkers, scientists and artists and to events of national importance;
> (c) products of archaeological excavations (including regular and clandestine) or of archaeological discoveries;
> (d) elements of artistic or historical monuments or archaeological sites which have been dismembered;
> (e) antiquities more than one hundred years old, such as inscriptions, coins and engraved seals;
> (f) objects of ethnological interest;
> (g) property of artistic interest, such as:
>
>> (i) pictures, paintings and drawings produced entirely by hand on any support and in any material (excluding industrial designs and manufactured articles decorated by hand);
>> (ii) original works of statuary art and sculpture in any material;
>> (iii) original engravings, prints and lithographs;
>> (iv) original artistic assemblages and montages in any material;
>
> (h) rare manuscripts and incunabula, old books, documents and publications of special interest (historical, artistic, scientific, literary, etc.) singly or in collections;
> (i) postage, revenue and similar stamps, singly or in collections;
> (j) archives, including sound, photographic and cinematographic archives;
> (k) articles of furniture more than one hundred years old and old musical instruments.
> (UNESCO 1970)

cultural relativism the theory that ethics and values differ from society to society and that no universally applicable norms exist.

deontic a general reference pertaining to anything having to do with the concept of necessity or duty.

deontological ethics from Greek, *deon*, moral duty; the theory that rightness or wrongness of an action is determined by rules of conduct rather than outcome; the view of obligation as immediately perceived and therefore independent of any reasons that may be given in support of one duty as against another.

descriptive ethics a methodology that describes how people act. It explains their actions in terms of their value judgments and assumptions (Brown 1990). A department of empirical science, descriptive ethics attempts to discover and describe the moral beliefs held by a particular culture.

duty defined (subjectively) as a moral obligation to do or to omit something.

end value (see intrinsic value.)

egalitarianism the belief there is common quality in all people and that they should be treated equally.

equity relating to justice and the function of the judge to supplement the generalities of law by giving attention to cases or situations that are exceptions to the rule.

ethical absolutism a concept that supports the notion that there is only one correct response to every ethical (moral) problem.

ethical egoism refers to a normative view about how people ought to act. It presents the idea that, regardless of how people act, they have no obligation to do anything except what is in their own interest – the maximizing of personal good as an end.

ethical hedonism a doctrine that places personal pleasure as the highest good. The level of pleasure is measured in "hedons."

ethical objectivism the theory that ethical values exist independently of human comprehension and that they must be found and used as principles of human conduct. Opposite to ethical subjectivism.

ethical relativism "the doctrine that the moral rightness and wrongness of actions vary from society to society and that there are no absolute universal moral standards binding on all men at all times. Accordingly, it holds that whether or not it is right for an individual to act in a certain way depends on or is relative to the society to which he belongs" (Pojman 1990: 18).

ethical subjectivism the assumption that the only measure for ethical actions is the individual; based on this concept, ethical right or wrong is self-determined and has no interpersonal evaluative meaning. Opposite to ethical objectivism.

ethics from the Greek word *ethike < ethikos*, ethical *< ethos*, character (American Heritage 1991).

ethnocentrism the belief of any people that their ways, religion, culture, government, or language are superior to all others.

extrinsic value value as a means to an end rather than a value unto itself (a contributory value). A part of the hierarchy of values that distinguishes between values as "ends" and "means." The value of material possessions is normally considered to be extrinsic in that it is a means to an end rather than an end unto itself. (See intrinsic value.)

fairness the concept of "treating people equally and making decisions based on notions of justice" (Guy 1990: 16).

fiduciary pertaining to holding something in trust; denoting a trustee or trusteeship.

good for the purposes of this theoretical discussion, "good" is to convey the notion of an act, idea, or results that are accepted as satisfying the desired outcome by the museum profession and which reflect the currently endorsed standard of "best practice." At the same time, "good" is to describe responsible adherence to the highest standards of professional probity.

governing body "used . . . to signify the superior authority concerned with the policy, finance and administration of the museum" (ICOM 1990: 24).

hedon a Greek word meaning "pleasure" and relating to the doctrine of hedonism.

hedonistic calculus a concept developed by Jeremy Bentham (1748–1832), whereby pleasures and pains are evaluated by measurement alone without reference to quantitative differences. According to his plan, moral worth of an action could be judged by reference to: (a) intensity (of the pleasure or pain), (b) duration, (c) probability, (d) promptitude, (e) fecundity, (f) purity, and (g) social extent.

honesty telling the truth in act and deed without deceiving or distorting.

hypothetical imperative one aspect of the system of ethics based on the imperative that is conditional on the desire to achieve a particular value (good). The means/end theory that asks the question "if" – if a person desires X , then they

must do Y. Immanuel Kant (1724–1804), the German philosopher, is associated with the imperative theory.

ICOFOM International Committee for Museology, one of the standing committees of ICOM.

ICOM the International Council of Museums – the international non-governmental organization of museums and professional museum workers established to advance the interests of museology and other disciplines concerned with museum management and operations. Address: ICOM Maison de l'Unesco, 1 rue Miollis, 75732 Paris Cedex 15, France (ICOM, 1990: 3).

ICOM *Statutes* adopted by the 16th General Assembly of ICOM in The Hague, September 5, 1989, the ICOM *Statutes* describe and define ICOM organization, its role, membership, method, and objectives.

ICTOP International Committee for the Training of Personnel, one of the standing committees of ICOM.

ideology in social ethics "a set of moral principles and accompanying beliefs so far as these have been determined by the social situation and social habits of the moral agent" (Wheelwright 159: 300).

integrity an attitude of ethical soundness used to describe a human quality founded on careful judgment, a sense of obligation, and reasoned application of principles while maintaining a faithful commitment to personal beliefs. "Integrity is loyalty to one's convictions and values; it is the policy of acting in accordance with one's values, of expressing, up-holding and translating them into practical reality" (Rand 1964: 51).

intrinsic value the Greek philosopher Plato (427–347 BC) was among the first to recognize that objects desired by people fall into three classes: those desired as an end in themselves (intrinsic or end value), those desired as a means to an end (extrinsic, means value, or instrumental value), and those desired both as ends in themselves and as means to further ends. Intrinsic is a value that is self-contained in that it is not required to serve any other purpose in order to have value. This topic was considered at great length in the book *Utilitarianism* by John Stuart Mill published in 1863 (Taylor 1975). (See extrinsic value.)

intuitionism the theory that universal ethical principles and basic truths are known by intuition rather than reason and that these values are discernible by everyone. G. E. Moore (1873–1958), the English philosopher, is associated with the theory of intuitionism. He is known for *Principia Ethica* published in 1903.

means value (see extrinsic value.)

metaethics describing the critical examination of the ideas and reasoning processes of ethics. *Meta* is a Greek word meaning "beyond" or "about," it connotes self-reflection or self-evaluation in the form of a critical assessment of ethics as a science. Metaethics is a twentieth-century term that is not found in the works of classical philosophers.

mission statement a written document that states a museum's institutional philosophy, scope, and responsibility.

moral philosophy that part of philosophy concerned with the study and principles of behavior.

morality the quality of human acts or actions by which they are called right or wrong.

morals concerned with right and wrong and the distinction between them. Morals come from the Latin *moralis < mos*, custom (American Heritage 1991).

musealized originally used with reference to the idea of "ecomuseum" – a specific conceptual model of a museum based on a territory where natural and cultural environment were considered at the same time memory and patrimony of a specific social group. That model was developed in the 1960s, as opposed to the "traditional" museum, based on a building (or set of buildings) full of collections, worked by specialists and admired by visitors.

The main idea implied in the term "musealized" was the possibility of turning a parcel of territory, with all its total environment, into a museum. Instead of taking fragments of nature and of culture from their original context, to form museum collections, a formal process of "musealization" would make it possible to turn portions of the environment into museums. That is what museum theorists have called, from then on, "musealization *in situ*."

Museum theorists have over time extended the significance of the term "musealized" to refer to the specific conceptualization of a parcel of reality (be it a territory, community, non-material trait or cultural pattern, collection, or object) within the realm of museology, not only on a theoretical level but also in what refers to museum practice. The word is presently used with reference to all kinds of museums and to all realities concerning the field of museology (Scheiner 1994).

museum "a museum is a non-profit making, permanent institution in the service of society and of its development, and open to the public which acquires, conserves, researches, communicates and exhibits, for purposes of study, education and enjoyment, material evidence of people and their environment" (ICOM 1990: 3).

museum collections an identifiable selection of objects having some significant commonality.

naturalistic fallacy the assumption that because something is a certain way, it should be that way.

Nicomachean Ethics one of three treatises on ethics formulated by Aristotle (384–322 BC). The others are the *Eudemian Ethics* and the *Magna Moralia*. The names *Nicomachean* and *Eudemian* are said to identify the original editors of the works, namely Aristotle's son Nicomachus and his pupil Eudemus.

normative ethics establishing a set of rules (norms) for ethical activities and the study of how people ought to act, the analysis of value judgments, and assumptions that justify those actions (Brown 1990).

personal conduct referring to the voluntary activity of a person. When a person has two or more options a decision must be made, this act of choice involves some form of personal criteria.

philosophical ethics (see normative ethics.)

principle of utility a concept that promotes the doctrine that a person ought to do that which brings the greatest pleasure to the greatest number of people.

profit maximization the business theory of gaining the most return on an investment with the least amount of risk. May be viewed museologically as gaining the greatest benefit from the objects in the collections without placing them in a situation that causes deterioration, loss, or irreparable damage.

psychological egoism the doctrine that all people are selfish in everything they do, and that the only motive from which anyone acts is self-interest.

psychological hedonism a theory that identifies the "good" life with the pursuit of happiness (pleasure) and avoiding pain or unhappiness (displeasure). It assumes that whenever a person acts voluntarily, he or she is partly motivated by a hope of some form of pleasure. (See ethical hedonism.)

reason signifies the choice of the right means to an end that is to be achieved (Russell 1955).

responsibility the belief that there are certain acts or actions that a rational human being can and must perform and that the rational human being can be held accountable for failure to accomplish those acts or actions.

rule-governed "thinking and acting on the basis of rules and principles, with only secondary regard to circumstances or exceptions" (Solomon 1992: 255).

rule deontology one division of the deontological

system of thought (the other is act deontology). Rule deontology accepts the premise of universalizability, that is, the principle that ethical judgments must apply to all people in the same way under the same circumstances. Rule deontologists believe that following established rules will result in right decisions.

rule utilitarianism the notion that to act according to the general rules of ethical conduct will tend to increase good (happiness) and diminish bad (unhappiness or misery). The assumption is that the pursuance of accepted ethical rules leads to a greater utility for society than any available alternative.

self-interest associated with the doctrine of ethical egoism and the idea that each person should promote their own well-being and interests.

selfishness relating to the theory of psychological egoism, which views all persons as selfish in all things they do and the only motive for acts or action as self-interest. Ayn Rand (1905–82), author of *Atlas Shrugged* and *The Fountainhead*, is associated with this theory.

teleological ethics the theory that the outcome (rather than the intention) of an act or action determines its ethical nature, that is, an act is right or good if it produces the best consequences and that no act is intrinsically good.

truth "to say of what is that it is, and of what is not that it is not, is true" (Aristotle 1941: 1011b). "Truth is that explanation of things which causes us the smallest amount of mental exertion (apart from this, lying is extremely fatiguing)" (Nietzsche 1924: 279).

universalism the theory that ethical principles must apply universally to all people in the same way under the same circumstances otherwise an act or action cannot be considered an ethical principle. Opposite to relativism.

utilitarianism doctrine that the rightness (correctness) of actions is to be judged by their outcome or consequences.

values beliefs that model human assessments of relative worth and importance. Values influence and shape both goals and activities (Martin and Henningan 1982). That which a person wants or whatever engages a person's support or opposition.

virtue ethics a theory supporting the idea that it is important not only to do the right thing, but also to have the requisite dispositions, motivations, and emotions in being good and doing right. It is not only about action but about emotion, character, and habit. The theory includes both moral and nonmoral virtues.

volunteer a person who performs or gives a service or assistance of his or her free will without consideration of financial remuneration.

Bibliography

Allen, B. (1993) *Truth in Philosophy*, Cambridge, MA, and London: Harvard University Press. ISBN 0–674–91090–7.

Almond, B. and Hill, D. (eds) (1991) *Applied Philosophy: Morals and Metaphysics in Contemporary Debate*, New York and London: Routledge. ISBN 0–415–06015–X.

Aristotle (1980) *Nicomachean Ethics* (trans. and intro. D. Ross), Oxford: Oxford University Press. ISBN 0–19–281518–0.

Aristotle (1985) *Nicomachean Ethics*, (trans. and ed. T. Irwin), Indianapolis: Hackett Publishing Company, Inc. ISBN 0–915145–65–0.

Armstrong, D. M. (1973) *Belief, Truth, and Knowledge*, London and New York: Cambridge University Press. ISBN 0–521–08706–6.

Association of Art Museum Directors (1981) *Professional Practices in Art Museums, Report of the Ethics and Standards Committee*, Savannah, GA: Association of Art Museum Directors. LCCN 81–66765.

Bahm, A. J. (1974) *Ethics as a Behavioral Science*, Springfield, IL: Charles C. Thomas Publisher. ISBN 0–398–03043–X.

Banner, W. (1968) *Ethics: An Introduction to Moral Philosophy*, New York, Charles Scribner's Sons. LCCN 68–17349.

Beauchamp, T. L. (1989) *Case Studies in Business, Society, and Ethics* (2nd edn), Englewood Cliffs, NJ: Prentice-Hall. ISBN 0–13–119355–4.

Blanshard, B. (1941) *The Nature of Thought* (2 volumes), New York: The Macmillan Company. LCCN 64–1650.

Bowne, B. P. (1892) *The Principles of Ethics*, New York, Cincinnati, and Chicago: American Book Company. (No identification number).

Brandt, R. B. (1979) *A Theory of the Good and the Right*, New York and Oxford: Oxford University Press. ISBN 0–19–824550–5.

Brentano, F. (1973) *The Foundation and Construction of Ethics* (trans. and ed. by E. Schneewind), New York: Humanities Press, Inc. ISBN 0–391–00254–6.

Brink, D. O. (1989) *Moral Realism and the Foundations of Ethics*, Cambridge: Cambridge University Press. ISBN 0–521–35080–8.

Broadie, S. (1991) *Ethics with Aristotle*, New York and Oxford: Oxford University Press. ISBN 0–19–506601–4.

Broudy, H. S. (1981) *Truth and Credibility, The Citizen's Dilemma*, New York: Longman Inc. ISBN 0–582–28208–X.

Brown, M. T. (1990) *Working Ethics: Strategies for Decision Making and Organizational Responsibility*, San Francisco and Oxford: Jossey-Bass Publishers. ISBN 1–55542–280–2.

Bryce, H. J. (1992) *Financial and Strategic Management for Nonprofit Organizations* (2nd edn), Englewood Cliffs, NJ: Prentice-Hall, Inc. ISBN 0–13–377573–9.

Callahan, D. and Engelhardt, H. T. (eds) (1981) *The Roots of Ethics*, New York and London: Plenum Press. ISBN 0–306–40796–5.

Callahan, J. C. (1988) *Ethical Issues in Professional Life*, New York and Oxford: Oxford University Press. ISBN 0–19–505362–1.

Caplan, A. L. and Callahan, D. (eds) (1981) *Ethics in Hard Times*, New York and London: Plenum Press. ISBN 0–306–40790–6.

Cassara, E. (ed.) (1971) *Universalism in America*, Boston: Beacon Press. ISBN 0–8070–1664–0.

Chisholm, R. M. (1982) *The Foundations of Knowing*, Minneapolis: University of Minnesota Press. ISBN 0–8166–1103–3.

Curtler, H. M. (1993) *Ethical Argument: Critical Thinking in Ethics*, New York: Paragon House Publishers. ISBN 1–55778–513–9.

Danford, J. W. (1990) *David Hume and the Problem of Reason*, New Haven, CT, and London: Yale University Press. ISBN 0–300–04667–7.

Davis, J. W., Hockney, D. J., and Wilson, W. K. (eds) (1969) *Philosophical Logic*, Dordrecht-Holland: D. Reidel Publishing Company. LCCN 78–437276.

Dewey, R. E., Gramlich, F. W., and Loftsgordon, D. (1961) *Problems of Ethics*, New York: The Macmillan Company. LCCN 61–5086.

Edson, G. and Dean, D. (1994) *The Handbook for Museums*, New York and London: Routledge. ISBN 0–415–09952–8.

Edwards, P. (1967) *Encyclopedia of Philosophy*, 8 vols, New York: Macmillan and Free Press. LCCN 67–10059.

Ellis, B. (1990) *Truth and Objectivity*, Cambridge and Oxford: Basil Blackwell, Ltd. ISBN 0–631–15397–7.

Everett, W. G. (1918) *Moral Values: A Study in the Principles of Conduct*, New York: Henry Holt & Company. LCCN 18–3232.

Fagothey, A. (1972) *Right and Reason: Ethics in Theory and Practice* (5th edn), St Louis, MO: The C. V. Mosby Company. ISBN 0–8016–1544–5.

Finnis, J. (1983) *Fundamentals of Ethics*, Washington, DC: Georgetown University Press. ISBN 0–87840–404–X.

Fisk, M. (1980) *Ethics and Society*, New York: New York University Press. ISBN 0–8147–2564–3.

Fleishman, J. L. and Payne, B. L. (1980) *Ethical Dilemmas and the Education of Policymakers*, New York: Institute of Society, Ethics and the Life Sciences. ISBN 0–916558–05–3.

Foot, P. (ed.) (1967) *Theories of Ethics*, New York and Oxford: Oxford University Press. LCCN 68–74186.

Frankena, W. K. (1973) *Ethics*, Englewood Cliffs, NJ: Prentice-Hall, Inc. LCCN 63–10527.

Fried, C. (1978) *Right and Wrong*, Cambridge, MA, and London: Harvard University Press. ISBN 0–674–76905–8.

Fuller, B. A. G. (1947) *A History of Philosophy* (revised), New York: Henry Holt & Company. (No identification number).

Fuller, M. B. (1991) *Truth, Value and Justification*, Aldershot and Brookfield: Avebury. ISBN 1–85628–151–5.

Garnett, A. C. (1960) *Ethics: A Critical Introduction*, New York: Ronald Press Company. LCCN 60–6144.

Garrett, T. M. (1968) *Problems and Perspectives in Ethics*, New York: Sheed & Ward. LCCN 68–13850.

Gathercole, P. and Lowenthal, D. (eds) (1990) *The Policies of the Past*, London: Unwin Hyman Ltd. ISBN 0–04–445018–4.

Gauthier, D. P. (ed.) (1970) *Morality and Rational Self-Interest*, Englewood Cliffs, NJ: Prentice-Hall, Inc. LCCN 78–113847.

Gelven, M. (1990) *Truth and Existence*, University Park and London: The Pennsylvania State University Press. ISBN 0–271–00707–9.

Glenn, P. J. (1930) *Ethics: A Class Manual in Moral Philosophy*, St Louis, MO, and London: B. Herder Book Company. LCCN 36–24354.

Goldman, A. H. (1980) *The Moral Foundations of Professional Ethics*, Totowa, NJ: Rowman & Littlefield. ISBN 0–8476–6274–8.

Goodpaster, K. (ed.) (1976) *Perspectives on Morality: Essays by William K. Frankena*, Notre Dame, Ind., and London: University of Notre Dame Press. ISBN 0–268–01519–8.

Gowans, C. W. (1987) *Moral Dilemmas*, New York and Oxford: Oxford University Press. ISBN 0–19–504272–7.

Greenfield, J. (1989) *The Return of Cultural Treasures*, Cambridge: Cambridge University Press. ISBN 0–521–333199.

Guy, M. E. (1990) *Ethical Decision Making in*

Everyday Work Situations, New York and London: Quorum Books. ISBN 0–89930–418–4.

Halberstam, J. (1993) *Everyday Ethics*, New York and London: Penguin Books. ISBN 0–670–84247–8.

Harding, C. G. (1985) *Moral Dilemmas*, Chicago: Precedent Publishing, Inc. ISBN 0–913750–35–2.

Hare, R. M. (1952) *The Language of Morals*, Oxford: The Clarendon Press. ISBN 0–19–881077–6.

Hartle, A. E. and Kekes, J. (eds) (1987) *Dimensions of Ethical Thought*, New York, Berne, and Paris: Peter Lang Publishing, Inc. ISBN 0–8204–0590–6.

Heermance, E. L. (1924) *Codes of Ethics*, Burlington, VT: Free Press Printing Company. LCCN 24–30201.

Herman, R. D. and Associates (1994) *The Jossey-Bass Handbook of Nonprofit Leadership and Management*, San Francisco: Jossey-Bass Publishers. ISBN 1–5542–651–4.

Holmes, R. L. (1992) *Basic Moral Philosophy*, Belmont, CA: Wadsworth Publishing Company. ISBN 0–534–19656–X.

Horwich, P. (1990) *Truth*, Oxford and Cambridge: Basil Blackwell, Ltd. ISBN 0–631–17315–3.

Hudson, W. D. (ed.) (1969) *The Is/Ought Question*, New York: St Martin's Press. LCCN 79–106390.

International Council of Museums (1990) *Statutes and Code of Professional Ethics* (revised), Paris: ICOM. LCCN 93–158524.

James, W. (1909) *The Meaning of Truth*, New York: Longmans, Green, & Company. ISBN 0–781–23480–8.

Jaspers, K. (1959) *Truth and Symbol* (trans. and intro. J. T. Wilde, W. Kluback, and W. Kimmel), New York: Twayne Publishers. LCCN 59–8386.

Jevons, F. B. (1914) *Philosophy: What Is It?*, Cambridge: Cambridge University Press. LCCN 14–10910.

Joachim, H. H. (1906) *The Nature of Truth*, Oxford: The Clarendon Press. LCCN 07–2578.

Johnson, L. E. (1992) *Focusing on Truth*, London and New York: Routledge. ISBN 0–415–07252–2.

Kainz, H. P. (1988) *Ethics in Context*, Washington, DC: Georgetown University Press. ISBN 0–87840–461–9.

Kant, I. [1785] (1993) *Grounding for the Metaphysics of Morals* (trans. J. W. Ellington, 3rd edn), Indianapolis: Hackett Publishing Company, Inc. ISBN 0–87220–167–8.

Kemp, J. (1970) *Ethical Naturalism: Hobbes and Hume*, London and New York: Macmillan/St Martin's Press. LCCN 78–108404.

Kultgen, J. (1988) *Ethics and Professionalism*, Philadelphia: University of Pennsylvania Press. ISBN 0–8122–8094–6.

Kupperman, J. J. (1970) *Ethical Knowledge*, New York: Humanities Press, Inc. ISBN 0–04170026–0.

Lamont, W. (1981) *Law and the Moral Order*, Aberdeen: The University Press. ISBN 0–08–025742–9.

Landesman, C. (ed.) (1970) *The Foundations of Knowledge*, Englewood Cliffs, NJ: Prentice-Hall, Inc. LCCN 76–117012.

Lea, F. (1975) *The Ethics of Reason: An Essay in Moral Philosophy*, London: Brentham Press. ISBN 0–9503459–6–2.

Lewis, C. W. (1991) *The Ethics Challenge in Public Service*, San Francisco and Oxford: Jossey-Bass Publishers. ISBN 1–55542–383–3.

Leys, W. A. R. (1952) *Ethics for Policy Decisions: the Art of Asking Deliberative Questions*, New York: Prentice-Hall, Inc. LCCN 52–8388.

MacIntyre, A. (ed.) (1965) *Hume's Ethical Writings*, Notre Dame and London: University of Notre Dame Press. ISBN 0–268–01074–9.

—— (1966) *A Short History of Ethics*, New York: The Macmillan Company. LCCN 66–14209.

Mackie, J. L. (1980) *Hume's Moral Theory*, London and Boston: Routledge & Kegan Paul. ISBN 0–7100–0524–5.

Malaro, M. (1987) *A Legal Primer on Managing Museum Collections* (2nd edn), Washington, DC: Smithsonian Institution Press. ISBN 0–87474–656–6.

Margolis, J. (1971) *Values and Conduct*, Oxford: Clarendon Press. LCCN 75–140911.

Marion, J. (1989) *The Best of Everything*, New York: Simon & Schuster. ISBN 0–671–66783–1.

Martin, H. and Hennigan, P. (eds) (1982) *Applying Professional Standards and Ethics in the '80s*, Washington, DC: American Society for Public Administrations Publishers. ISBN 0–936678–04–6.

McDowell, B. (1991) *Ethical Conduct and the Professional's Dilemma*, New York and London: Quorum Books. ISBN 0–89930–596–2.

McInerney, P. K. and Rainbolt, G. W. (1994) *Ethics*, New York: HarperCollins Publishers, Inc. ISBN 0–06–467166–6.

McKechnie, J. L. (general supervisor) (1977) Webster's New Twentieth Century Dictionary of the English Language (2nd edn), William Collins/World Publishing Co., Inc. ISBN 0–529–04852–3.

Merryman, J. and Elsen, A. (1987) *Law, Ethics, and the Visual Arts* (2nd edn, vols I and II), Philadelphia: University of Pennsylvania Press. ISBN 0–8122–8052–2 (set).

Messenger, P. (ed.) (1989) *The Ethics of Collecting Cultural Property*, Albuquerque: University of New Mexico Press. ISBN 0–8263–1167–9.

Meyer, K. (1973) *The Plundered Past*, New York: Atheneum. ISBN 0–689–1–522–3.

Moore, G. E. (1903) *Principia Ethica* (republished 1988), Buffalo, NY: Prometheus Books. ISBN 0–87975–498–2.

Mount, E. (1990) *Professional Ethics in Context*, Louisville, KY: Westminster/John Knox Press. ISBN 0–664–25143–9.

Munitz, M. K. (ed.) (1958) *A Modern Introduction to Ethics*, Glencoe, IL: The Free Press. LCCN 58–6489.

Murray, M. V. (1963) *Problems in Conduct*, New York and London: Holt, Rinehart & Winston, Inc. LCCN 63–8817.

Pahel, K., and Schiller, M. (eds) (1970) *Readings in Contemporary Ethical Theory*, Englewood Cliffs, NJ: Prentice-Hall, Inc. LCCN 78–87265.

Parfit, D. (1984) *Reasons and Persons*, Oxford: Clarendon Press. ISBN 0–19–824615–3.

Patterson, C. H. (1949) *Moral Standards: An Introduction to Ethics*, New York: The Ronald Press Company. LCCN 49–2957.

Pepper, S. C. (1960) *Ethics*, New York: Appleton-Century-Crofts, Inc. LCCN 60–6796.

Phelan, M. (1982) *Museums and the Law*, Vol. 1, AASLH Management Series, Nashville, TN: American Association for State and Local History. ISBN 0–910050–60–0.

Pojman, L. P. (1990) *Ethics: Discovering Right and Wrong*, Belmont, CA: Wadsworth Publishing Company. ISBN 0–534–12378–3.

Polka, B. (1990) *Truth and Interpretation: An Essay in Thinking*, New York: St Martin's Press, Inc. ISBN 0–312–04218–3.

Rachels, J. (1993) *The Elements of Moral Philosophy* (2nd edn), New York: McGraw-Hill, Inc. ISBN 0–07–051098–9.

Rand, A. (1964) *The Virtue of Selfishness*, New York: The New American Library. LCCN 65–299.

—— (1990) *The Voice of Reason: Essays in Objectivist Thought* (ed. by L. Peikoff), New York: Meridian. ISBN 0–453–00634–5.

Rapoport, A. (1953) *Operational Philosophy*, New York: Harper & Brothers. LCCN 53–8550.

Rawls, J. (1971) *A Theory of Justice*, Cambridge, MA: The Belknap Press of Harvard University Press. LCCN 73–168432.

Reidenbach, R. E. and Robin, D. P. (1989) *Ethics and Profits*, Englewood Cliffs, NJ: Prentice-Hall, Inc. ISBN 0–13–2902140–1.

Rescher, N. (1987) *Ethical Idealism*, Berkeley, Los Angeles, and London: University of California Press. ISBN 0–520–05696–5.

Rohr, J. A. (1978) *Ethics for Bureaucrats*, New York and Basle: Marcel Dekker, Inc. ISBN 0–8247–6756–X.

Rosenthal, D. M. and Shehadi, F. (eds) (1988) *Applied Ethics and Ethical Theory*, Salt Lake City: University of Utah Press. ISBN 0–87480–289–X.

Rouner, L. S. (ed.) (1983) *Foundations of Ethics*, Notre Dame, Ind., and London: University of Notre Dame Press. ISBN 0–268-00963–5.

Russell, B. (1955) *Human Society in Ethics and Politics*, New York: Simon & Schuster. LCCN 55–5945.

Schaub, E. L. (1968) *Philosophy Today* (reprint series), Freeport, NY: Books for Libraries Press. LCCN 68–22944.

Schilpp, P. A. (1968) *The Philosophy of C. I. Lewis*, London: Cambridge University Press. LCCN 67–10007.

Sellars, W. and Hospers, J. (eds) (1952) *Readings in Ethical Theory*, New York: Appleton-Century-Crofts, Inc. LCCN 47–5415.

Simon, Y. R. (1991) *Practical Knowledge* (ed. by R. Mulvaney), New York: Fordham University Press. ISBN 0–8232–1316–1.

Solomon, R. (1992) *Ethics and Excellence: Cooperation and Integrity in Business*, New York and Oxford: Oxford University Press. ISBN 0–19–506430–5.

Sommers, C. H. (1986) *Right and Wrong: Basic Readings in Ethics*, New York: Harcourt Brace Jovanovich, Publishers. ISBN 0–15–577110–8.

Spinoza, B. [1677] (1989) *Ethics and Improvement of the Understanding* (trans. by R. H. M. Elwes), New York: Prometheus Books. ISBN 0–87975–528–8.

—— [1677] (1993) *Ethics and Treatise on the Correction of the Intellect* (trans. A. Boyle), London: Orion Publishing Group. ISBN 0–460–87347–4.

Sprigge, T. L. S. (1990) *The Rational Foundations of Ethics*, London and New York: Routledge. ISBN 0–415–05519–9.

Taylor, P. W. (1975) *Principles of Ethics: An Introduction*, Belmont, CA: Dickenson Publishing Company, Inc. ISBN 0–8221–0142–4.

Titus, H. H. (1947) *Ethics for Today* (2nd edn) New York: American Book Company. LCCN 47–5415.

Titus, H. H. and Keeton, M. T. (eds) (1966) *The Range of Ethics*, New York, American Book Company. LCCN 66–788.

Tomberlin, J. (ed.) (1992) *Philosophical Perspectives, 6 Ethics, 1992*, Atascadoro, CA:

Ridgeview Publishing Company. ISBN 0–924922–58–3.

Tsanoff, R. A. (1955) *Ethics* (revised), New York: Harper & Brothers. LCCN 55–6958.

van Mensch, P. (ed.) (1989) *Professionalising the Muses*, Amsterdam: AHA Books. ISBN 90–5246–013–2.

Van Wyk, R. N. (1990) *Introduction to Ethics*, New York: St Martin's Press. ISBN 0–312–03682–5.

Vivas, E. (1950) *The Moral Life and the Ethical Life*, Chicago: The University of Chicago Press. LCCN 50–10775.

Weil, S. (1983) *Beauty and the Beasts: On Museums, Art, the Law, and the Market*, Washington, DC: Smithsonian Institution Press. ISBN 0–8747–958–1.

—— (1990) *Rethinking the Museum and Other Meditations*, Washington, DC: Smithsonian Institution Press. ISBN 0–87474–948–4.

Westermarck, E. (1971) *The Origin and Development of the Moral Idea*, (vols I and II, revised), Freeport, NY: Books for Libraries Press. ISBN 0–8369–6706–2.

Wheelwright, P. (1959) *A Critical Introduction to Ethics* (3rd edn), New York: The Odyssey Press, Inc. LCCN 59–1511.

Williams, B. (1985) *Ethics and the Limits of Philosophy*, Cambridge, MA: Harvard University Press. ISBN 0–674–26857–1.

Williams, G. (1951) *Humanistic Ethics*, New York: Philosophy Library, LCCN 51–14849.

Williams, S. (1977) *The International and National Protection of Movable Cultural Property, A Comparative Study*. Dobbs Ferry, NY: Oceana Publications, Inc. ISBN 0–379–20294–8.

Index